# Explaining and Exploring Mathematics

## Teaching 11- to 18-year-olds for understanding and enjoyment

Christian Puritz

 Routledge
Taylor & Francis Group

LONDON AND NEW YORK

First published 2017
by Routledge
2 Park Square, Milton Park, Abingdon, Oxon OX14 4RN

and by Routledge
711 Third Avenue, New York, NY 10017

*Routledge is an imprint of the Taylor & Francis Group, an informa business*

*British Library Cataloguing in Publication Data*
A catalogue record for this book is available from the British Library

*Library of Congress Cataloging in Publication Data*
Names: Puritz, Christian.
Title: Explaining and exploring mathematics : teaching 11 to 18 year olds for understanding and
    enjoyment / Christian Puritz.
Description: Abingdon, Oxon ; New York, NY : Routledge, 2017.
Identifiers: LCCN 2016030449| ISBN 9781138680197 (hardback) | ISBN 9781138680210
    (pbk.) | ISBN 9781315563688 (ebook)
Subjects: LCSH: Mathematics—Study and teaching (Secondary)
Classification: LCC QA11.2 .P87 2017 | DDC 510.71/2—dc23
LC record available at https://lccn.loc.gov/2016030449

ISBN: 978-1-138-68019-7 (hbk)
ISBN: 978-1-138-68021-0 (pbk)
ISBN: 978-1-315-56368-8 (ebk)

Typeset in Gill Sans Std
by Swales & Willis Ltd, Exeter, Devon, UK

Printed and bound in Great Britain by
TJ International Ltd, Padstow, Cornwall

# Explaining and Exploring Mathematics

*Explaining and Exploring Mathematics* is designed to help you teach key mathematical concepts in a fun and engaging way by developing the confidence that is vital for teachers. This practical guide focuses on improving students' mathematical understanding, rather than just training them for exams. Covering many aspects of the secondary mathematics curriculum for ages 11–18, it explains how to build on students' current knowledge to help them make sense of new concepts and avoid common misconceptions.

Focusing on two main principles to improve students' understanding: spotting patterns and extending them to something new, and relating the topic being taught to something that the pupils already understand, this book helps you to explore mathematics with your class and establish a successful teacher-student relationship.

Structured into a series of lessons, *Explaining and Exploring Mathematics* is packed full of practical advice and examples of the best way to answer frequently asked questions such as:

- Do two minuses really make a plus?
- Why doesn't $3a + 4b$ equal $7ab$?
- How do you get the area of a circle?
- Why do the angles of a triangle add up to $180°$?
- How can you integrate $\frac{1}{x}$ and calculate the value of e?

This book will be essential reading for all trainee and practising teachers who want to make mathematics relevant and engaging for their students.

**Christian Puritz** studied maths at Wadham College, the University of Oxford and completed his PhD at Glasgow University, UK. Following on from his studies, he taught mathematics at the Royal Grammar School, High Wycombe, UK for more than thirty years. He currently offers home tuition for children of all abilities.

# Contents

# Introduction

So, what do you say to a pupil who asks why $x^{-1}$ means $\frac{1}{x}$? Sadly, I fear that too often the reply will be something like "It's a definition: just make sure that you know it and get plenty of practice with negative and fractional indices because they'll be in the exam." Which leaves the enquirer wondering why $x^{-1}$ should be defined in that way, as well as adding to the number of unconnected and seemingly arbitrary facts that have to be remembered and practised for the exam.

The point of this book is that merely being trained to know and use facts in an exam is not the same as being educated; and the purpose of exams is to check that education has taken place and has been successful. To teach mathematics includes understanding as a vital ingredient. Without that, training has taken place rather than education. I am also convinced that with understanding, plus plenty of practice, the pupil is much better prepared for the exam anyway.

I am not arguing for anything like full mathematical rigour in the teaching process: for instance, in teaching decimal multiplication I ask for the answers to $2 \times 3$ and to $20 \times 3$ to show that multiplying one factor in a product by 10 multiplies the answer by 10. I don't try to appeal to the fact that multiplication is associative, far less try to prove that – it would only baffle pupils at that stage. Just seeing what happens when you do $20 \times 3$ instead of $2 \times 3$ is far more illuminating to someone beginning to grapple with multiplying decimals.

The two main principles I have used to help pupils' understanding are: 1) spotting patterns and then extending them to something new, and 2) relating the topic being taught to something that the pupils already understand, from the world around them or from what they have previously learned. Both of these occur, for example, in the chapter on negative numbers. To let the class see that subtracting a negative number is the same as adding a positive number they are asked to look at the answers to $7 - 3, 7 - 2, 7 - 1, 7 - 0$ and to spot the pattern of answers increasing by 1, then to continue it to deal with $7 - - 1, 7 - - 2$ and so on. This is reinforced by asking "How much is a temperature of $7°$ higher than $2°$? Than $1°?\ldots$ Than $-2°$?" The pupils see that answering those questions entails subtraction, and they already know that $-2°$ is further below $7°$ than $2°$ is. Further practical reinforcement is provided by imagining that one has a bank account with $-£1000$ in it, and that a kind uncle offers to take away this account and transfer it into his own name. It is obvious that this is the same as a gift of £1000 from that uncle. The fact currently being taught is thus seen to follow logically from what the pupils already know and understand, instead of being a new piece of isolated and incomprehensible information to be remembered by rote.

During my own time as a teacher I wrote articles on various topics for maths teaching journals. The substance of these is included in this book, but I have rewritten them, and the other chapters which are new, as lessons given by a teacher to a class of three pupils. This has added variety and flexibility to the treatment and hopefully made the book more readable; but please be aware that the chapters are *not* intended to be actual model lessons! Some of them are too long to be a single lesson, and would in real life be interspersed with spells of doing exercises. Also the pupils stay focused throughout, often show an unusual rapidity in taking things in and only make instructive mistakes, while the teacher hopefully makes none, unlike real teachers, including the author! (Did you know that there are three sorts of maths teachers: those who can count and those who can't?)

Also some of the more advanced topics, included for the sake of enjoyment for the reader, I have myself only taught to small groups of talented pupils, or even never taught at all. The lesson format is simply a literary device, hopefully a useful one.

An important ingredient in a successful teacher-pupil relationship is confidence on the teacher's part that he or she is capable of doing the job well; and a vital part of that confidence is the teacher's own full understanding of the material being taught, plus an enjoyment of mathematics and the rich variety of topics and problems it provides. My hope is that this book will contribute to that understanding and enjoyment for the teacher, and thus also for the learners.

# Part I
## 11–14 years old

# Decimals and multiplication by 10, etc.

| | |
|---|---|
| Teacher: | "Look at this number, 3528. What is the 3 actually worth?" |
| Mike: | "Three thousand; and the 5 is 500." |
| Nadeem: | "The 2 is 20, two 10s, and the 8 is units, just 8." |
| Teacher: | "Good. What happens as you move from left to right in a number like 3528?" |
| Linda: | "Each time you move right the value is less, ten times smaller." |
| Teacher: | "Right; so what about 3528.79? The dot after the 8 is the decimal point, which comes after the units." |
| Nadeem: | "So the 7 has to be ten times smaller than if it were in the units." |
| Linda: | "That makes it $\frac{7}{10}$, doesn't it?" |

If a pupil can't see that yet, it can help to draw a rectangular chocolate bar with lines to divide it into ten equal pieces, shade one piece and ask "What would you call this?", hopefully leading to the fact the shaded piece is one tenth. At the next stage one of the unshaded tenths can be divided into ten smaller parts, followed by the question "How many of these smaller parts would make a whole bar? So what do you call each smaller part?"

| | |
|---|---|
| Mike: | "Yes, and then the 9 is ten times smaller again, so it's $\frac{9}{100}$." |
| Teacher: | "Good, you're getting the idea. The pattern of each step to the right giving a value ten times smaller continues on into the fractional part of the number. The way we write numbers using just ten digits and making the value of each depend on its position was invented centuries ago in India, copied by the Arabs and brought by them to Europe, where previously the Roman numerals were used; they are still used sometimes for dates, but the place value system is much better for doing sums. What is 528 × 10?" |
| Linda: | "That easy, 5280." |

Teacher:    "Yes; now why does putting a 0 on the end make the number ten times bigger?"

Mike:       "It's because the 0 now occupies the units place, making the other digits move one place to the left, thus becoming ten times bigger."

Teacher:    "That's right. The introduction of a symbol for zero was an important step. The Babylonians had a place value system based on 60 (which is why we still have 60 minutes – minute parts – in an hour and 60 seconds – second minute parts – in a minute; but they didn't have a proper symbol for 0, so for instance the numbers 3 and 3 × 60 = 180 looked the same, just as in our system 3 could be three or thirty or three hundred if we didn't have 0."

Nadeem:     "So what about 528.79 × 10?"

Teacher:    "OK, the 5, 2 and 8 each move one place to the left to make them 10 times bigger, but then so do the 7 and the 9."

Mike:       "So it's 5287.9?"

Teacher:    "Yes; the 7 was worth $\frac{7}{10}$ and is now 7 units or just 7, while the 9 was $\frac{9}{100}$ and changes to $\frac{9}{10}$. Every digit moves one place to the left."

Linda:      "Or can you just move the decimal one place to the right; that has the same effect, doesn't it?"

Teacher:    "Yes indeed. Now what about 528.79 × 100?"

Mike:       "You move the digits or the decimal point twice, gives 52879."

Teacher:    "Right, and what if you divide 528.79 by 10?"

Nadeem:     "You have to move the digits to the right, makes 52.879."

Linda:      "Or you can move the decimal point to left, can't you? It makes the same answer."

Teacher:    That's right. Can you do 0.046 ÷ 100?"

Linda:      "You move the point two places left; but there's only one digit before the decimal point."

Mike:       "You could think of it as 000.046 ÷ 100, then that give 0.000 46."

Teacher:    "That's right. You see that the digits 4 and 6 have moved two places to the right, which makes their value 100 times smaller. Now it's time for some practice."

# Multiplying and dividing by decimals

| Teacher: | "You all know 2 × 3 = 6. What about 20 × 3? And 2 × 30?" |
|---|---|
| Linda: | "They're both 60." |
| Teacher: | "Yes. And 20 × 30? What are we seeing from these results?" |
| Nadeem: | "20 × 30 = 600." |
| Mike: | "And every time you make one of the numbers ten times bigger the answer gets ten times bigger." |
| Teacher: | "Good. So what happens if you make one of the numbers ten times smaller? What about 0.2 × 3?" |
| Linda: | "It would make the answer ten times smaller; that would be 0.6, would it?" |
| Mike: | "And would 0.2 × 0.3 be 0.06?" |
| Teacher: | "Yes, that's right. In a multiplication, making one of the numbers ten times bigger or smaller does the same to the answer. So let's see how we can do a sum like 0.004 × 1.2." |
| Nadeem: | "You start with 4 × 12 = 48, then 4 × 1.2 = 4.8." |
| Mike: | "And 0.4 × 1.2 = 0.48, and 0.04 × 1.2 = 0.048." |
| Linda: | "So 0.004 × 1.2 = 0.0048, does it? And do we have to do all this every time? Isn't there a quicker method?" |
| Teacher: | "Yes, there is. Start again with 4 × 12 = 48. Just two whole numbers multiplied, no decimal point involved. Next we did 4 × 1.2 = 4.8; we now have a decimal point on each side, and just one figure after it in 1.2, and just one figure after it in the answer 4.8." |
| Mike: | "Then in 0.4 × 1.2 = 0.48 there are two figures after decimal points in 0.4 and 1.2 and also two figures after the decimal point in the answer." |

| Nadeem: | "And in $0.04 \times 1.2 = 0.048$ there are three figures after the decimal point on each side, and then four on each side in $0.004 \times 1.2 = 0.0048$." |
|---|---|
| Teacher: | "That's right; that gives you the quick way to know where to put the decimal point in the answer. Try $0.05 \times 0.003$." |
| Linda: | "Start with $5 \times 3 = 15$, and there are five figures after the decimal point, two in 0.05 and three in 0.003, so the answer must be 0.00015; is that right?" |
| Teacher: | "Yes, you've got the idea. Now try $0.8 \times 2.5$" |
| Nadeem: | "$8 \times 25 = 200$, and we need two figures after the decimal point. Is that 2.00? Can't we just call that 2?" |
| Teacher: | "Yes that's right. The two 0s are needed when you are doing the count of how many figures go after the decimal point; but once that is established you can drop them." |
| Mike: | "Does 2.00 ever mean anything different from 2?" |
| Teacher: | "Yes; but that's in a situation where you are giving an approximate value of a number. Suppose the exact value is 2.003468. What would that be correct to the nearest whole number?" |
| Mike: | "Just 2." |
| Teacher: | "Yes, and what if you were giving it to two decimal places?" |
| Linda: | "That would be 2.00; it's the same size as 2, but it's giving more information about what the actual number is." |
| Teacher: | "That's right. Now tell me about the sums $300 \times 2$, $30 \times 20$ and $3 \times 200$, and what they show." |
| Nadeem: | "They're all 600." |
| Mike: | "And they show that in a multiply sum if you make one number ten times bigger and the other number ten times smaller the answer doesn't change." |
| Teacher: | "Good. That can help with a sum like $0.003 \times 5000$." |
| Linda: | "It's the same as $0.03 \times 500$." |
| Mike: | "Or $0.3 \times 50$." |
| Linda: | "Or $5 \times 3$, that's 15. But could we do it the original way counting figures after the decimal point?" |
| Teacher: | "Yes; but you would start with $3 \times 5000 = 15000$ and then have three digits after the decimal point, making 15.000, which of course is 15. Don't try to start with $5 \times 3 = 15$ and then count figures; that would go badly wrong." |

Nadeem: "We also need to divide by decimals, don't we? Does that involve counting figures?"

Teacher: "No. To start with, if you are dividing by a whole number, say $1.296 \div 8$, it's just like doing $1296 \div 8$, except that you put a decimal point in the answer exactly above the decimal point in 1.296; so as $1296 \div 8 = 162$, so $1.296 \div 8 = 0.162$. If you are diving by a decimal, say $1.296 \div 0.08$, use the following idea: $6 \div 2 = 3$. What about $60 \div 20$ and $600 \div 200$ and $6000 \div 2000$? And what do those answers tell us?"

Mike: "They are all 3 as well."

Linda: "So in a divide sum, if you make both numbers ten times bigger or a hundred times bigger the answer doesn't change."

Teacher: "That's right; so to divide by a decimal, make the decimal into a whole number, see how many times you made it bigger and then change the other number in exactly the same way. So for $1.296 \div 0.08$ what do we do?"

Mike: "Change 0.08 to 8; that's 100 times bigger."

Nadeem: "Then make 1.296 a hundred times bigger to be 129.6."

Linda: "Then do $129.6 \div 8$; that's 16.2."

Teacher: "That's right. You can also use the method in the opposite way: To do $0.15 \div 300 \ldots$"

Linda: "Would you make them both a hundred times smaller, to $0.0015 \div 3 = 0.0005$?"

Teacher: "Yes, that's it! So now you know what to do to multiply and divide by decimals."

# 3 Adding fractions

Teacher: "We're going to try adding fractions; for instance $\frac{2}{5}+\frac{1}{15}$."

Linda: "I know how to do that! I learned it at my last school. You just do $\frac{2\times15+5\times1}{5\times15}$, that's $\frac{35}{75}$."

Nadeem: "Do you know why that works?"

Linda: "No; that's just what I was taught to do."

Teacher: "And would you know how to add up three fractions, say $\frac{2}{5}+\frac{1}{15}+\frac{3}{10}$?"

Linda: "No, we didn't learn that yet."

Mike: "Isn't it easier just to add the top numbers and the bottom numbers and make $\frac{3}{20}$?"

Teacher: "It's easy enough, but does $\frac{3}{20}$ really look big enough to be the result of adding $\frac{2}{5}$ and $\frac{1}{15}$? It's actually less than $\frac{2}{5}$ but more than $\frac{1}{15}$: that is not the way to add fractions! I want to show you a way you will understand, and that will work equally well for more than two fractions. Let's start with a simpler one: $\frac{2}{7}+\frac{3}{7}$. Have a look at the diagram on this page. The whole chocolate bar has been divided into seven equal pieces. What fraction is shaded with lines from bottom left to top right?"

Mike: "Two pieces so that's two sevenths."

Teacher: "Yes; and how much is shaded the other way, from top left to bottom right?"

Linda: "Three sevenths. So the total shaded is five sevenths. Is that to show that $\frac{2}{7} + \frac{3}{7} = \frac{5}{7}$ ?"

Teacher: "That's right. Whenever two fractions have the same denominator (the number on the bottom) you can just add the numerators (the numbers on the top.)"

Nadeem: "So the problem is when the denominators are different."

Teacher: "Yes, that's what we need to look at now. The good news is that we can express a fraction in different ways with different numbers on top and bottom without actually changing the fraction. Have a look at this next bar. How much of it is shaded?"

Mike: "Two fifths."

Teacher: "Yes. Now look at it again below."

Linda: "It's still two fifths but each fifth has been divided into three."

Nadeem: "It's now in fifteen parts of which six are shaded. So $\frac{2}{5} = \frac{6}{15}$ ."

Teacher: "That's right. Notice that each of the original fifths was cut into three smaller pieces and so the whole bar was divided into three times as many pieces. $2 \times 3 = 6$ and $5 \times 3 = 15$."

Mike: "So if you had divided each fifth into 4 pieces there would now be $2 \times 4 = 8$ shaded pieces and $5 \times 4 = 20$ pieces altogether, making $\frac{2}{5} = \frac{8}{20}$ ?"

Teacher: "Yes indeed; if you multiply the 2 and the 5 each by the same number, you get another fraction that equals $\frac{2}{5}$. The same applies to any other fraction, and indeed to any division. Think of $6 \div 2 = 3$. What is $60 \div 20$? And what about $6000 \div 2000$?"

Mike: "They are both 3 as well."

Teacher: "That's right; and a fraction is really a division sum written in a different way: $2 \div 5 = \frac{2}{5}$. We can also do the process in reverse: if you start with $\frac{24}{36}$ for instance . . . '"

Linda: "Can you divide 24 and 36 each by 12 and make it $\frac{2}{3}$?"

Teacher: "That's exactly it. Now coming back to our addition sum, $\frac{2}{5} + \frac{1}{15}$, we can replace this by $\frac{6}{15} + \frac{1}{15}$, making $\frac{7}{15}$ ."

Linda: "Is that the same as the answer I gave, $\frac{35}{75}$?"

Nadeem: "Yes, you just divide top and bottom by 7."

Teacher: "Yes, Linda's method gets the right answer, but sometimes in a needlessly more complicated form."

Mike: "What about the sum with three fractions, $\frac{2}{5}+\frac{1}{15}+\frac{3}{10}$?"

Teacher: "Right. The problem with that one is that turning $\frac{2}{5}$ into $\frac{6}{15}$ is not so useful, because we still have the two denominators 15 and 10. We need to find a number that is in the 5 times table and in the 15 times table and in the 10 times table. We call that a common multiple of 5, 15 and 10."

Linda: "So it's in 5, 10, 15, 20 . . . and in 15, 30, 45, 60 . . . and in 10, 20, 30, 40 . . ."

Nadeem: "How about 60?"

Teacher: "60 is a common multiple, but there is a smaller one."

Mike: "It's 30."

Teacher: "Right. 30 is the lowest common multiple (LCM) of 5, 15 and 10, so it is also the lowest common denominator that the three fractions can have."

Linda: "So we replace $\frac{2}{5}$ by $\frac{2\times6}{5\times6}=\frac{12}{30}$ . . ."

Nadeem: "And $\frac{1}{15}$ by $\frac{2}{30}$ and $\frac{3}{10}$ by $\frac{9}{30}$ . . ."

Mike: "So it makes $\frac{12}{30}+\frac{2}{30}+\frac{9}{30}=\frac{23}{30}$."

Teacher: "Right, you've got it! Now we'll try $\frac{3}{5}+\frac{4}{7}$. Which is the first number that's in the 5 times table and the 7 times table?"

Nadeem: "I think that must be $5\times7=35$."

Teacher: "That's right; because 5 and 7 have no common factor you have to multiply them to get the LCM."

Linda: "Then it becomes $\frac{3\times7}{35}+\frac{5\times4}{35}=\frac{41}{35}$; that's the same way I learned at my last school!"

Teacher: "Yes, in that example where you could only get a common multiple by multiplying the two denominators, that method gives the simplest answer. At least now I hope you understand why that is a correct method."

Linda: "I do; but should the answer be left as $\frac{41}{35}$ with the top more than the bottom? Isn't that a top-heavy fraction?"

| Teacher: | "Yes, also known as an improper fraction, though there isn't anything wrong about it. But it is more than 1, so would often be expressed as a mixed number." |
|---|---|
| Mike: | "1 is the same as $\frac{35}{35}$ and $41-35 = 6$ so $\frac{41}{35} = 1\frac{6}{35}$." |
| Teacher: | "That's it. Now try $7\frac{2}{9} - 4\frac{5}{6}$." |
| Linda: | "Can we just do $7 - 4 = 3$?" |
| Teacher: | "Yes; when you add or subtract mixed numbers you can keep the whole numbers separate from the fractions. Later when you multiply and divide it will be different; but not with subtraction." |
| Nadeem: | "We need a number in the 9 times table: 9, 18, 27, 36 . . . and in the 6 times table: 6, 12, 18, 24 . . ." |
| Mike: | "That's 18, the LCM of 9 and 6. So then $\frac{2}{9} - \frac{5}{6} = \frac{4}{18} - \frac{15}{18}$." |
| Linda: | "How do we do that? It's going to be negative!" |
| Teacher: | "Yes, but altogether you have $3 + \frac{4}{18} - \frac{15}{18}$, so the answer won't be negative. Write the 3 as $2 + 1$ and turn the 1 into a fraction; can you see what fraction?" |
| Mike: | "It needs to have denominator 18, so it must be $\frac{18}{18}$." |
| Nadeem: | "So that makes $2 + \frac{18}{18} + \frac{4}{18} - \frac{15}{18}$." |
| Linda: | "That's $2\frac{7}{18}$." |
| Teacher: | "Well done all! You've got the idea." |

# Multiplying and dividing by fractions; and by 0

Nadeem: "Sir, I tried to do 19 ÷ 8 and I got 2, remainder 3, but Linda made it $2\frac{3}{8}$ and Mike said it's 2.375. Which of those is right?"

Teacher: "They could each be right, depending on the context. Let's say first you are sharing 19 marbles among 8 children. How many does each get?"

Linda: "They get 2 each and there are 3 marbles left over."

Teacher: "That's right. No one would want a fraction of a marble; you can't do anything with it. But what if it were 19 muesli bars to be shared among 8?"

Nadeem: "They get 2 each, then you can divide each of the remaining 3 into 8 pieces, so each child gets $2\frac{3}{8}$."

Teacher: "And if it were money, with £19 to be shared out among 8?"

Mike: "That's when you'd use decimals and make it £2.375; but actually you can't do that these days as there are no halfpenny coins any more. So to be totally fair you'd give each £2.37 and have 4p left over."

Teacher: "That's right; division of money doesn't usually work out exactly to 2DP. But you see the point: a quotient and remainder is sometimes the best answer, as with marbles where fractions are useless; otherwise, for such items as muesli bars or money, give a whole number plus a fraction or a decimal."

Nadeem: "What if there is no context given – you are just told to work out 19 ÷ 8?"

Teacher: "Then treat it like muesli bars, give $2\frac{3}{8}$, as that's an exact answer.

But we are going to do multiplying and dividing by fractions, so now look at the following sums:

12 × 4 = 48

12 × 2 = 24

12 × 1 = 12

What is happening to the multipliers and the answers?"

Linda:      "They are both being halved each time; 4 to 2 to 1 and 48 to 24 to 12."

Teacher:    "Right. And what are the next two lines going to be?"

Nadeem:     "$12 \times \frac{1}{2} = 6$ and $12 \times \frac{1}{4} = 3$."

Mike:       "So multiplying by a half is the same as dividing by 2."

Linda:      "And multiplying by a quarter is the same as dividing by 4."

Teacher:    "Yes. What do you think multiplying by one third or one fifth would do?"

Nadeem:     "That would be like dividing by 3 or by 5."

Teacher:    "Good. So what about $12 \times \frac{2}{3}$ ?"

Mike:       "That should be twice as big as $12 \times \frac{1}{3}$, so that's $12 \div 3 \times 2 = 8$."

Teacher:    "Right. So what does multiplying by $\frac{5}{8}$ do to a number?"

Linda:      "It divides it by 8 and then multiplies by 5."

Teacher:    "OK. So can you do $\frac{3}{7} \times \frac{5}{8}$ ?"

Linda:      "You'd have to divide $\frac{3}{7}$ by 8 – make it 8 times smaller, and then multiply by 5."

Nadeem:     "You can make it smaller by making the denominator bigger, from 7 to $7 \times 8 = 56$."

Mike:       "And then multiply the numerator by 5 to make the answer 5 times bigger."

Linda:      "So that's $\frac{3 \times 5}{7 \times 8} = \frac{15}{56}$. You just have to multiply the two numerators and the two denominators; is that it?"

Teacher:    "Yes; multiplying is about the most straightforward process with fractions – easier than adding – because basically a fraction is just a division sum, and division is so closely related to multiplication, as we'll see shortly. What about $5\frac{1}{3} \times 1\frac{1}{8}$ ?"

Mike:       "Is it just $5 \times 1 + \frac{1}{3} \times \frac{1}{8}$ ? That would be $5\frac{1}{24}$."

Teacher:    "No. If you want to keep the whole numbers and fractions separate (which is the best way when you are adding or subtracting) you have to think of it as $\left(5 + \frac{1}{3}\right) \times \left(1 + \frac{1}{8}\right)$, which includes $5 \times \frac{1}{3}$ and $\frac{1}{8} \times 1$ when you multiply it all out. But that makes it rather complicated, because you have to add fractions with different denominators. It's better when multiplying to turn mixed numbers into improper fractions."

Nadeem: "So that's $\frac{16}{3} \times \frac{9}{8} = \frac{144}{24}$."

Linda: "That cancels down to 6, doesn't it?"

Teacher: "Yes, and there's a better way to manage the calculation. Think of it as $\frac{16 \times 9}{3 \times 8}$ and then ask 'What can I divide the top and bottom by?'"

Mike: "You can divide them both by 8; that makes $\frac{2 \times 9}{3 \times 1}$."

Linda: "And by 3, so you get $\frac{2 \times 3}{1 \times 1} = 6$."

Teacher: "Good; that's the way to do it if possible, rather than doing all the multiplications on top and bottom and then trying to see if you can cancel."

Nadeem: "Can we do division as well?"

Teacher: "OK. Suppose you have just multiplied a number by 5, say $12 \times 5 = 60$. What would you do to undo that and get back to the number you started with?"

Linda: "You'd have to divide by 5; $60 \div 5$ gets you back to 12."

Teacher: "Yes. Could you do it by a multiplication? Can you multiply 60 by something and get 12?"

Mike: "Yes, we did that before: multiplying by $\frac{1}{5}$ is the same as dividing by 5."

Teacher: "That's right. Multiplying by $\frac{1}{5}$ makes a number 5 times smaller, which is the same as dividing by 5. So now, what if you started with 60 and multiplied it by $\frac{1}{5}$?"

Nadeem: "That makes 12."

Teacher: "Yes. Could you undo that process and get back to 60?"

Mike: "Easy; multiply by 5."

Linda: "You could also do it by dividing by $\frac{1}{5}$, couldn't you? Or does it make sense to divide by $\frac{1}{5}$?"

Nadeem: "You could share £60 among 5 people, but you can't share £12 among a fifth of a person; it just doesn't make sense."

Curiously, sharing among a mixed number of entities seems less problematic. Suppose for example that £60 000 is to be shared equally among $6\frac{2}{3}$ battalions. How much does each battalion get? The reader would presume that a battalion normally consists of 3 companies, but that in this case one of the battalions only has 2; so we divide the money among $6 \times 3 + 2 = 20$ companies, giving £3000 per company and hence $3 \times £3000 = £9000$ per complete battalion. Effectively we have done $60000 \div \frac{20}{3} = (60\ 000 \div 20) \times 3$, which incidentally is the same as $60\ 000 \times \frac{3}{20}$, illustrating the usual rule "invert and multiply." However, intuition does not easily allow the same sharing approach when faced with division by a proper fraction such as $\frac{1}{5}$.

Teacher: "That's right; but dividing doesn't always have to mean sharing. Suppose you have 12 kg of rice and you're making it into parcels. If there are 4 kg in each parcel how many parcels does it make?"

Linda: "Easy; 3 parcels: $12 \div 4 = 3$."

Teacher: "OK. What if there are 2 kg in each parcel? Or 1 kg? Or $\frac{1}{2}$ kg?"

Mike: "That would be $12 \div 2 = 6$ parcels, or $12 \div 1 = 12 \ldots$"

Nadeem: "Or with $\frac{1}{2}$ a kg in each parcel it's 24 parcels; so $12 \div \frac{1}{2} = 24$. Oh, so I guess you can divide by $\frac{1}{5}$, and $12 \div \frac{1}{5} = 60$."

The two interpretations of division, sharing and parcelling, are related to the asymmetry in the original definition of multiplication. We think of 3 4s, or $3 \times 4$, as $4 + 4 + 4$, effectively 3 parcels of 4 added up, while 4 3s is $3 + 3 + 3 + 3$, 4 parcels of 3. It is not obvious from the definition that the two answers should be the same, as the two factors' roles are quite different. But think of a rectangular array of dots with either 4 rows and 3 columns or 3 rows and 4 columns; a 90° turn transforms one into the other. I have read of a future mathematician (I cannot recall who!) being greatly excited to discover as a child that swapping round the two factors does not change the answer of a multiplication, and then being disappointed that his teacher responded to this discovery with such nonchalance!

Teacher: "That's right. Multiplying by 5 exactly undoes multiplying by $\frac{1}{5}$, and hence is the same as dividing by $\frac{1}{5}$. What about dividing by $\frac{3}{5}$? Try starting with 12 kg of rice again."

Linda: "When the parcels were $\frac{1}{5}$ kg each there were 60 parcels. Now the parcels are 3 times as big, so there will be 3 times less, only 20."

Mike: "So to divide by $\frac{3}{5}$ we multiply by 5 and divide by 3. That's the same as multiplying by $\frac{5}{3}$, isn't it?"

Teacher: "Yes; and think about it: suppose you multiply a number by $\frac{3}{5}$ and then multiply the answer by $\frac{5}{3}$. What have you done altogether?"

Nadeem: "That's multiplying by $\frac{3}{5} \times \frac{5}{3}$, which makes 1; so it leaves the number unchanged."

Note that Nadeem is taking for granted the *associative* property of multiplication: that $(a \times b) \times c$ is always the same as $a \times (b \times c)$, which justifies the use of expressions like *abc* or $a \times b \times c$ being written without brackets. At this level that property can be assumed as known from experience.

Teacher: "Exactly. The numbers $\frac{3}{5}$ and $\frac{5}{3}$ are called *reciprocals*. Multiplying by one of them can be undone by multiplying by the other."

Mike: "So to divide by $\frac{7}{8}$ you would turn it upside down and multiply by $\frac{8}{7}$ ?"

Teacher: "Yes. Multiplying by $\frac{b}{a}$ exactly undoes multiplication by $\frac{a}{b}$. Each is the reciprocal of the other."

Linda: "So dividing by a small fraction can give a big answer?"

Teacher: "Yes, because it undoes multiplying by a small fraction; thus $600 \times \frac{1}{200} = 3$, which is much smaller than 600, and $3 \div \frac{1}{200} = 3 \times 200 = 600$, much bigger than 3."

Nadeem: "What about dividing by 0? Does $12 \div 0 = 12$, because you're not really dividing by anything?"

Teacher: "Think of those 12 kg of rice being made up into parcels. We saw before that if each parcel had $\frac{1}{5}$ kg there would be 60 parcels. What if each parcel had only 1 g, that's $\frac{1}{1000}$ of a kg?"

Linda: "There would be 12 000 parcels: $12 \div \frac{1}{1000} = 12 \times 1000 = 12\,000$."

Nadeem: "Oh, and if each parcel had just one millionth of a kg, there would be twelve million parcels. So if each parcel had 0 kg then there would be an infinite amount of parcels; you could never use up the 12 kg."

Teacher: "That's right. We sometimes say $1 \div 0 = \infty$, the 8 on its side being the symbol for infinity. But $\infty$ is not a number; it's an extra symbol that is a shorthand for the fact that $1 \div x$ increases without limit if $x$ is made closer and closer to 0. Think of it another way: division is meant to undo multiplication: if I tell you that I've multiplied a number by $\frac{3}{5}$ and got an answer of 9, can you work out what number I started with?"

Mike: "It's $9 \div \frac{3}{5} = 9 \times \frac{5}{3} = 15$."

Teacher: "That's right. But what if I tell you I multiplied a number by 0 and got 12; can you tell me the number I started with?"

Linda: "There's no such number! You can't get 12 by multiplying a number by 0. You can only get 0."

Teacher: "That's right. That means that 12 cannot be divided by 0. Now what if I tell you I multiplied a number by 0 and got 0; can you tell me the number I started with?"

Nadeem:  "Well, it could be any number."

Mike:    "So 12 ÷ 0 is impossible and 0 ÷ 0 can be any number."

Teacher:  "That's right. Multiplying by 0 turns every number into 0, so there's no way it can be undone. Now here are some examples for you to try."

## Exercise

**1**  Find, if possible, the unit price in £ per litre for:

    a    $2\frac{1}{2}$ litres of milk costing £1.20

    b    $\frac{1}{50}$ litre of bubblejet printer ink costing £18.60

    c    0 litres of orange juice costing 50p

    d    0 litres of petrol costing £0.

**2**  Find, if possible, the speed of each of the following:

    a    A car that goes 24 miles in $\frac{3}{4}$ of an hour

    b    Light travelling 1200 km in $\frac{1}{250}$ of a second

    c    A spaceship that goes 200 km in 0 sec

    d    A helicopter that flies 0 km in 0 sec.

# Using patterns with negative numbers, or do two minuses really make a plus?

**5**

| | |
|---|---|
| Teacher: | "What's −3 − 8?" |
| Linda: | "Is it 11? Two minuses make a plus, don't they?" |
| Teacher: | "Sometimes they do, but often they don't. I don't recommend using that saying at all. I'll tell you what to remember instead. To begin with, be prepared to think of a practical situation, either a temperature scale or a bank account. What if the temperature starts at −3 and then goes down 8?" |
| Mike: | "That would bring it down to −11." |
| Teacher: | "Good. Or if you had −£3 in your bank account: what does that mean?" |
| Linda: | "It means you took out £3 when there was no money in the account, so now you owe the bank £3." |
| Teacher: | "Right, so now, starting with −£3 you take out £8. How much does that leave?" |
| Linda: | "That would be −£11." |
| Teacher: | "Yes, so you can see that way as well that −3 − 8 = −11 . Now what about 15 + −4?" |
| Nadeem: | "I can't see how you can add a negative temperature or add a negative amount to a bank account." |
| Teacher: | "OK, for this one let's suppose you have two bank accounts, with £15 in one and −£4 in the other. How much do you have in the bank altogether?" |
| Nadeem: | "That's £11, because you could use £4 from the £15 to cancel the debt in the other account." |
| Teacher: | "Yes, so 15 + −4 is the same as 15 − 4. What about −8 + −12?" |

Mike: "That means you're in debt on both accounts, a total debt of £20, so it's −20."

Teacher: "Yes; and what would −8 − 12 be?"

Linda: "That's 12 lower than −8, which is −20; same as −8 + −12."

Teacher: "Good. So here is the first principle to use with negative numbers:
**Adding a negative number is the same as taking away a positive number**.
Now we're going to look at taking away a negative number. Let's first look at:

$$7 - 3 = 4$$
$$7 - 2 = 5$$
$$7 - 1 = 6$$
$$7 - 0 = 7.$$

What is happening to the answers?"

Nadeem: "They're getting one bigger each time, because you're taking away less."

Teacher: "Right, so what should the next line be?"

Nadeem: "It starts with 7 − −1, and the next number on the right hand side has to be 8, so is that the answer? And would 7 − −2 be 9, and so on?"

Teacher: "That's right. If you find that a bit odd, think of temperature. How much higher is 7° than 2°?"

Linda: "5° of course; just do 7 − 2."

Teacher: "That's right; and how much higher is 7° than −2°?"

Mike: "That's 9°, same as 7 + 2; you go 7 down from 7 to 0 and then another 2 down to −2."

Teacher: "Good. Another way to think of it: imagine that you have two bank accounts and one of them has −£2000 in it, meaning that on that account you owe the bank £2000. Now suppose that a rich and kind uncle offered to take from you the account with −£2000 and have it transferred to his own name. What effect does that have on your total wealth?"

Linda: "You'd be £2000 better off than before; taking away the minus £2000 is just like giving you £2000."

Teacher: "Yes, and that's the second principle to use:
**Taking away a negative number is the same as adding a positive number**."

The use of the pattern in the series of subtraction sums has made the children find for themselves how to take away a negative number, while the explanations in a practical context help them to see that it all makes sense. These are important parts of the teaching/learning process, without which many children come to regard maths as a game in which the teacher knows the arbitrary rules, while the child's unhappy lot is to try to pick up what they are and to memorise them for tests and exams!

Teacher: "Now let's have a look at multiplication. What is $-4 \times 3$?"

Nadeem: "That would be three lots of $-4$, must be $-12$."

Teacher: "Right; multiplying a negative and a positive number together gives a negative answer; probably just what you would expect. Now look at this:

$$-4 \times 3 = -12$$

$$-4 \times 2 = -8$$

$$-4 \times 1 = -4$$

$$-4 \times 0 = 0.$$

What is happening to the answers?"

Linda: "Getting smaller?"

Mike: "Getting closer to 0, but if those were temperatures, they are getting higher."

Teacher: "Yes, and if they were bank balances they are also getting higher, closer and closer to coming out of debt. Now what are the next three lines?"

Nadeem: "$-4 \times -1 = 4$

$-4 \times -2 = 8$

$-4 \times -3 = 12$."

Teacher: "Good; those results preserve the pattern you've seen of answers steadily increasing as you decrease the number that $-4$ is being multiplied by. Now think of the number line with 0 in the centre and positive numbers on the right and negatives on the left. If you multiply all the numbers by $-1$ what happens to all the positive numbers, and can you describe that in a geometric way?"

Linda: "They go negative, so it's like the positive side of the number line has turned through $180°$."

Teacher: "Good; and if you do that to the whole number line what happens to the negative numbers?"

Mike: "They go to the positive side; so that shows how multiplying a negative number by $-1$ makes a positive number."

Teacher:     "Right. Now can you tell me the answer to $12 \div -4$?"

Nadeem:     "We had $-4 \times -3 = 12$, so $12 \div -4$ must be $-3$; that's the same as $-12 \div 4$ isn't it?"

Teacher:     "Right, and what about $-12 \div -4$?"

Linda:       "That must be 3, because we had $-4 \times 3 = -12$ earlier."

Teacher:     "Good; so what happens when we multiply or divide by a negative number?"

Mike:        "If you start with a positive number you get a negative answer, and if you start with a negative number the answer is positive."

Teacher:     "Right, so here is the third rule to remember:
             **Multiplying or dividing by a negative number causes a change of sign**."

Giving this a practical context is not so easy, because multiplication is rather more sophisticated than addition. I am reminded of an illustration given by one of the famous maths teachers (C. V. Durell?) of the early 20th century. He saw a car driving, let's say northward. The car did a half turn and began to drive southward, then stopped, engaged the reverse gear and began to drive northward again, while still facing south. The half turn and the engaging of reverse gear each had the effect of multiplying the velocity by $-1$, i.e. reversing the direction of travel. When both were done, the two reversals cancelled each other, illustrating $-1 \times (-1) = 1$.

This visualisation incidentally (at a later stage!) gives an approach to the square root of $-1$. What operation when done twice results in a half turn? Answer: a quarter turn, in either direction. Hence we get the imaginary axis in the Argand diagram, at right angles to the real axis, with the two square roots of $-1$ at the points $(0, 1)$ and $(0, -1)$. They are called $i$ and $-i$ respectively, because their sum is 0, but the labels could easily have been assigned in the other way: neither is more negative than the other.

Another possible illustration of multiplying by a negative number involves times and rates. Suppose the water surface in a harbour is at mean sea level at noon, and is rising steadily at $v$ cm/min. Then the height $h$ cm above mean sea level at time $t$ minutes past noon is given by $h = v \times t$. Suppose $v = 3$. Then at time $t = 2$ the height is 6 cm, while at $t = -2$ (2 minutes before noon) it is $-6$ cm, i.e. 6 cm below mean sea level. If instead $v = -3$, then the water level is actually falling at 3 cm/min, which means that before noon the water was higher than mean sea level; so for $t = -2$ the calculation $-3 \times (-2)$ is right to give the positive answer 6. This illustration does take some setting up, and would not be worth the effort with every class.

Having learned to cope with negative numbers and the four rules, at a later stage comes the opening of **brackets with a minus sign in front**. Again, we want to lead the children to see that the rules they have to learn are the outcome of common sense.

Teacher:     "What is $30 + (8 + 3)$? And how about $30 + 8 + 3$?"

Linda:      "They're both 41, aren't they? Does the bracket make a difference?"

Teacher:    "You're right, there's no difference. Now what about 30 − (8 + 3) and
             30 − 8 + 3?"

Mike:       "They're not the same. 30 − (8 + 3) = 30 − 11 = 19 and 30 − 8 + 3 =
             22 + 3 = 25."

Nadeem:     "To get the same answer without the brackets you have to do 30 − 8 − 3."

Teacher:    "That's right; if you want to take away 8 + 3 you take away 8 and also take
             away 3. Now what about 20 − (9 − 2)?"

Linda:      "That's 20 − 7 = 13, or you could do 20 − 9 + 2, because taking away 9 is
             taking away too much when you are supposed to be taking away only 9 − 2,
             so you add back 2."

Teacher:    "Good. Here's a practical example: You pay 20p for a chocolate bar that
             is normally 9p, and expect 11p change. However, there is a special offer: a
             discount of 2p. This gives you 2p *more* change than usual. So how would you
             write $a − (b + c)$ and $a − (b − c)$ without brackets?"

Nadeem:     "$a − (b + c) = a − b − c$ and $a − (b − c) = a − b + c$."

Teacher:    "That's right, and gives us the rule:

            **A minus sign in front of a bracket causes all the signs inside to be
            changed when the brackets are removed.**

            Do notice that, when the terms inside the bracket had the same sign as each
            other (i.e. $b + c$) then they still have the same sign as each other, now $−b − c$,
            when the bracket is removed. And if the signs were different to start with
            ($b − c$) then they are still different, $−b + c$, after the bracket is removed."

## What about "two minuses make a plus"?

It depends on the context! In $10 − (−3) = 10 + 3$ and in $−10 × (−3) = 30$ they do, but in
$−10 − 3 = −13$ they don't.

I find it safer to teach and encourage the use of the rules above. If the children have seen
that they make sense, and have had some practice in their use, they should soon be handling
negative number arithmetic with confidence and reasonable ease.

# Use hundreds and thousands, not apples and bananas!

Helping beginners make sense of algebra

| | |
|---|---|
| Mike: | "Sir, why can't $3a + 4b$ be simplified to make $7ab$?" |
| Linda: | "My last teacher told us that 3 apples plus 4 bananas don't make 7 apples bananas." |
| Teacher: | "That's true; but did he also tell you that 2 apples times 3 bananas makes 6 apples bananas? Because $2a \times 3b$ does actually make $6ab$." |
| Nadeem: | "That's confusing. How can you have 6 apples bananas? It doesn't make sense." |
| Teacher: | "You're quite right, it doesn't make sense. That's because letters in algebra don't stand for kinds of fruit. Do you know what they stand for?" |
| Mike: | "They stand for numbers, don't they? But why do we need letters to stand for numbers when we've got 1, 2, 3 and so on already?" |
| Teacher: | "Good question! Why use letters for numbers?" |
| Linda: | "We've learned to use $\pi$ in the formula for a circle's circumference; is that because the actual number is so long and complicated?" |
| Teacher: | "Yes, in fact that number when written as a decimal goes on for ever, and even the version stored on a calculator has over ten digits and would be tedious to write out. But that's a rather special case. |
| | Mostly we use letters either to stand for numbers we don't know yet, or because we are looking at some number pattern and don't want to tie ourselves down to any particular number. Suppose we are told that a number was multiplied by 5, then 9 added and the answer was 144. Let's use a letter to represent the number; we often use $x$ in this sort of problem." |

Nadeem: "So then we have $5 \times x + 9 = 144$."

Teacher: "Yes, that's called an equation, and finding the value of $x$ is called solving the equation. We normally write $5 \times x$ as $5x$; if a number and a letter, or two letters, are next to each other without a sign then that means they are multiplied: it's a convention that saves a lot of writing! The technique for finding $x$ is to keep doing things that make the equation simpler, till at the end it is just $x =$ something; then it's been solved. What is happening to $x$ in the equation we are solving?"

Mike: "It's being multiplied by 5 and then 9 is added. Should we divide by 5?"

Teacher: "You could: that would change the $5x$ to just $x$; but you have to do that division by 5 to each side, to keep the sides equal. Think of a football game among friends, with just 9 on each side. If two more friends arrived and they both joined one team to make it up to 11, would that be fair?"

Nadeem: "Of course not; the teams would then be unequal. Instead one should be added to each team to make 10 against 10."

Mike: "And if you divide by 5 you get $x + 9 \div 5 = 144 \div 5$, which looks more complicated."

Teacher: "Yes. Think of how you dress in the morning, putting socks on and then shoes. What order do you take in taking them off?"

Linda: "Shoes off first of course; you can't take the socks off with the shoes on!"

Teacher: "Right; and when two or more things are being done to $x$ it's best to start by undoing the last, then the next to last and so on."

Mike: "So we take off 9 to make $5x = 144 - 9 = 135$."

Nadeem: "Then we can change $5x$ back to $x$ by dividing by 5: $x = 135 \div 5 = 27$."

Teacher: "Good, and you can check the answer by working out $5 \times 27 + 9$."

Linda: "It makes $135 + 9 = 144$."

Teacher: "Right. Now coming back to the other reason for using letters for numbers; that's when we are investigating patterns that we think work for all numbers, and we want to express them without being tied to particular numbers. For instance what is 200 plus 300? And 2000 plus 3000?"

Nadeem: "Easy: 500 and 5000. And 2 000 000 plus 3 000 000 makes 5 000 000."

Teacher: "Quite right; and also two dozen plus three dozen makes five dozen. These are illustrating the fact that two times any number plus three times the same number makes five times that number. This can be expressed by letting $n$ stand for any number and saying $2 \times n + 3 \times n = 5 \times n$, which can be shortened to

$2n + 3n = 5n$, using the agreement that $2n$ means the same as $2 \times n$. What about $3n + 4n$?"

Linda:      "That's $7n$ because $3 + 4 = 7$; you just add the two numbers in front of $n$."

Teacher:    "Good; and that can be expressed by saying that $xn + yn =$ what?"

Mike:       "$x + yn$?"

Teacher:    "Not quite. Think of $2 + 3 \times 100$. What is that?"

Mike:       "It could be 500 or it could be 302, depending on whether you add first or multiply first."

Linda:      "Isn't there a rule called BIDMAS to tell you what order to do things in? That's Brackets, Indices, Divide, Multiply, Add, Subtract."

Teacher:    "Quite right; that's again an agreement among users of maths to avoid ambiguity in a sum like $2 + 3 \times 100$."

Linda:      "So you'd do the times first and get 302, which is not what we wanted."

Nadeem:     "To get it right you put brackets and make it $(2 + 3) \times 100$."

Teacher:    "That's right; and likewise you use brackets to express $xn + yn$ as $(x + y)n$. We use letters to stand for numbers so as not to be tied down to particular numbers. $xn + yn = (x + y)n$ is true no matter what numbers $x$, $y$ and $n$ stand for."

Mike:       "So what about $3a + 4b$?"

Teacher:    "OK, let's look at that. If $a$ is 1000 and $b$ is 100, what is $3a + 4b$?"

Mike:       "That would be $3000 + 400 = 3400$."

Teacher:    "Right; is that the same as $7 \times 1000 \times 100$? Because that's what $7ab$ would be."

Mike:       "No, it's not really 7 times anything. In fact the answer 3400 shows the 3 and the 4 still there."

Teacher:    "That's right; and if you made $a = 1\ 000\ 000$ and $b = 1000$, what is $3a + 4b$ then?"

Nadeem:     "3 004 000, that's 3 000 000 and 4000; the 3 and 4 are still visible."

Teacher:    "Right, so can you see that you shouldn't expect to simplify $3a + 4b$ to 7 times something?"

Linda:      "Yes; but is it different if you multiply, say $2a$ by $3b$?"

Teacher:    "Well, what is $2 \times 100$ times $3 \times 1000$?"

Linda:      "It's 600 000 which is $6 \times 100 \times 1000$; so $6ab$ is right, is it?"

| Teacher: | "Yes; in fact you have $2 \times a \times 3 \times b$. You can rearrange that to make $2 \times 3 \times a \times b$ which gives $6ab$." |
|---|---|
| Mike: | "So you say can generally that $ma \times nb = mnab$, but you can't do anything with $ma + nb$. What about simplifying $5x + x$?" |
| Teacher: | "Well, what is 500 plus 100? And 5000 plus 1000?" |
| Mike: | "They're 600 and 6000. So $5x + x = 6x$, does it?" |
| Teacher: | "Yes; after all $x$ is the same as $1x$ or $1 \times x$, and you know what to do with $5x + 1x$." |
| Linda: | "And what about $2x + 3$?" |
| Nadeem: | "If $x$ is 100 you get 203, or if $x$ is 1 000 000 you get 2 000 003, so the 3 stays separate from the 2; it doesn't make 5 of anything." |
| Teacher: | "Good; and likewise $5a^2 + 2a$ can't be combined into 7 times something. To see that, try it with $a = 10$; what does $5a^2 + 2a$ make then?" |
| Mike: | "$5a^2$ is $50^2 = 2500$, is that right?" |
| Linda: | "No, that's wrong! BIDMAS says you do the index first, so it's $5 \times 10^2$ which is 500, and then you add 20 to make 520; and it's not a multiple of 7 so you can't combine $5a^2$ and $2a$ to make 7 times something." |
| Teacher: | "That's right. Now see if you can simplify $39a + 8b - 12a - 7b + 5a - 2b$." |
| Nadeem: | "Is it $22a + 3b$? I took $12a + 5a$ away from $39a$ and $7b - 2b$ away from $8b$." |
| Teacher: | "No. To deal with $39a - 12a + 5a$ suppose you have £39 000 in the bank and you draw out £12 000 and then put in £5000. What's the combined effect of those two transactions?" |
| Nadeem: | "It's the same as taking out £7000, leaving £32 000." |
| Teacher: | "That's right. It's not the same as taking out £12 000 + £5000. And if you take out £700 and then take out £200, what does that do?" |
| Nadeem: | "It means you've taken out £900 altogether. So in fact $39a + 8b - 12a - 7b + 5a - 2b$ should simplify to $32a - b$ should it?" |
| Teacher: | "That's right; and you could see what to do once you had numbers like thousands or hundreds instead of the letters $a$ and $b$. Whenever you get stuck in algebra, try replacing some of the letters with numbers, often you then know what to do. Now we are ready to try another equation: $15x - 48 = 72 - 25x$." |
| Mike: | "It's got $x$ occurring on both sides. Can we get rid of the $-25x$?" |
| Linda: | "You could add $25x$ to undo taking away $25x$. That makes $15x - 48 + 25x = 72$, so that $40x - 48 = 72$." |

Nadeem: "Then add 48 and get $40x = 72 + 48 = 120$. So then $x = 3$."

Teacher: "Well done. How would you check that?"

Mike: "$15 \times 3 - 48 = 72 - 25 \times 3$, so $45 - 48 = 72 - 75$, so $-3 = -3$. It works!"

Teacher: "But you were not meant to be proving that $-3 = -3$; we know that already. You were to show that the two sides are equal when $x = 3$. A better way is to work out the two sides separately: $15 \times 3 - 48 = 45 - 48 = -3$ and $72 - 25 \times 3 = 72 - 75 = -3$ Now observe that the two sides have the same value $-3$ when $x = 3$. But you're doing well with equations: let's try one with fractions: $\dfrac{2x+5}{3} - \dfrac{x+8}{12} = \dfrac{4}{3}$ ."

Linda: "Do we start by combining the fractions into one, using a common denominator?"

Teacher: "You could, but as you are solving an equation with two sides instead of just simplifying an expression you have a more convenient option: get rid of the fractions by multiplying both sides of the equation by whatever it takes to do that."

Mike: "That has to be a multiple of 3 and 12, so should it be $3 \times 12 = 36$ ? But no, 12 is enough."

Nadeem: "So then $12 \times \dfrac{2x+5}{3} - 12 \times \dfrac{x+8}{12} = 12 \times \dfrac{4}{3}$ , or $4(2x + 5) - x + 8 = 16$ "

Teacher: "No, you've got to watch out there. The fraction line in $\dfrac{x+8}{12}$ acts as a bracket: the whole of $x + 8$ is to be divided by 12. When you multiply by 12 you don't have the fraction line anymore, but the $x + 8$ is still to be treated as a unit and taken away from the $4(2x + 5)$. You now have to put brackets round to show that. And remember what happens when you next remove the brackets with a minus sign in front."

Linda: "The signs change, so now it's $4(2x + 5) - (x + 8) = 8x + 20 - x - 8 = 16$."

Mike: "So $7x + 12 = 16$, $7x = 4$. Now what? Does $x = 4 \div 7$? But 4 doesn't divide by 7, does it?"

Teacher: "Not to give a whole number, but suppose you have 4 chocolate bars to divide among 7 children; how would you do that?"

Linda: "Divide each bar into 7 equal pieces – I guess each piece is one seventh – and then each kid gets four of those, that's $\dfrac{4}{7}$. So $x = \dfrac{4}{7}$, does it?"

Teacher: "That's right. The fraction line is just another way of showing that you divide 4 by 7. Now let's see if we can solve the equation $ax + bx = c$ to get $x$ in terms of the other letters."

Silence.

Teacher:   "OK. Let's replace all the letters except $x$ by numbers."

Linda:   "We could make it $5x + 3x = 9$ maybe? Then that's $8x = 9$ so $x = \dfrac{9}{8}$."

Teacher:   "Good. Now look at what you did. How did $5x + 3x$ turn into $8x$?"

Mike:   "The 8 is just $5 + 3$, so with $ax + bx$ make it $(a + b)x$ ."

Nadeem:   "Then $(a + b)x = c$, so $x = \dfrac{c}{a + b}$ ."

Teacher:   "Well done! So you can see how replacing letters by specific numbers can often help you see what to do. How about $\dfrac{x}{bc} + \dfrac{x}{ca} + \dfrac{x}{ab} = 1$?"

Mike:   "You have to multiply by enough to clear all the fractions: that's just abc , isn't it?"

Linda:   "So you get $ax + bx + cx = abc$ , that makes $(a + b + c)x = abc$."

Nadeem:   "So then $x = \dfrac{abc}{a + b + c}$ ."

Teacher:   "That's right, well done all of you. Now we'll try a game: Think of a number, any number you like. Double it. Add 12. Add the number you first thought of. Divide by 3. Subtract the number you first thought of.

Now let 1 stand for A, 2 for B and so on. Turn your final answer into a letter, and think of a European country starting with that letter. Then think of an animal that starts with the last letter of the country, and a colour that starts with the last letter of the animal."

Pause.

Linda:   "I've got an orange kangaroo in Denmark."

Nadeem:   "So have I!"

Mike:   "Mine is an amber koala but it's still in Denmark."

Teacher:   "So, what numbers did you start with and what was your final answer?"

They had started with 7, 11 and 20, but all finished with 4, hence Denmark, etc.

Teacher:   "OK. How was it that you started with different numbers but all ended with 4? Here's where using a letter to stand for an unspecified number can help. Suppose you start with $n$. Then what happens?"

Mike:   "You double it, that makes $2n$, then add 12, so that's $2n + 12$."

Linda:   "Then you add $n$ again, so that's $3n + 12$."

Nadeem: "Then dividing by 3 makes $n + 4$ and taking away $n$ leaves 4: so that's why we all got the same answer!"

Teacher: "That's right; and it's the fact that $n$ can stand for 7 or 11 or 20 or just any number at all shows you that the final answer doesn't depend on what number you chose to start with.

Now here's a challenge for you. You remember the Fibonacci type sequence where each term is made by adding the previous term to the one before that, like for instance 4, 7, 11, 18, 29 ... Well, another such sequence starts with 17, and the 8th term is 526. Can you find the terms in between? Start by letting the second term be $x$. That's a letter standing for a definite number, but you don't know yet what that number is. Then the third term is $17 + x$."

Linda: "Then the fourth is $17 + x + x$ or $17 + 2x$."

Mike: "And the fifth is $17 + 2x + 17 + x = 34 + 3x$."

Teacher: "That's right; just carry on that way till the 8th and then you have an equation as the 8th term is to be 526. I'll leave the rest to you. Enjoy!"

# Angles and polygons

Mike:        "Why are there 90° in a right angle?"

Nadeem:      "Easy! It's a quarter of 360°."

Linda:       "But where does the 360 come from?"

Teacher:     "From history rather than from mathematics itself. The ancient Babylonians used a number system with a base 60 instead of 10. That's why an hour is divided into 60 minutes (minute parts) and a minute into 60 seconds (second minute parts; some people used third and fourth minute parts for even smaller subdivision.) Also 360, as well as being a multiple of 60 and having lots of factors, is close to the number of days in a year; so the circle was divided into 360 equal parts. The earth going round the sun travels just under one degree each day. So a full turn is 360°, a half turn is 180° and a right angle or quarter turn 90°."

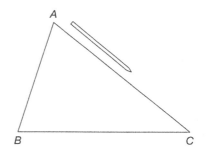

Mike:        "I've heard that the angles of a triangle always add up to 180°. Is there a reason for that?"

Teacher:     "Have a look at the triangle ABC. I've put my pencil along AC, pointing from A to C. Now I'm going to turn the pencil through the angle A of the triangle. Which way will it point then?"

Linda:       "From A to B?"

Teacher:     "That's right; see the next diagram. Then I'm going to turn the pencil through angle B and lastly through angle C. What does that do?"

Nadeem: "It will point from C to B and then from C to A."

Teacher: "Yes, look at it in the final position. How does that compare the original position?"

Linda: "It's pointing in the opposite direction to the way it was at the start."

Mike: "So that's a 180° turn. Aha! That's how the angles have to add up to 180°."

Nadeem: "Could we use that method with the pencil for a quadrilateral or a pentagon?"

Teacher: "Why not try it?"

Linda: "I've done it with a quadrilateral, and the pencil ended up turning right round and facing the same way as when it started."

Nadeem: "So that makes the angles of a quadrilateral add up to 360°."

Mike: "I've done it with a pentagon, and the pencil ends up facing the opposite way to the way it started; so is that 180°? That can't be right, can it?"

Teacher: "Try that again and watch carefully as the pencil goes round."

Mike: "Oh, I see. It turned right round and then did another half turn; so that's 540°."

Teacher: "Yes, and you could continue with a hexagon and so on. But there's a simpler way. If you take a quadrilateral and draw a diagonal, what do you get?"

Linda: "It divides into two triangles."

Nadeem: "And their angles add up to 180° each, so that makes 360°."

Mike: "And if you start with a pentagon you can draw two diagonals and make three triangles, so the angles add up to $3 \times 180° = 540°$."

Teacher: "Yes; and if you go on to a hexagon, you draw one more diagonal and make four triangles, and so it goes on, with the triangles increasing by 1 whenever the number of sides increases by 1. If you start with $n$ sides..."

Nadeem: "You have $n - 2$ triangles, so that angles add up to $(n - 2) \times 180°$."

Teacher: "Yes, and that's a useful result. For instance, how big is each angle in a regular dodecagon, with 12 sides"

Linda: "The angle sum is $(12 - 2) \times 180°$, that's 1800°, so divide by 12 and each angle is 150°."

Teacher: "Good. There's another way to do that which uses a very simple result about exterior angles. This assumes that the polygon is convex, meaning that all the angles are less than 180°. When each side is extended we get exterior angles like the marked angle *CBP*. Now, suppose my pencil starts pointing along *AB* and then goes right round the polygon (like a car going round a roundabout). At *B* it turns through the exterior angle *CBP*, then at *C* it turns through the next exterior angle, and so on, till it reaches *A* and turns through the last exterior angle. What then?"

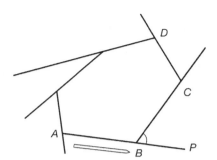

Nadeem: "It's gone through one complete turn."

Linda: "So the exterior angles add up to 360°?"

Mike: "And it doesn't matter how many sides there are?"

Teacher: "That's right; that makes it a very simple result to remember: the exterior angles always add up to 360°. Now can you see how to use that to find an interior angle of a regular dodecagon?"

Linda: "Each exterior angle would be $360 \div 12 = 30°$."

Mike: "And then each interior angle is $180 - 30 = 150°$. Same answer we got before."

Teacher: "Yes, it should be the same answer! If you add up all the interior angles and all the exterior angles for an *n*-sided polygon, what do you get?"

Nadeem: "That's $(n - 2) \times 180° + 360° = 180n - 360 + 360$ degrees."

Linda: "That's $180n°$. Of course, it should be that, because at each corner the interior and exterior angles add up to 180°, and there are *n* corners."

Teacher: "Yes, so that all fits together. Now there is also a special result for the exterior angles of a triangle. In the diagram *ACD* is an exterior angle, and is divided into two parts by the line *CK* drawn parallel to *BA*. What can you say about the angles marked *x* and *y*?"

Nadeem: "*x* is the same as ∠*A*, because of the parallel lines."

Teacher: "Yes; they are called alternate angles, because they are on alternate sides of the line *AC* that meets the two parallels."

Mike: "And *y* = ∠*B*; they are corresponding angles."

Teacher: "Good; they are in corresponding positions, each above and to the right, at the points *B* and *C*. So what follows about the angle *ACD*?"

Linda: "It's $x + y = \angle A + \angle B$. Didn't we see that when you turned the pencil from $CA$ to $BA$ and then to $BC$? You had turned it through the angles $A$ and $B$ and from facing along $CA$ it was facing along $BC$ which is the same direction as $CD$."

Teacher: "That's right; either way we find each exterior angle of a triangle equals the sum of the two other interior angles. Can you see how this gives another proof that the interior angles add up to 180°?"

Linda: "Yes, because $x + y + \angle ACB$ makes a straight line."

Mike: "And that's the same as $\angle A + \angle B + \angle C$."

Nadeem: "We also get again the sum of the exterior angles being 360°, because it has to be twice the sum of the interior angles."

Teacher: "Good! Now see if you can work out before next lesson how many sides a polygon has if each interior angle is 168°."

# 8 Special quadrilaterals

Teacher: "The quadrilateral in the diagram has been drawn in such a way that the diagonals bisect each other, meaning that the point K where they meet is the midpoint of each of them. So if the whole figure is rotated 180° about K, what would happen?"

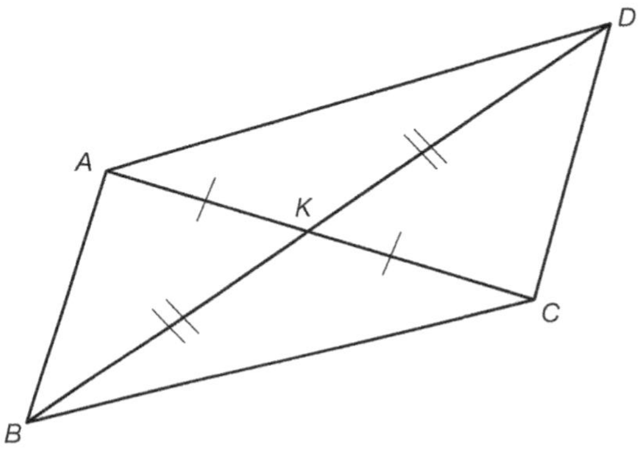

Linda: "Then A would go to C and C to A."

Nadeem: "And B and D would change places too."

Mike: "But no lengths would change, so CD must be the same length as AB, and likewise AD = BC."

Teacher: "That's right. And what can you say about the directions of the lines?"

Nadeem: "If you turn a line through 180° it's just facing in the opposite direction."

Linda: "So AB and CD must be parallel, and likewise AD and BC."

Teacher: "That's right. We call this sort of quadrilateral a *parallelogram*. The opposite sides are parallel and equal, and the diagonals bisect each other. What can you say about the angles?"

Mike: "Angles ABC and BAD must add up to 180° as they are allied angles with AD parallel to CD."

Linda: "And BAD is also allied to ADC with BA parallel to CD, so then angles ABC and ADC must be equal."

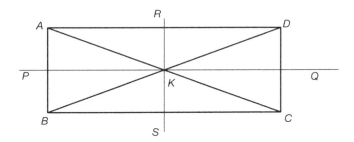

Teacher: "Yes, the opposite angles in a parallelogram are equal, and adjacent angles are supplementary. Now let's consider a *rectangle*, the special case, where one of the angles is a right angle."

Mike: "They must all be right angles then."

Nadeem: "So the figure has lines of symmetry; is that what PQ and RS are drawn there for?"

Teacher: "Yes, PQ is parallel to AD and BC and is midway between them, and RS is midway between the other pair of sides. You can reflect the figure in PQ; what happens then?"

Linda: "A and B swap places, and so do D and C."

Mike: "So the diagonals AC and BD reflect into each other. They must be equal then"

Teacher: "That's right. Diagonals of a rectangle are equal, as well as still bisecting each other. You can also prove that from the fact that triangles ABD and DCA are congruent. Can you see why?"

Nadeem: "They share the side AD, they have equal sides AB and DC, and they have equal right angles at A and D; that's two sides and the included angle, SAS."

Mike: "It also follows from Pythagoras's theorem, as each diagonal squared equals the sum of the squares of two adjacent sides of the rectangle."

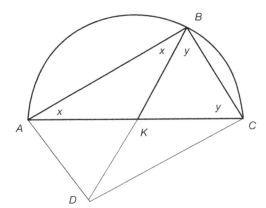

Teacher: "That's right. The rectangle is by far the most common two dimensional man-made shape: think of doors, windows, pictures and so on. Also, since the half diagonals are all equal, a circle of centre K and radius KA will pass through all four corners of the rectangle. This also applies to a right-angled triangle such as ABC in the diagram. If the other triangle ADC is added, we get a rectangle, and a circle passes through the four corners. Just looking at triangle ABC we find that, if the angle at B is a right angle, the circle on AC as diameter will pass through B."

Mike: "So does that mean that, if B is any point on the circle with diameter AC, the angle ABC will be 90°?"

Teacher: "It doesn't quite mean that, because we started with a right-angled triangle in the first place. However, your question can be addressed using the figure. If we *don't* yet assume that ABC is a right angle, but instead assume that the semicircle has AC as diameter, then what can we say about the triangles AKB and BKC?"

Linda: "They are isosceles because of the equal radii."

Nadeem: "And that's why the two angles marked x are equal, and the two angles marked y."

Mike: "Between them those angles make all the angles of triangle ABC; so $2x + 2y$ has to be 180°. Oh, then $x + y = 90°$, which shows that ABC has to be a right angle."

Teacher: "Yes; that result is summarised by saying that the angle in a semicircle is a right angle; but it does work the other way too: if you start knowing ∠ABC is a right angle, then you can deduce

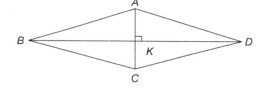

that B lies on the circle whose diameter is AC. But next we're going to look at a parallelogram whose diagonals are perpendicular, while still bisecting each other of course."

Linda: "That means you can reflect it in BD and A and C would swap places."

Mike: "That makes triangles ABK and CBK congruent, so BA = BC. And likewise AD = CD."

Nadeem: "So all the sides are equal, since the opposite sides are equal anyway."

Teacher: "Right; this shape is called a *rhombus*. Can you say anything more about angles?"

Mike: "The symmetry about BD shows that BD bisects the angles at A and D."

Linda: "And we could equally reflect in AC, so that must bisect the angles at A and C."

Teacher:   "Good. A rhombus has all four sides equal, the diagonals are perpendicular and they bisect the angles."

Nadeem:   "Can the sides as well as the diagonals be perpendicular?"

Mike:   "That makes it a square, doesn't it?"

Teacher:   "Yes indeed; a square is a rectangle that's also a rhombus, so sides are all equal and diagonals are equal and bisect the angles, which are right angles; so each diagonal makes a 45° angle with each side."

Nadeem:   "Are there quadrilaterals that have just one axis of symmetry?"

Linda:   "What about a kite?"

Teacher:   "Yes; that has one diagonal as an axis of symmetry, so the other diagonal is perpendicular to that diagonal and is bisected by that diagonal. The other possibility is that an axis of symmetry bisects two opposite sides at right angles. Those two sides are then parallel, making the quadrilateral a *trapezium*, and the other two sides are equal, as each is the mirror image of the other; so it is called an isosceles trapezium.

There is also another way that a quadrilateral can be special. I want you to draw a circle, then draw a fairly irregular quadrilateral *ABCD* with all the points on the circle; that makes the quadrilateral *cyclic*. Measure and note down the sizes of the angles at the corners; then do that again with more cyclic quadrilaterals. See if you notice anything about how the angles are related (apart from their total being 360°, which you know is true for all quadrilaterals.) Then see if you can give a reason for what you notice by considering the diagram on the right."

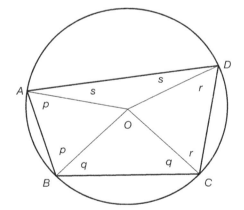

# **9** Basic areas

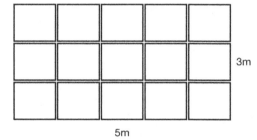

| | | |
Teacher: | "John has a kitchen with a rectangular floor measuring 5 m by 3 m. He wants to put new vinyl tiles on the floor, with each tile being a square of side 1 m. How many tiles will he need?"

Linda: | "Easy! I can see it's 15."

Nadeem: | "It's just 3 rows with 5 in each row."

Teacher: | "OK. So how many tiles would be needed for a rectangular floor measuring 7 m by 4 m?"

Mike: | "That's 4 rows with 7 in each row, so 28 tiles."

Teacher: | "Right. The number of 1m square tiles needed to cover a rectangle is called the *area* of the rectangle, measured in square metres or m$^2$; or for smaller shapes we use cm$^2$ or mm$^2$. So what is the area of a rectangle with length $l$ and width $w$?"

Linda: | "That's just $l \times w$ isn't it?"

Teacher: | "Yes; so what about a square whose side has length $l$?"

Mike: | "The area is $l \times l$ which is $l^2$."

Teacher: | "That's right; and we actually say '$l$ squared' instead of '$l$ to the power 2' because this is what we do to get the area of a square."

Nadeem: | "So is $l$ cubed used to get the volume of a cube?"

Teacher: | "Yes indeed. Now before we leave rectangles, look at this diagram. What is the area of the whole rectangle?"

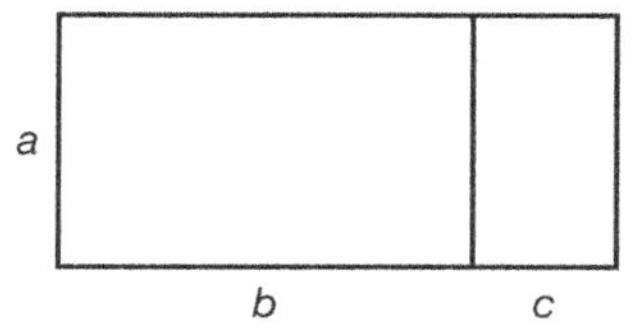

Linda: "It has length $b + c$ and width $a$, so the area must be $(b + c) \times a$, or $a(b + c)$."

Mike: "But it's also two rectangles together, so it's $ab + ac$."

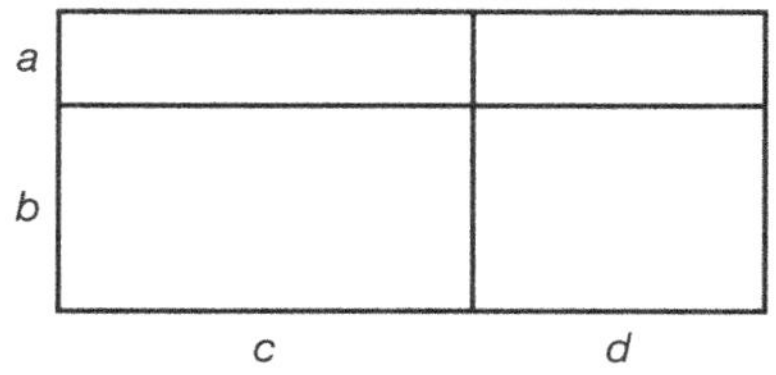

Nadeem: "So that means that $a(b + c)$ is always the same as $ab + ac$, does it?"

Teacher: "Yes indeed, and this equality is used a lot in algebra. Now look at the next diagram. What can you say about the area here?"

Nadeem: "It's $(a + b)(c + d)$, and it's also $ac + ad + bc + bd$."

Teacher: "That's right, and it shows how we can multiply out two brackets. Now let's look at a parallelogram."

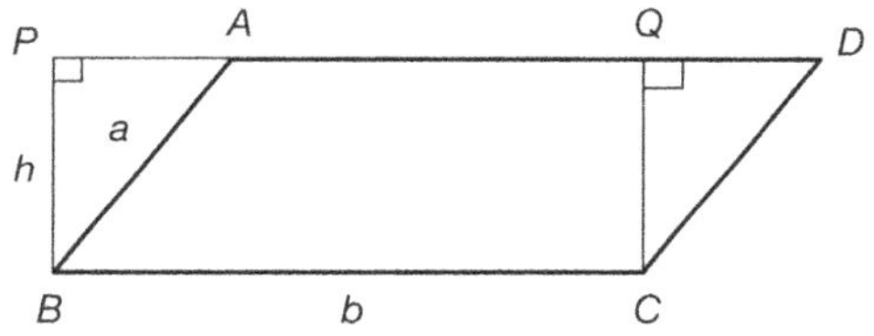

Mike: "Is the area $a \times b$?"

Teacher: "Imagine making the parallelogram out of Meccano rods, freely jointed at the corners. You could keep $BC$ fixed and turn $AD$ around it. Would that make the area change?"

Linda: "Yes, you could make the area almost 0 if you made the angle $ABD$ really small."

Mike: "Oh, so the area can't be $a \times b$ because $a$ and $b$ don't change when you do the turning."

Nadeem: "Is the area of $ABCD$ the same as the area of the rectangle $PBCQ$?"

Teacher: "Yes. Can you see why?"

Mike: "The rectangle has got the extra triangle $PAB$ while the parallelogram has the triangle $QDC$."

Linda: "And those triangles are equal because $AB$ and $CD$ are equal and parallel, and so $\angle PBA = \angle QCD$, and also they both have a right angle; that makes the triangles congruent."

Nadeem: "So the area is $b \times h$ not $b \times a$."

Teacher: "That's right. The area of a parallelogram is base times height, where the base is any side and the height has to be perpendicular to the base. Now what about a triangle? Have a look at the diagram."

Mike: "The triangle has been 'gift-wrapped' in a rectangle."

Linda: "And I think it takes up half the area of the rectangle, because the diagonal AB bisects the rectangle PADB and so does AC bisect AQCD."

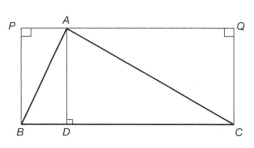

Nadeem: "So the triangle is just half the area of the rectangle, that's half of BC × BP."

Teacher: "Yes, it's also $\frac{1}{2} \times BC \times AD$, usually expressed as half the base times the height; the base can be any side of the triangle, and the height must be perpendicular to the base, as with a parallelogram."

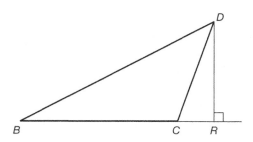

Linda: "We could have done that from the parallelogram diagram, because AC bisects the parallelogram △ABC is just half of ABCD."

Teacher: "Yes, we could. Also the other diagonal BD bisects the parallelogram, so the area of △BCD is also half the base times the height; though if you were to draw the triangle on its own and take BC as base you would have to extend the base to draw the height DR perpendicular to BC. Next we'll look at a trapezium, which has two parallel sides of length a and b, a distance h apart, as in the diagram."

Nadeem: "If you do a × h that's too small; it's just the area ABRS."

Linda: "And b × h is PCDO, that's too big."

Mike: "Could it be half way in between?"

Linda: "That's an idea. a × h = ABSR is too small by the areas of triangles ACR and BDS."

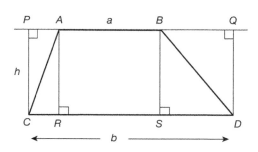

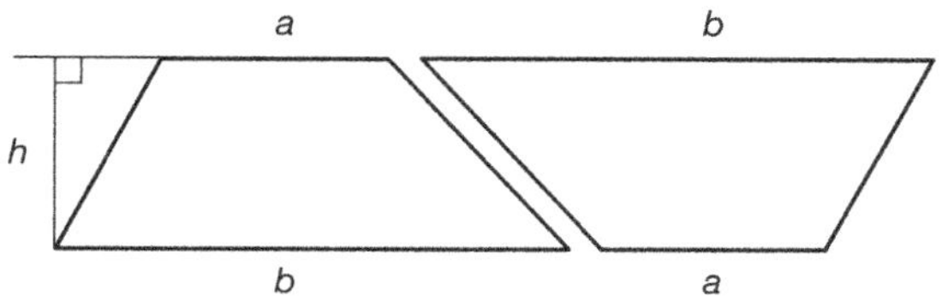

Nadeem: "And $b \times h = PCDOQ$ is too big by triangles $PCA$ and $QDB$."

Mike: "And $ACR = PCA$ because they are halves of rectangle $PARC$."

Linda: "And $BDS = QDB$, halves of $BQDS$."

Teacher: "Good! You're on the right lines. The area is halfway between $a \times h$ and $b \times h$ for just the reasons you've given."

Mike: "So it would be the average of those, $\frac{1}{2}(ah + bh)$."

Teacher: "Yes; that can also be written as $\frac{1}{2}(a+b)h$. You can see this also by turning a second copy of the trapezium upside down and putting the two together, as in the diagram."

Linda: "They make a parallelogram with area $(a + b)h$ and the trapezium is just half that."

Teacher: "That's right. Next time we'll look at area of a circle."

# Circles and π

Teacher: "Have a look at this diagram. We're trying to find a way to work out the area inside a circle given its radius, and also the length of the circle, its circumference. The circle has radius $r$ and the square $ABCD$ has been drawn round it. Can you tell me the area of this square?"

Mike: "Is it $2r^2$?"

Teacher: "How did you get that?"

Mike: "Well it's a square with side $2r$, so you have to multiply that by itself."

Teacher: "Yes, but does $2r \times 2r$ make $2r^2$?"

Nadeem: "No, it makes $4r^2$, doesn't it?"

Linda: "Or could you write it with a bracket, $(2r)^2$?"

Teacher: "Yes, those are both correct; but $2r^2$ is $2 \times r \times r$ which is too small. That's because the index $^2$ has priority over the multiplication by 2, according to BIDMAS."

Nadeem: "You can see that it's $4r^2$ because it divides into 4 squares of side $r$."

Teacher: "That's right. Now what about the figure $PQRS$? What shape is it, and what is its area?"

Linda: "It's a square isn't it?"

Teacher: "Yes; how do you know that?"

Linda: "The sides are diagonals of equal squares, so they are all the same length."

Mike:   "And the angles are right angles, because diagonals of a square bisect its angles so make 45° with the sides."

Nadeem:   "And each diagonal divides its square into two equal triangles, so overall *PQRS* is half of *ABCD*, which makes $2r^2$."

Teacher:   "Good; and *PQRS* is inside the circle, which is inside *ABCD*. So the area of the circle is somewhere between $2r^2$ and $4r^2$. Any idea what it might be?"

Mike:   "Maybe $3r^2$?"

Teacher:   "That sounds plausible, and actually is not far wrong. But do we really have a reason to think the circle area is exactly halfway between the two squares' areas?"

Nadeem:   "Is it $kr^2$ with *k* being a constant somewhere near 3?"

Teacher:   "That's right! And now we're going to look at the problem in a different way. In this second diagram I've drawn a polygon inside the circle and joined two adjacent corners to the centre to make a triangle *OEF*, and drawn *OM* perpendicular to *EF*. What is the area of △*OEF*?"

Linda:   "It's half base times height, that's ½ *EF* × *OM*."

Teacher:   "Right; now what about the area of the whole polygon? We'll assume it's regular, made up of *n* triangles all congruent to △*OEF*."

Mike:   "That would make $n \times \frac{1}{2} \times EF \times OM$,."

Teacher:   "Yes, and we can rewrite that as ½ × *n* × *EF* × *OM*."

Nadeem:   "*n* × *EF* is the perimeter of the polygon, so we've got half the perimeter times *OM*."

Teacher:   "Right. Now let's see what happens if we make *n* get bigger and bigger without limit. What happens to the area of the polygon, its perimeter and *OM*?"

Linda:   "The area gets nearer and nearer to the whole area inside the circle, and its perimeter approaches the circumference."

Mike:   "And *OM* tends to the radius of the circle."

Teacher:   "Good; so what does that tell us about the area of the circle?"

Nadeem:   "It must be half the circumference times the radius."

Teacher:   "Right. Now let's call the circumference *C*. We have two formulae for the area. One is $kr^2$ as found previously. The other is ½*Cr*. These must be equal to each other; so what does that tell us about *C*?"

Mike: "If $\frac{1}{2}Cr = kr^2$ then $Cr = 2kr^2$ so $C = 2kr$."

Teacher: "That's right. We now have the formulae $kr^2$ and $2kr$ for the area and circumference of the circle; but still have not found what $k$ is. It is in fact a very important number in mathematics, used also in many different contexts that have nothing to do with circles, and it's been given the symbol $\pi$; that's the Greek lower case letter $P$, the first letter of the word perimeter."

Linda: "So the area is $\pi r^2$ and the circumference is $2\pi r$."

Teacher: "That's right. Note that both formulae involve 2, $\pi$ and $r$."

Mike: "So how can we remember which is which?"

Teacher: "That's easy if you bear in mind that to get an area you always have to multiply two lengths together. The area formula involves $r^2$ which is $r$ times $r$, making the area of a small square like *APOS*; then multiplying that by $\pi$ makes a bigger area, that of the circle. In $2\pi r$ the length $r$ is just being multiplied by a number, $2\pi$, not by another length, to make a bigger length."

Nadeem: "How can we find $\pi$? We need its value to be able to use the formulae."

Teacher: "Yes. Nowadays you can simply press the special $\pi$ button on your calculator, giving 3.141592654; but it actually goes on and on for ever; it's been found to millions of decimal places using computers and advanced methods. In my school days, before we had calculators, we often used $\frac{22}{7}$ or $3\frac{1}{7}$ which is surprisingly accurate for such a simple approximation. In fact, try working out the length of the equator taking the earth's radius as 4000 miles, using $\frac{22}{7}$ and also using your $\pi$ button."

Linda: "It makes 25 143 miles, to the nearest mile, using $\frac{22}{7}$ ."

Mike "And 25 133 using the $\pi$ button."

Teacher: "That's right; only about 10 miles difference in over 25 000. The ancient Greek mathematician Archimedes proved that $\pi$ is between $3\frac{10}{71}$ and $3\frac{1}{7}$ ."

Nadeem: "Is there any way we could calculate $\pi$ ourselves?"

Teacher: "Yes, you can do it using Pythagoras's theorem. But that will have to wait for another day. (See Chapter 20.) However, using just a regular hexagon, you can show that $\pi > 3$. Any idea how you would do that?"

# Starting trigonometry

Mike: "Sir, if you know the angles of a triangle and know the length of one of the sides, is there a way to calculate the other sides?"

Teacher: "Yes there is! And we're going to start investigating that. To begin with we will be concentrating on right-angled triangles. I want you to draw on graph paper something like this diagram: a pair of axes, a quarter circle of any convenient radius, the tangent at A and then a number of lines like OPT, but with the angle $\theta$ being 0°, then 10°, then 20° and so on up to 90°. For each line OPT you will read the lengths MP, OM and AT and then work out and make a table of the following ratios: $\frac{MP}{OP}, \frac{OM}{OP}, \frac{MP}{OM}$ and $\frac{AT}{OA}$. Give each answer to 2 decimal places."

Linda: "We don't need to do the line OPT for $\theta = 0°$ do we?"

Teacher: "That's right, because it will just lie along OA which you've already drawn."

After a while...

Nadeem: "Sir, when I get to $\theta = 70°$ I can't locate T; it's too high up to be on the page."

Linda: "I had that at 60°."

Teacher: "Yes, don't worry about that; just leave it if T goes off the page."

Mike: "And with 90° we can't even do $\frac{MP}{OM}$, because you showed us that we can't divide by 0."

Teacher:     "That's right; so leave that blank as well."

One set of results was as follows:

| $\theta$ | MP/OP | OM/OP | MP/OM | AT/OA |
|------|------|------|------|------|
| 0° | 0 | 1 | 0 | 0 |
| 10° | 0.18 | 0.99 | 0.18 | 0.18 |
| 20° | 0.34 | 0.94 | 0.35 | 0.36 |
| 30° | 0.50 | 0.87 | 0.57 | 0.57 |
| 40° | 0.64 | 0.76 | 0.84 | 0.84 |
| 50° | 0.76 | 0.64 | 1.19 | 1.19 |
| 60° | 0.86 | 0.5 | 1.72 | 1.73 |
| 70° | 0.94 | 0.34 | 2.76 | — |
| 80° | 0.98 | 0.17 | 5.76 | — |
| 90° | 1 | 0 | — | — |

Nadeem:     "The last two columns are almost the same. Is that because triangle OAT is just an enlarged version of OMP?"

Linda:       "And we used different values for the radius OP but got very similar results."

Teacher:     "Yes, when two triangles are similar, so one is just an enlargement of the other, then ratios of corresponding pairs of sides are equal. So in a right-angled triangle the size of one of the angles determines the ratios of pairs of sides. The ratio $\frac{MP}{OP}$ is called the *sine* of the angle, written as sin $\theta$ for short. $\frac{OM}{OP}$ is the *cosine*, cos $\theta$, and the last two columns have the *tangent* (because one way of defining it involved the length of the tangent AT), tan $\theta$. You have a button for each of these on your scientific calculators."

Nadeem:     "I get tan 80° = 5.671..., not 5.76 as measured."

Linda:       "And tan 70° should be 2.747..., not 2.76."

Teacher:     "Remember that you used your protractors to make the angles; and the tangent particularly grows very fast at large angles; in fact 2.76 is the correct tangent for around 80.15° instead of 80°."

Nadeem:     "How did you get that, Sir? Just by trial?"

Teacher:     "No; you often need, instead of finding the tangent for a known angle, to find what angle has a particular tangent; so you want the inverse of the tangent function, called tan⁻¹; so I pressed SHIFT then tan then 2.76 to get $\tan^{-1}(2.76)$, the angle whose tangent is 2.76."

For the use of ⁻¹ to indicate an inverse function, see Chapter 18 on negative and fractional indices.

Mike: "So can we use sine, cos and tan whenever we're working in a right-angled triangle?"

Teacher: "Yes indeed. What we do is label the three sides of the triangle, in our mind at least, as HYP for hypotenuse, OPP for opposite and ADJ for adjacent."

Nadeem: "The hypotenuse is the longest side, opposite the right angle. But what does adjacent mean? And opposite what?"

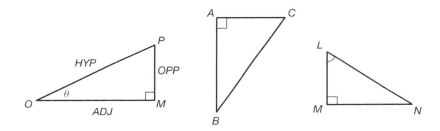

Teacher: "Adjacent means next to; the houses adjacent to your home are where your next door neighbours live. Both adjacent and opposite refer to a *marked angle*, other than the right angle, in the triangle. In triangle *OPM* the angle at *O* is marked with the letter $\theta$. *MP* is the side opposite $\theta$ while *OM* is adjacent to $\theta$. (*OP* is of course also adjacent to $\theta$, but it is already named as the hypotenuse.) Can you label the sides in triangle *ABC*?"

Linda: "*BC* is the hypotenuse; is *AB* the opposite?"

Mike: "You can't say which is the opposite; there isn't a marked angle."

Teacher: "That's right. There has to be a marked angle. It is marked either because we know how big it is, and will be using it in our calculation, or because it is the angle we want to find."

Linda: "So *AB* would be the opposite if the marked angle was at *C*; otherwise *AB* would be the adjacent."

Mike: "So the sine of *C* would also be the cosine of *B*; is that right? Does that explain how the first two columns in the lists we made were about the same but in opposite order?"

Teacher: "Yes, well spotted. In fact that's the reason for the name cosine: it's the sine of the other angle, i.e. of the complement, namely of 90° minus the marked angle."

Nadeem:   "And in triangle *LMN* the opposite is *MN* and the adjacent is *LM* because *L* is the marked angle."

Teacher:   "That's right. Now the sine of the marked angle is the ratio $\frac{OPP}{HYP}$, the cosine is $\frac{ADJ}{HYP}$ and the tangent is $\frac{OPP}{ADJ}$. The list of letters SOHCAHTOA summarises these; but shortly we'll be rewriting that in a somewhat different way. First, let's practise using them. In triangle *LMN*, if $\angle L = 60°$ and $LN = 8$ cm, what is *LM*?"

Linda:   "*LN* is the HYP and *LM* is the ADJ, so we use $\cos 60° = \frac{LM}{LN} = \frac{LM}{8}$."

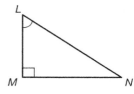

Nadeem:   "So then $LM = \cos 60° \times 8 = 0.5 \times 8 = 4$ cm. That's a simple answer! Is there some reason why it doesn't have lots of decimal digits?"

Teacher:   "That's because with $\angle L$ being 60° the triangle is half an equilateral triangle, as you would see if you reflected it in *MN* to make the other half. But notice that from $\cos = \frac{ADJ}{HYP}$ we deduced ADJ = cos × HYP. Next, if instead we have $LM = 5$ cm and $\angle L = 50°$, what is *LN*?"

Mike:   "We're still using cosine: $\cos 50° = \frac{5}{LN}$, so $\cos 50° \times LN = 5$, so $LN = \frac{5}{\cos 50°}$ which comes to 7.7786…cm."

Teacher:   "Good; that can be rounded to 7.78 cm; note that this time, from ADJ = cos × HYP you deduced $HYP = \frac{ADJ}{\cos}$. The three ways of using the relationship between cos, ADJ and HYP can be symbolised by writing

A  to remind us that $C = \frac{A}{H}$, $A = C \times H$ and $H = \frac{A}{C}$
C  H

The same applies to the other ratios, so SOHCAHTOA can be written as

O       A       O
S  H    C  H    T  A . Finally, if $LM = 3$ and $MN = 4$ cm, what is angle *L*?"

Nadeem:   "This time we are given ADJ and OPP, so we need TOA: $\tan L = \frac{4}{3}$. Oh, so we have to use SHIFT tan, do we?"

Linda:   "That's right: $L = \tan^{-1}\frac{4}{3}$ which comes to 53.13010…°."

Teacher:   "That's right; we usually give angles to 1 decimal place, so 53.1°. You now have the ability to work out lengths and angles in right-angled triangles."

# Square of a sum and sum of squares, leading to Pythagoras' theorem

Teacher: "Start with two numbers. Add them up and square the answer. Then square the numbers first and add the squares. Which answer is bigger?"

Nadeem: "Aren't they the same?"

Linda: "I've tried it with 3 and 7. I get $(3 + 7)^2 = 100$ and $3^2 + 7^2 = 9 + 49 = 58$, so the first answer is bigger, by 42."

Mike: "And with 5 and 8 I get 169 and 89. The first is bigger by 80."

Nadeem: "OK, they're not equal. With 2 and 3 I get 25 and 13, a difference of 12."

Linda: "The first one always seems bigger, and the difference seems related to the product of the two numbers: 42 is twice $3 \times 7$, 80 is twice $5 \times 8$ and 12 is twice $2 \times 3$."

Note: More numerical experimentation could be useful here.

Teacher: "Good; it looks as if there may be a pattern there. But can we know whether that pattern works for every pair of numbers?"

Nadeem: "Should we use letters? That's how we know we're not dealing with any particular numbers, isn't it?

Linda: "So call the numbers $a$ and $b$. Then we are comparing $(a + b)^2$ with $a^2 + b^2$, are we?"

Teacher: "That's right: so now look at the diagram. What can you say about the whole area?"

Mike: "It's a square of side $a + b$, so that's $(a + b)^2$."

Linda: "And part of it is $a^2$, the square in the bottom left, and $b^2$ on the top right."

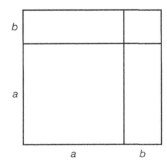

Nadeem: "And the rest is two rectangles making 2*ab*. So that's why we found that as the difference between the square of the sum and the sum of squares!"

Linda: "I suppose we could have done it anyway by treating $(a + b)^2$ as $(a + b)(a + b)$ and just multiplying out the brackets; it makes $a^2 + ab + ba + b^2$."

Teacher: "That's right. So now you can see that this pattern works for all numbers. I'm now going to divide that big square up in a different way, still using lengths *a* and *b*, as in the second diagram. What can you say about the four triangles at the corner, like $\triangle APS$?"

Nadeem: "They're all right-angled, with sides *a* and *b*, so they must be congruent, all the same."

Teacher: "What can you conclude about *PQRS*?"

Linda: "The sides must all be equal, so it must be a square."

Mike: "No, hang on; equal sides make it a rhombus. What about the angles?"

Nadeem: "Well, $\angle APS = \angle PQB$ so $\angle APS + \angle BPQ = 90°$; that makes $\angle SPQ = 90°$."

Teacher: "Good. That means *PQRS* is a square. Let's call the side *c*. We're going to look at how *c* is related to *a* and *b*, using areas."

Nadeem: "The square then has area $c^2$, and each triangle has area $\frac{1}{2}ab$, so the whole area is $c^2 + 2ab$."

Linda: "But the whole area is still $(a + b)^2 = a^2 + b^2 + 2ab$."

Mike: "Then $c^2$ must be the same as $a^2 + b^2$!"

Teacher: "Well done all of you! You've just proved Pythagoras' theorem, perhaps the most important theorem in the whole of mathematics."

For a somewhat similar approach, but using squared paper and some numerical work to begin with, see the worksheet on "Introducing vectors and Pythagoras" in the geometry book of my *Venture Mathematics Worksheets* series (Puritz 2005, St Albans: Tarquin).

Another approach (among many; there are lots of proofs of this theorem; the one that follows may be more suitable with older pupils) is to let angle $A$ be the right angle in $\triangle ABC$, and draw the perpendicular $AD$ from $A$ to $BC$. This divides the main triangle into two that are similar to each other and to $\triangle ABC$, whose hypotenuses are $AB$ and $AC$. Because they are similar, the area of each is in a fixed ratio to the area of the square on its hypotenuse, and hence, since $\triangle ABD + \triangle ADC = \triangle ABC$ it follows that $AB^2 + AC^2 = BC^2$.

# 13 The difference of two squares

The humble identity $a^2 - b^2 = (a - b)(a + b)$ deserves more emphasis than it usually gets. This is probably because it is generally seen as part of algebra, viewed as an abstract formal game not clearly related to arithmetic. In text books it is included in the chapter on factorisation, and the exercises usually just practise variations like $64u^2 - 49v^2$ or even $(3x + y)^2 - (x - 5y)^2$.

These formal exercises undoubtedly deserve a place, but to confine oneself to them is to miss a great deal about the identity. As a fact of arithmetic it is not at all obvious, but it can be discovered with surprise by pupils quite early on, and can then be given an appealing geometric proof, and also one based on looking at multiplication. It has lots of applications, including speeding up certain mental calculations and giving an easy proof of the important fact that the product of two numbers with a given sum is greatest when the numbers are equal. It is also the basis of many further problems and investigations, of which a few are given here.

Teacher: "What do you think $\dfrac{57^2 - 43^2}{57 - 43}$ would come to?"

Mike: "Maybe $57 - 43 = 14$?"

Linda: "I've done it on my calculator and got 100!"

Nadeem: "That's $57 + 43$! What's going on?"

Teacher: "OK, now try working out $\dfrac{8^2 - 5^2}{8 - 5}$, $\dfrac{14^2 - 6^2}{14 - 6}$ and $\dfrac{61^2 - 27^2}{61 - 27}$"

Linda: "That's 13, 20 and 88. It's always just the two numbers added up!"

Teacher: "So what do you think $\dfrac{a^2 - b^2}{a - b}$ comes to?"

Nadeem: "It looks like $a + b$. But does that always work?"

Teacher: "Good question. How can we answer that?"

Mike: "Try more numerical examples?"

Teacher: "You could, and if you kept getting the same result, you would be more inclined to believe that it's always true. But does that make you sure?"

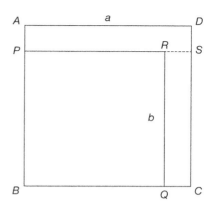

Linda: "Not really; and we still can't see why it's true, if it is."

Teacher: "Quite right, we need a way that doesn't depend on specific examples.

The diagram shows a big square office of side $a$. It is bigger than I need and is also used by people going through to other offices. So I got the builders to put up partition walls, making a smaller square office with side $b$ and a corridor. What's the area of the corridor?"

Mike: "That's $a^2 - b^2$."

Teacher: "Right, now if I want to buy heavy duty carpet for the corridor, what width do I need?"

Nadeem: "That would be $a - b$."

Teacher: "Yes, and what length of carpet is needed?"

Linda: "The top bit has length $a$ and then down the side is length $b$ so that's $a + b$ altogether."

Teacher: "So, if the width $a - b$ and the length is $a + b$ what's the area of the corridor?"

Mike: "$(a + b) \times (a - b)$."

Linda: "So $a^2 - b^2$ also equals $(a - b)(a + b)$."

Nadeem: "And that's why $\dfrac{a^2 - b^2}{a - b} = a + b$."

Teacher: "That's right. Now can you use what you know to work out $36^2 - 34^2$ without a calculator?"

Mike: "That's $2 \times 70 = 140$."

Teacher: "Good, and what about $59^2 - 41^2$?"

Linda: "$18 \times 100 = 1800$."

Teacher: "And $0.64^2 - 0.36^2$?"

Nadeem: "$0.28 \times 1 = 0.28$."

Teacher: "Good. Now look at the picture of a ring road. If you are given that the road is 8 m wide and that the length of the dotted circle along its middle is 300 m, could you work out the area of all the tarmac?

Mike: "If it was a straight road it would be 8 × 300 = 2400 m²? That seems the sensible way to try, but does it give the actual answer with a curved road?"

Teacher: "Worth trying anyway! Now let's see if it really does give the right answer. Let's take the radii of the outer and inner boundary circles to be $R$ and $r$ respectively. Then what is the area?"

Nadeem: "It's the difference between two circles, so $\pi(R^2 - r^2)$; but we don't know $R$ and $r$, so how does that help?"

Teacher: "Can you rewrite that formula, using what you found out today?"

Nadeem: "Yes, it's equal to $\pi(R + r)(R - r)$. But how does that help?"

Linda: "$R - r$ is the width of the road, so that's 8 m. But what about the $\pi(R + r)$?"

Teacher: "Well, can you express the length of the central broken circle in terms of the radii?"

Linda: "Its radius is half way betwee the outer and the inner radius, that's the average of $R$ and $r$, which is $\frac{1}{2}(R+r)$, so the length $2\pi\frac{1}{2}(R+r)$. Oh, that does make exactly $\pi(R + r)$! So we can treat the ring as if it were a straight road with length equal to the dotted circle's length."

Teacher: "That's right. And that's also the average of the lengths of the inner and outer circles."

# Another look at $(a - b)(a + b)$

We've so far looked at starting with $a^2 - b^2$, but it is also worth looking at $(a - b)(a + b)$ as the starting point.

Teacher: "Which is bigger, and by how much: $8^2$ or $7 \times 9$? $5^2$ or $4 \times 6$? $11^2$ or $10 \times 12$?"

Linda: "The first is bigger, always just by 1."

Teacher: "Can you see why that is?"

Nadeem: "If you go from $8^2 = 8 \times 8$ to $7 \times 8$ you lose 8. Then if you go to $7 \times 9$ you gain 7; so altogether you've lost 1. Likewise from $11 \times 11$ to $10 \times 11$ to $10 \times 12$ you lose 11 and then gain 10."

Teacher: "Well explained! Now what about $9^2$ compared with $6 \times 12$, or $7^2$ compared with $4 \times 10$?"

Mike: "The square is bigger by 9 both times. You go from $9 \times 9$ to $6 \times 9$ and lose 3 nines, then go from $6 \times 9$ to $6 \times 12$ and gain three 6s, so overall you lose three 3s; or from $7 \times 7$ to $4 \times 7$ lose three 7s, then from $4 \times 7$ to $4 \times 10$ gain three 4s, lose three 3s again overall."

Teacher: "Well done. So how would $(n - 5)(n + 5)$ compare with $n^2$?"

Linda: "I guess it's less by five 5s = $5^2$ this time. Hang on; haven't we just recently learned that $(a - b)(a + b)$ is the same as $a^2 - b^2$? Of course! We could have used that from the start!"

Teacher: "That's right. Now suppose you had 100 m of fencing and wanted to make a rectangular paddock. What's the maximum area you could make it?"

Nadeem: "Make it square, $25 \times 25$ makes 625 m$^2$. But does that count as rectangular?"

Teacher: "Yes it does. A square is a special kind of rectangle. If it was not allowed to be square I would have specified an oblong rectangle. But how do you know that making it square gives maximum area?"

Nadeem:   "You could try $24 \times 26 = 624$, or $23 \times 27 = 621$ m²."

Mike:     "You don't need just numerical examples; if you change from 25 by 25 then the width has to be less than 25, say $25 - x$, and the length then would be $25 + x$, making the area $(25 - x)(25 + x)$ which is $25^2 - x^2$, and that's always less than $25^2$ except when $x = 0$."

Teacher:  "Good. The same approach shows that, if two numbers can vary but always have the same sum, then their product is biggest when they are equal. Now can you see a quick way to calculate $21 \times 29$?"

Linda:    "It's $(25 - 4)(25 + 4)$ which is $25^2 - 4^2 = 625 - 16 = 609$."

Teacher:  "Good. Now use the same approach to find $79 \times 81$, $37 \times 43$, $96 \times 104$, $2.6 \times 3.4$ and $0.43 \times 0.57$. Then you can try this question: 3 is prime and $3 + 1$ is square. Is there any other square that is just 1 greater than a prime number?"

# Number museum

## How many factors?

Teacher: "Can you tell me what is meant by a *factor* of a number? Or tell me all the factors of 12?"

Linda: "Are they 12, 24, 36, 48 and so on?"

Teacher: "No, those are the *multiples* of 12, the numbers in the 12 times table."

Nadeem: "The factors of 12 are the numbers that divide exactly into 12: 2, 3, 4 and 6."

Mike: "Those are the numbers that have 12 as a multiple. What about 1 and 12 itself? Are they not factors too?"

Teacher: "Yes, they are. A factor of *n* is any whole number that can be multiplied by a whole number to make *n*. That includes 1 and *n* itself. The idea of a factor of *n* is that you can use it to make *n* by multiplying by another number. Think of a factory: a place where things are made."

Linda: "But you don't really make 12 by doing 12 × 1. You have to have 12 already!"

Teacher: "Yes, and that's why the other factors 2, 3, 4, and 6 are called *proper* factors; you use them to make 12 without having 12 already. However, 1 and 12 are still factors of 12 because you can divide 12 by them without leaving a remainder. Now do you know what is meant by a prime number?"

Mike: "It's a number that can't be divided by any number except itself and 1."

Linda: "So that makes 1 the first prime number, does it?"

Teacher: "No. A prime number is one that has exactly two factors, itself and 1. That rules out 1, which has just one factor. There's a good reason to rule out 1. The prime numbers can be used to make all the other numbers, called composite numbers, by multiplying; for instance $360 = 2 \times 2 \times 2 \times 3 \times 3 \times 5 = 2^3 \times 3^2 \times 5$. The number 1 is no use in that process. (If we were trying to make numbers by adding instead of multiplying, then 1 would be the only prime: you can make every other whole number by just adding up 1 enough times!)"

Linda:      "So the prime numbers are 2, 3, 5, 7, 11, 13, 17…"

Nadeem:     "Does anyone know how many prime numbers there are?"

Teacher:    "Yes, that is known. Just think of any finite collection of prime numbers. Suppose you multiply all those numbers together and then add 1, what can you say about the answer you'd get?"

Mike:       "It wouldn't be divisible by any of the prime numbers you started with. So I guess it would be a new prime number, or if not, it must be made by multiplying prime numbers that weren't in the original set."

Teacher:    "That's right; and that shows that any finite collection of primes can't contain them all, so there are infinitely many prime numbers. That was proved by the Greek mathematician Euclid many centuries ago."

Nadeem:     "How do we find if a number is prime or not?"

Mike:       "It couldn't end in an even digit or in 5, otherwise it would be a multiple of 2 or of 5."

Teacher:    "That's right. Do you know how to test for divisibility by 3?"

Nadeem:     "You have to add the digits I think; but why does that work?"

Teacher:    "OK, let's say we start with 7458. That's $7 \times 1000 + 4 \times 100 + 5 \times 10 + 8$. Now what is $1000 - 1$ and what is $100 - 1$?"

Linda:      "They're 999 and 99 of course."

Teacher:    "That's right, and of course $10 - 1 = 9$. So then $7458 = 7 \times 999 + 7 \times 1 + 4 \times 99 + 4 \times 1 + 5 \times 1 + 5 \times 9 + 5 \times 1 + 8$ which is $(7 \times 999 + 4 \times 99 + 5 \times 9) + 7 + 4 + 5 + 8$. Can you see what follows from that?"

Mike:       "The first part in brackets must be a multiple of 9, and the rest is just the sum of the digits of the original number."

Nadeem:     "So the original number 7458 is the same as the sum of the digits plus a multiple of 9; so if you divide the original number by 9 you get the same remainder as if you divide the digit sum by 9."

Teacher:    "That's right. Here the digit sum comes to 24. When you divide that by 9 the remainder is 6 (which is actually the digit sum of 24); thus when the original number is divided by 9 the remainder is also 6, which means that 7458 is a multiple of 9, plus 6; so it is divisible by 3 though not by 9. There is a similar test for divisibility by 11, in which you alternate the signs attached to the digits; so for 7458 you do $7 - 4 + 5 - 8 = 0$. If the answer is a multiple of 11, positive, 0 or negative, then so is the original number."

Mike:       "How does that work?"

| Teacher: | "It's based on the facts that $10 = 11 - 1$, $100 = 99 + 1$, $1000 = 1100 - 99 - 1$, $10000 = 11000 - 1100 + 99 + 1$ and so on." |
|---|---|
| Linda: | "What about testing for other primes?" |
| Teacher: | "Here is a way you can check whether a number has factors while riding a bicycle, if your mental arithmetic is reasonable. Let's try 1219. The digit sum 13 is not a multiple of 3, so nor is 1219, and it's not a multiple of 2 or 5 either. To test for 7 you don't need to divide 1219 by 7 in your head. You multiply 7 by 3 to give 21 and add this to 1219 making 1240. If 1240 is a multiple of 7 then so is 124 and hence so is 62 and so is 31; clearly they are not multiples of 7, so neither is 1219. The 11 test fails; try 13. Multiply 13 by 3 to give 39 and take this away from 1219, leaving 1180, which is $118 \times 10 = 59 \times 2 \times 10$, clearly not a multiple of 13, hence neither is 1219." |
| Nadeem: | "So you keep trying to bring the original number up or down to a multiple of 10 so that you've then got a simpler number to work with, is that right?" |
| Teacher: | "That's right; and you continue so long as the prime factors you are trying are not more than the square root of the original number." |
| Mike: | "For 17, do $1219 + (17 \times 3 = 51) = 1270$, then $127 - 17 = 110$, and 11 is not a multiple of 17, so neither is 1219." |
| Linda: | "For 19, $1219 - 19 = 1200$; that's clearly not a multiple of 19." |
| Nadeem: | "With 23 we have to multiply by 3 again, is that right?" |
| Teacher: | "Yes; you either leave the potential prime factor as it is and add it to or subtract it from 1219, or you do that with 3 times the prime added to or taken from 1219, whatever gives you a multiple of 10, which then means you are looking at a much smaller number and repeating the process if necessary." |
| Nadeem: | "So $1219 - (3 \times 23 = 69) = 1150$; then $115 = 5 \times 23$. Aha! That means 23 is a factor of 1219. So 1219 is not a prime." |
| Teacher: | "Well done. $1219 = 23 \times 53$ in fact. Now I want you to make a number museum starting with 1 and working to 100, or further if you can. For each number express it as a product of powers of primes, (unless the number is a prime itself), then list all the factors of the number, then write down how many factors there are; we're going to investigate how to find the number of factors without always having to list them. So, what would you write for 24?" |
| Mike: | "24, then $2^3 \times 3$, then 1, 2, 3, 4, 6, 8, 12, 24, then 8, as there are 8 factors." |
| Teacher: | "Good; get on with that." |

Later on ...

Teacher: "OK, what sort of numbers have just one or just two factors?"

Linda: "Only 1 has just one factor, and every prime has two factors."

Teacher: "Right. What about numbers with three or four factors?"

Nadeem: "Numbers with three factors are 4, 9, 25, 49. They are squares."

Linda: "And squares of primes. 16 is a square but has five factors, and 36 has nine."

Mike: "Numbers with four factors are 6, 8, 10, 14, 15, 21, 22, 27 ... Most of those are products of just two primes, like $14 = 2 \times 7$."

Nadeem: "But 8 and 27 aren't; they are cubes of primes."

Teacher: "OK. Let's try with some letters for primes. If $p$ is prime, what factors has $p$, and what about $p^2$, $p^3$, and how about $p^n$ for any positive integer $n$?"

Linda: "$p$ has just 1 and $p$. $p^2$ has 1, $p$ and $p^2$. $p^3$ has 1, $p$, $p^2$ and $p^3$, that's four factors."

Mike: "And $p^n$ has 1, $p$, $p^2$, $p^3$, ... $p^n$; that's $n + 1$ factors for $p^n$."

Teacher: "Good. What about $pq$ if $p$ and $q$ are both primes and not equal?"

Nadeem: "The factors are 1, $p$, $q$ and $pq$; that's four factors. So that's why the numbers with four factors were partly products of two primes and partly cubes of primes. So what about $p^2 q^2$?"

Linda: "That has 1, $p$, $p^2$, $q$, $pq$, $pq^2$, $q^2$, $pq^2$ and $p^2 q^2$; nine factors altogether."

Teacher: "Good. Can you see how to deal with $p^a q^b$ if $p$, $q$ are unequal primes and $a$, $b$ are positive integers?"

Mike: "You can take any of the $a + 1$ factors of $p^a$ and multiply by any of the $b + 1$ factors of $q^b$. So does that make $a + 1 + b + 1$ factors?"

Teacher: "Imagine you are in a restaurant for a meal, and the menu offers 3 starters and 5 main courses. How many different two course meals can you have?"

Linda: "You can have starter 1 followed by any of 5 main courses; or starter 2 followed by any of 5 ... So it must be $3 \times 5 = 15$ different two course meals."

Teacher: "That's right. And if there were 4 choices of dessert, how many three course meals?"

Nadeem: "Any of the 15 two course meals, each with 4 choices of dessert, so there'd be $15 \times 4 = 60$ three course meals."

Mike: "Aha; if we have to make a series of choices, and the number of alternatives for each choice is given, then we have to multiply those numbers of alternatives together. So for the factors of $p^a q^b$ we need a factor of $p^a$ times a factor of $q^b$, and that makes $(a + 1)(b + 1)$ choices. Does that generalise to numbers with three or more prime factors raised to various powers?"

Teacher:  "Yes indeed. If the number has the form $p^a q^b r^c \ldots$ then the number of factors is $(a + 1)(b + 1)(c + 1) \ldots$ with as many brackets as there are prime factors. To finish for now, here's a problem: A class has 32 boys and there are 32 lockers numbered 1 to 32. One day when they can't think of anything better to do, the lockers are all closed, and the first boy opens them all. Then the second boy closes every second locker, numbers 2, 4, 6 to 32. Then the third boy changes the state (open to shut or shut to open) of every third locker, numbers 3, 6, 9 up to 30. They continue this way until the 32nd boy just changes the state of the 32nd locker. Which lockers are open at the end of all that?"

# Part II
## 14–16 years old

# The difference of two squares revisited

Teacher: "You've seen that $a^2 - b^2$ can be *factorised*, that is expressed as a product of two factors $a - b$ and $a + b$. Can you do something like that with $a^2 + b^2$?"

Paula: "Maybe $(a + b) \times (a + b)$? That would be $(a + b)^2$."

Qasim: "That's not the same. We know it's $a^2 + b^2 + 2ab$."

Teacher: "Good; remember that result, or at least remember that squaring and adding two numbers does *not* give the same result as adding and then squaring! Most schoolboys (and girls) are convinced that all functions are additive, namely that $f(a + b) = f(a) + f(b)$ is true, whatever $f$ is; but in fact that's not true in general! But to come back to trying to factorise $a^2 + b^2$ Any other ideas? . . . No? Well now consider the equation $x^2 - 25 = 0$. How would you solve that?"

Paula: "Can't you just say $x^2 = 25$ so $x = 5$?"

Ricky: "What about $x = -5$? That squares to 25 as well."

Teacher: "Good. Now can anyone see another way that uses factorising of $x^2 - 25$?"

Qasim: "It's the same as $x^2 - 5^2 = (x - 5)(x + 5) = 0$. Then what?"

Teacher: "OK; now how can two numbers multiply to give 0?"

Paula: "One of them must be 0, otherwise the answer would be positive or negative, not 0."

Qasim: "Aha, so then $x - 5 = 0$ or $x + 5 = 0$, making $x = 5$ or $-5$."

Teacher: "Right! Now let's look at another equation, $x^2 + 64 = 0$. Any ideas?"

Ricky: "Then $x^2 = -64$. But hang on, both $8^2$ and $(-8)^2$ make 64 not $-64$."

Paula: "There isn't any number that has a negative square. So that equation can't be solved."

Teacher: "That's right. The equation has no solution. So what about factorising $x^2 + 64$?"

| Qasim: | "If we could factorise it like we factorised $x^2 - 25$ we'd be able to solve it, but that's impossible; so it must be impossible to factorise $x^2 + 64$." |
|---|---|
| Teacher: | "That's right; and that puts paid to our trying to find factors for $a^2 + b^2$. By the way, if you go further in maths you may learn about an extended number system that does include square roots for negative numbers. If you look at the number line with 0 in the centre, positive numbers on the right and negatives on the left, can you think of a geometric operation that is equivalent to multiplying numbers by $-1$?" |
| Paula: | "That turns positives into negatives and vice versa; it could be a 180° rotation." |
| Teacher: | "That's right; now could you do that operation in two equal stages?" |
| Qasim: | "You could do a 90° turn, but which way? Clockwise or anticlockwise I guess." |
| Teacher: | "That's right; so the square roots of negative numbers then lie on a line at right angles to the original number line, and you get a number plane instead of just a line; it's called the complex number plane, and the complex numbers are effectively two dimensional vectors, but they can also be multiplied and divided like the ordinary numbers. However, that's for the future. |
| | Now let's look at the sequence of square numbers: 0, 1, 4, 9, 16, 25 . . . What do you notice about the differences between successive squares?" |
| Ricky: | "They're 1, then 3, then 5, then 7 and so on; successive odd numbers. But does that continue in the same way?" |
| Paula: | "Can we try it with algebra? If we call one number $n^2$ then the next is $(n + 1)^2$ . . ." |
| Qasim: | "And then the difference is $(n + 1)^2 - n^2$ and that's the same as $(n + 1 + n) \times (n + 1 - n) = 2n + 1$, which makes the sequence of odd numbers when you put $n = 0, 1, 2, 3, 4$ and so on." |
| Teacher: | "Yes, in fact the difference between the squares is equal to the sum of the two unsquared numbers, $n$ and $n + 1$, and that's always odd. So what is $3001^2 - 3000^2$?" |
| Paula: | "That's $3001 + 3000 = 6001$." |
| Teacher: | "Right; and what happens when you add up a number of successive odd numbers, $1 + 3 + 5 + 7$ . . ." |
| Ricky: | "$1 + 3 = 4, 1 + 3 + 5 = 9, 1 + 3 + 5 + 7 = 16$; it looks like the answers are always square numbers." |
| Paula: | "Why is that then? Is it to do with the odd numbers being differences of squares?" |

Teacher:     "Yes; look at it this way: $1 + 3 + 5 + 7 = 1^2 - 0^2 + 2^2 - 1^2 + 3^2 - 2^2 + 4^2 - 3^2$."

Paula:       "That comes down to $4^2 - 0^2 = 4^2$, because all the other squares are added and then subtracted."

Teacher:     "Exactly. In the same way the sum of the first $n$ odd numbers adds up to $n^2$, because each odd number is the difference between two successive square numbers. So what is $1 + 3 + 5 + 7 + 9 + \ldots + 99$?"

Qasim:       "Is it $99^2$? That would be 9801."

Ricky:       "No, you have to work out how many odd numbers there are in the sum and square that."

Paula:       "Yes, the $n$th odd number is $2n - 1$, so if that is 99, $n = 50$ and the sum is $50^2 = 2500$."

Teacher:     "That's it; well done. This also leads to a way of factorising large numbers that works well when the number has factors that are not far from each other, and was a method used by mathematicians such as Euler in the heroic days of number theory without any calculating aids. It needs an extensive table of squares, or nowadays a calculator with square root button. Let's take 6319. Is that a square?"

Ricky:       "No, its square root is a long decimal between 79 and 80."

Teacher.     "Right, now add 1 to make 6320. Is that square? No? OK, add 3 and try 6323. Still not square? Add 5 next, to give 6328. How much have we added so far?"

Qasim:       "$1 + 3 + 5 = 9$; and we still don't have a square."

Teacher:     "OK, add 7, then 9, then 11 and so on. See what happens."

After a while,

Paula:       "I got up to adding 17 and reached 6400. That's a square, it's $80^2$!"

Teacher:     "Right; so how much did you add altogether?"

Paula:       "17 is the 9th odd number, so the numbers I added totalled to $9^2$."

Teacher:     "So $6319 + 9^2 = 80^2$. How does that help?"

Ricky:       "Then $6319 = 80^2 - 9^2 = (80 - 9)(80 + 9) = 71 \times 89$."

Teacher:     "That's right, and so 6319 has been factorised; it's a product of those two prime numbers. For homework try factorising 4891, 3127, 2961 and 9523."

Answers:     $4891 = 67 \times 73$, $3127 = 53 \times 59$, $2961 = 47 \times 63$, $9523 = 89 \times 107$.

# The *m,d* method

## An alternative approach to quadratics

Teacher: "How would you find two numbers with a sum of 64 and product 999?"

Paula: "You could do it by trial, couldn't you?"

Ricky: "But there should be a more systematic way. Let one number be $x$; the other is then $64 - x$."

Qasim: "So then $x(64 - x) = 999$; that makes $64x - x^2 = 999$ so $0 = x^2 - 64x + 999$."

Paula: "But then to factorise the right hand side into two brackets like $(x - a)(x - b)$ you have to make $a + b = 64$ and $ab = 999$, and you're back to trial, which I wanted to do in the first place."

Qasim: "Or you can use completing the square, or the quadratic formula."

Teacher: "You're quite right; trying to solve by factors really takes you back to the original problem, and you do have the option to use the other techniques Qasim has mentioned. But there is a simpler approach I want to show you. Call the numbers $x$ and $y$, and think of them on a number line as in the diagram, with $m$ being the number halfway in between, and $d$ the distance of each from $m$."

Paula: "So then $x = m - d$ and $y = m + d$."

Qasim: "That makes $x + y = 2m = 64$, so $m = 32$."

Ricky: "And $xy = (m - d)(m + d) = m^2 - d^2 = 32^2 - d^2 = 999$."

Paula: "So $d^2 = 32^2 - 999 = 1024 - 999 = 25$. $d$ must be 5, that makes $x = 32 - 5 = 27$, $y = 32 + 5 = 37$."

Teacher: "Good; you're getting the hang of it right away. One point though: if $d^2 = 25$, does $d$ have to be 5, or is there another possibility?"

Ricky: "$d$ could be $-5$; that would make $x = 37$ and $y = 27$; but on the diagram $x$ is less than $y$."

Teacher: "Yes, it does look that way on the diagram, but you have to be aware of the other possibility. I asked at first about finding two numbers with sum 64 and product 999. The numbers are 27 and 37; the order doesn't matter. But if I had asked you to find where the graphs of $x + y = 54$ and $xy = 999$ meet, there would be two answers."

Qasim: "(27, 37) and (37, 27)?"

Teacher: "That's right, and you would need to give both. So whether there is just one answer or two depends on how the original problem is posed. For example, can you find the length and width of a rectangle with perimeter 922 cm and area 51408 cm²? Feel free to use your calculators for the details."

Ricky: "Let the length $l = m + d$ and the width $w = m - d$, so $2l + 2w = 4m = 922$, $m = 230.5$."

Paula: "And the area is $lw = (m + d)(m - d) = m^2 - d^2 = 230.5^2 - d^2 = 51408$."

Qasim: "So $d^2 = 230.5^2 - 51408 = 17220.25$; that makes $d = 41.5$, so $l = 272$, $w = 189$."

Paula: "Or could $d = -41.5$?"

Teacher: "Not in this case, because $l$ is the *length* and $w$ the *width* of a rectangle, so $l$ can't be less than $w$. Here is a case where there is just one solution to the problem as set. Now can you use the $m$, $d$ approach to solve $x - y = 18$, $x^2 + y^2 = 1844$?"

Ricky: "That makes $x > y$ so it doesn't make sense to say $x = m - d, y = m + d$ does it?"

Teacher: "It's not impossible, as $d$ can be negative, but it does make sense this time to let $x = m + d, y = m - d$."

Ricky: "So $x - y = 2d = 18, d = 9$."

Paula: "And $x^2 + y^2 = (m + d)^2 + (m - d)^2 = 2m^2 + 2d^2 = 1844$, so $m^2 = 922 - 9^2 = 841$."

Qasim: "So $m = 29$ or $-29$. That makes $(x, y) = (38, 20)$ or $(-20, -38)$."

Teacher: "Well done all of you. You can see this time the second solution is not just the first one with the numbers swapped. You'll see this even more with $5x - 8y = 96, xy = 2376$."

Ricky: "Are we still supposed to use the same method? With $x = m - d, y = m + d$ we get $5m - 5d - 8m - 8d = -3m - 13d = 96$ and $m^2 - d^2 = 2376$. That looks worse than the original problem!"

Teacher: "You're right; but that's not what we do. We let $u = 5x, v = 8y$ so that $uv = 40 \times 2376 = 95040$."

Qasim: "So let $u = m + d$, $v = m - d$, so $2d = 96$, $d = 48$ and $m^2 - d^2 = 95040$."

Paula: "Then $m^2 = 48^2 + 95040 = 97344$, so $m = \pm312$."

Ricky: "That makes $(u, v) = (312 + 48, 312 - 48) = (360, 264)$ or
$(-312 + 48, -312 - 48) = (-264, -360)$.

Teacher: "Yes, but what about $x$ and $y$?"

Paula: "$x = \dfrac{u}{5}$ and $y = \dfrac{v}{8}$ so $(x, y) = (72, 33)$ or $(-52.8, -45)$. They're completely different!"

Teacher: "Yes, that reflects the fact that the first equation $5x - 8y = 96$ is not symmetric in $x$ and $y$."

Qasim: "So can we use this method for any pair of equations?"

Teacher: "Well, try it on $5x - 8y = 96$, $x^2 + y^2 = 6273$."

Qasim: "Start with $u = 5x = m + d$, $v = 8y = m - d$ like in the last one."

Paula: "Then you have $\left(\dfrac{u}{5}\right)^2 + \left(\dfrac{v}{8}\right)^2 = 6273$, that's $\dfrac{(m+d)^2}{25} + \dfrac{(m-d)^2}{64} = 6273$."

Ricky: Of course you still have $2d = 96$ so $d = 48$ from the first equation, but even then the second equation looks heavy going."

Teacher: "Yes, it becomes a quadratic equation in $m$, so no better than if we had used the standard approach of solving the first equation for $y$ in terms of $x$ and substituting in the second equation. However, you can use the $m,d$ approach to factorise a quadratic, especially if the coefficient of $x^2$ is 1. Try it with $x^2 - 47x - 1800$"

Qasim: "The factors would be $(x + p)(x - q)$ with $p - q = -47$ and $pq = 1800$."

Paula: "So if $p = m - d$, $q = m + d$ then $-2d = -47$ so $d = 23.5$."

Ricky: "And $m^2 - d^2 = m^2 - 23.5^2 = 1800$, which makes $m^2 = 1800 + 23.5^2 = 2352.25$."

Paula: "Then $m = \pm48.5$. Does that give two different ways to do the factorisation?"

Teacher: "Not really. We can assume $p$ and $q$ are positive; the plus and minus signs in the two brackets were chosen with that in mind; so take $m = 48.5$."

Paula: "Then $p = 48.5 - 23.5 = 25$ and $q = 48.5 + 23.5 = 72$."

Qasim: "So the factors are $(x + 25)(x - 72)$."

Teacher: "Good. If you did use $m = -48.5$ you would just get $p = -72$ and $q = -25$, and just end up with the same factors but the other way round."

Ricky: "What if the coefficient of $x^2$ is not 1?"

Teacher: "It is possible to modify the method for that situation, but it's a bit cumbersome. If the aim is to solve an equation, then if it is difficult to spot the factors by trial, (or if it's not going to factorise anyway using whole numbers) it's best to divide both sides by the coefficient of $x^2$. For instance, can you find the width of a frame of area 100 cm² that surrounds a picture with length 30 cm and width 21 cm? (That's almost A4.)"

Qasim: "If the width is $w$ all round then the area is the perimeter times $w$, so $102w = 100$. That's easy; it's not a quadratic anyway!"

Ricky: "That's because it's wrong, silly! You've left out the squares in the four corners. It should be $4w^2 + 102w = 100$. Then divide by 4 to make $w^2 + 25.25w = 25$."

Qasim: "All right; do you never make mistakes? So it's $w^2 + 25.25 - 25 = 0$ and we want to factorise the left side to $(w - p)(w + q)$."

Paula: "So $q - p = 25.25$ and $pq = 25$. Let $q = m + d$, $p = m - d$ and get $2d = 25.25$ so $d = 12.625$."

Ricky: "And $m^2 - 12.625^2 = 25$, $m^2 = 184.390625$. Does that have an exact square root!"

Teacher: "No, it doesn't, so work to 3DP."

Ricky: "OK, taking the positive root $m = 13.579$."

Qasim: "So $p = 0.954$, $q = 26.204$ and the factors are $(w - 0.954)(w + 26.204)$."

Paula: "So the width is 0.954 cm to 3DP."

Teacher: "Good. The other way of course is to use the formula for solving a quadratic equation."

Qasim: "Can you use $m$, $d$ to derive the formula?"

Teacher: "Yes; why not try that now?"

Qasim: "Start with $ax^2 + bx + c = 0$, but how to factorise that?"

Ricky: "Can we divide by $a$, get $x^2 + \dfrac{bx}{a} + \dfrac{c}{a} = 0$? Then make the left side into factors: $(x + p)(x + q)$."

Paula: "Then $p + q = \dfrac{b}{a}$ and $pq = \dfrac{c}{a}$. So if $p = m - d$, $q = m + d$, $2m = \dfrac{b}{a}$ so $m = \dfrac{b}{2a}$."

Qasim: "And $m^2 - d^2 = \dfrac{b^2}{4a^2} - d^2 = \dfrac{c}{a}$. That makes $d^2 = \dfrac{b^2}{4a^2} - \dfrac{c}{a} = \dfrac{b^2 - 4ac}{4a^2}$."

Ricky: "So then $p = \dfrac{b}{2a} - \sqrt{\dfrac{b^2 - 4ac}{4a^2}}$; that's same as $\dfrac{b - \sqrt{b^2 - 4ac}}{2a}$."

Paula: "And $q = \dfrac{b + \sqrt{b^2 - 4ac}}{2a}$; is that right?"

Teacher:  "Yes; and then the roots of the equation are $-p$ and $-q$ which gives the formula $\dfrac{-b \pm \sqrt{b^2 - 4ac}}{2a}$ for the two roots. Now you can try the questions in the exercise."

The following exercise is taken from my article "The m-d Method" in the Mathematical Association's journal *Mathematics in School*, 33 (3), May 2004, page 8, with permission.

## Exercise

Find two numbers with sum and product given as follows:

1  Sum 20, product 91        2  Sum 56, product 768        3  Sum 17, product 70.81

Solve the equations:

4  $x + y = -15$, $xy = -154$        5  $x + y = 190$, $xy = 8881$        6  $x + y = 565$, $xy = 79\,156$

7  $x - y = 12$, $xy = 493$        8  $x - y = 27$, $xy = 1798$        9  $x - y = 60$, $xy = -576$

10  $x - y = -18$, $xy = 1855$        11  $x^2 + y^2 = 400$, $x + y = 28$        12  $x + y = 4$, $x^2 + y^2 = 3208$

13  $x^2 + y^2 = 2098$, $xy = 999$        14  $2x + 5y = 105$, $xy = 170$        15  $3x - 8y = 19$, $xy = 175$

16  $4x^2 + 9y^2 = 11\,925$, $xy = 525$

17  Find the length and width of a rectangle with perimeter 250 m and area 3526 m².

18  Find the length of the diagonal of a rectangle with area 660 m² and perimeter 142 m.

19  Find the area of a right-angled triangle with hypotenuse 41 m and perimeter 90 m.

20  Find the perimeter of a right-angled triangle with area 924 m² and hypotenuse 65 m.

Factorise:

21  $x^2 + 60x + 864$        22  $x^2 - 137x + 4680$        23  $x^2 + 130x + 4189$

24  $x^2 + 12x - 4453$        25  $x^2 - 100x - 5244$

Solve, correct to 3DP:

26  $x + y = 10$, $xy = 23$        27  $x^2 - 6x + 4 = 0$

28  The points $A$, $B$ are on the x-axis and y-axis respectively. The line $AB$ has length 70 and passes through the point (24, 24). Find the area of the triangle $OAB$.

29  A ladder 442 cm long leans against a vertical wall and just touches a cubical box of side 120 cm which is on the ground and in contact with the wall. Given that the ladder is leaning at more than 45° to the horizontal, find how far it reaches up the wall.

# Answers

**1** 7, 13　　**2** 24, 32　　**3** 7.3, 9.7　　**4** −22, 7 or 7, −22　　**5** 83, 107 or 107, 83
**6** 257, 308 or 308, 257　　**7** 29, 17 or −17, −29　　**8** 58, 31 or −31, −58
**9** 48, −12 or 12, −48　　**10** 35, 53 or −53, −35　　**11** 12, 16 or 16, 12　　**12** 42, −38 or −38, 42
**13** ±27, ±37 or ±37, ±27 (4 solutions)　　**14** 10, 17 or 42½, 4　　**15** 25, 7 or $-18\frac{2}{3}, -9\frac{3}{8}$
**16** ±15,　±35　or　±52½,　±10　　**17** 82m,　43m　　**18** 61m　　**19** 180m²
**20** 154m　　**21** $(x + 24)(x + 36)$　　**22** $(x - 65)(x - 72)$　　**23** $(x + 59)(x + 71)$
**24** $(x - 61)(x + 73)$　　**25** $(x - 138)(x + 38)$　　**26** 3.586, 6.414　　**27** 0.343, 11.657
**28** 1176　　**29** 408 cm.

# Negative and fractional indices

Paula:     "Sir, what does $3^{-2}$ mean?"

Teacher:   "Well, can you tell me what $3^4$ means?"

Paula:     "It's four 3s all multiplied together. I can understand that, but how can you have minus two 3s to multiply together?"

Teacher:   "Yes, it doesn't make sense that way, does it? Let's look at it another way. What is $1 \times 3^4$?"

Qasim:     "You multiply 1 four times over by 3, makes 81."

Teacher:   "Right, now look at this:

$$1 \times 3^4 = 81,$$
$$1 \times 3^3 = 27,$$
$$1 \times 3^2 = 9,$$
$$1 \times 3^1 = 3.$$

What is happening to the answers?"

Ricky:     "They're getting smaller, three times smaller from each number to the next. But why have you written $1\times$ at the start of each line?"

Teacher:   "That's so that in each case the index counts exactly how many times you multiply by 3. It gets 1 less from each line to the next, so the answer keeps getting divided by 3. Now what's the next line?"

Paula:     "$1 \times 3^0 = 0$?"

Teacher:   "Why 0? Is that what you get when you divide 3 by 3?"

Qasim:     "It should be $1 \times 3^0 = 1$, so that makes $3^0 = 1$?"

| | |
|---|---|
| Teacher: | "Yes; if you do no multiplication at all by 3 then you don't change anything, and that's the same as multiplying by 1. So what's the next line?" |
| Ricky: | "$1 \times 3^{-1} = -3$?" |
| Teacher: | "No, you're doing $3 \times -1$, that's not what raising to a power means, just like $3^2$ isn't $3 \times 2$. Stick to the pattern we saw, that when the power is reduced by 1 the answer becomes three times smaller." |
| Paula: | "It should be $1 \times 3^{-1} = \frac{1}{3}$. And is the next line $1 \times 3^{-2} = \frac{1}{9}$?" |
| Teacher: | "Good! That's right. So multiplying by 3 'minus once' means the same as dividing by 3, and multiplying $-2$ times means dividing twice by 3: $1 \div 3 \div 3$ makes $\frac{1}{9}$. So can you tell me what $2^{-3}$ is?" |
| Qasim: | "That should be $\frac{1}{2^3} = \frac{1}{8}$, is that right?" |
| Teacher: | "Yes. Can you tell me what $5^0$ and $10^{-4}$ equal?" |
| Paula: | "$5^0 = 1$ and $10^{-4}$ is $1 \div 10^4$. That makes $0.0001$." |
| Teacher: | "Good, it looks as if you're happy with negative indices now. Now let's try an index that's a fraction. What can you make of $1 \times 16^{\frac{1}{2}}$?" |
| Ricky: | "Maybe 8?" |
| Teacher: | "No, you're doing $16 \times \frac{1}{2}$ aren't you? Think of doing a multiplication by 16 in two equal stages. What would each stage be? It wouldn't be multiply by 8, because doing that multiplies by 64 not 16." |
| Ricky: | "Oh, it must be multiply by 4." |
| Teacher: | "That's right. What about $1 \times 25^{\frac{1}{2}}$ and $1 \times 100^{\frac{1}{2}}$?" |
| Qasim: | "Er, 5 and 10? It looks like the square root, is that right?" |
| Teacher: | "Yes, If you multiply by $\sqrt{n}$ and again by $\sqrt{n}$ you have multiplied altogether by $n$, so multiplying by $\sqrt{n}$ is half the job of multiplying by $n$, which is what multiplying by $n^{\frac{1}{2}}$ means. Now can you give a meaning to $1 \times 8^{\frac{1}{3}}$?" |
| Paula: | "That would be multiplying by 8 in three equal stages; each of those is multiplying by 2." |
| Ricky: | "So $n^{\frac{1}{3}}$ means the cube root of $n$; is that right?" |
| Teacher: | "Yes, well done! Now how about $1000^{-\frac{2}{3}}$?" |

The following note is taken directly from my article "Negative and Fractional Indices: Making Them Make Sense" in the Mathematical Association's journal *Mathematics in School*, 33 (2), March 2004, page 9, with permission.

The reader will have noticed that an important part of the foregoing treatment of indices is the replacing of a power such as $5^3$ by an expression like $1 \times 5^3$, designed to make the index equal to the number of multiplications rather than just the number of 5s. This has enabled us later to talk about "doing half a multiplication by 16," and making sense of that; whereas "multiplying half a sixteen together" (the exact counterpart to "multiplying three fives together") is irreparable nonsense.

This change really focuses on the operation of multiplying by a number. Suppose we define the notation $\{\times 16\}$ to mean the function $f$ given by $f(x) = 16x$; thus $\{\times 16\}(3) = 48$; indeed $\{\times 16\}(x)$ just means $16x$. Likewise, we'll define $\{+16\}(x)$ to mean $x + 16$, and so also for $-$ and $\div$. (I've chosen 16 as a specific number to keep things more concrete; what follows would apply equally with any other number.)

Using the standard notation for composition of functions, $f^2(x) = ff(x) = f(f(x))$, $f^3(x) = fff(x) = f(f(f(x)))$, and so on. $f^n(x)$ can be defined inductively as $f^n(x) = f(f^n(x))$. Also $f^{-1}(x)$ is the usual inverse of $f$, meaning that $f^{-1}f(x) = ff^{-1}(x) = x$.

If we apply this to the function $\{\times 16\}$, for example, we have $\{\times 16\}^2 = \{\times 256\} = \{\times 16^2\}$, and more generally $\{\times 16\}^n = \{\times 16^n\}$. Also $\{\times 16\}^{-1} = \{\div 16\} = \{\times 16^{-1}\}$. If we wanted to define $f^0$, we would require that $f^0(x) = x$ meaning that $f^0$ does nothing. This would make $\{\times 16\}^0 = \{\times 1\}$.

If, on the other hand, we think of the function $\{+16\}$ which adds 16 to its input, we find $\{+16\}^2 = \{+32\} = \{+(16 \times 2)\}$, $\{+16\}^n = \{+16n\}$, $\{+16\}^{-1} = \{-16\}$ and $\{+16\}^0 = \{+0\}$.

Coming to fractions, we would want $f^{\frac{1}{4}}(x)$ to be a function $g$ with the property $g^4(x) = f(x)$, and then $f^{\frac{3}{4}}$ would be $g^3$. Following this through we find $\{\times 16\}^{\frac{1}{4}} = \{\times 2\}$ and $\{\times 16\}^{\frac{3}{4}} = \{\times 8\}$, whereas $\{+16\}^{\frac{1}{4}} = \{+4\}$ and $\{+16\}^{\frac{3}{4}} = \{+12\}$. The learner's tendency to interpret $16^{\frac{3}{4}}$ as $\frac{3}{4}$ of 16, i.e. 12, arises probably from an inadequate awareness that it is $\frac{3}{4}$ of the $\times 16$ operation, rather than of $+16$, that is meant.

Geometrically $\{+16\}$ is a translation of the number line by 16 units to the right; three quarters of this is a translation by 12 units. Meanwhile $\{\times 16\}$ is an enlargement with a scale factor of 16, and three quarters of this is an enlargement with scale factor 8. In the complex plane, if $z = x + iy$ has modulus $r$ and argument $\theta$, then $\{+z\}$ is a translation of the plane by $x\mathbf{i} + y\mathbf{j}$, while $\{\times z\}$ is a rotation through $\theta$ combined with an enlargement with scale factor $r$. If $n$ is any real number, $\{\times z\}^n = \{\times z^n\}$ makes a rotation through $n\theta$ combined with an enlargement with factor $r^n$.

## A concluding problem

Given $a = 2\frac{1}{4}$ and $b = 3\frac{3}{8}$, prove (no calculator!) that $a^b = b^a$ and find other rational solutions of $x^y = y^x$. This equation was dealt with in the *Mathematical Gazette* some years ago. As a hint, try putting $y = tx$. Enjoy the challenge!

# A way to calculate π

Ricky: "I know we have a π button on our calculator, but how do we know the value of π?"

Teacher: "There are lots of ways to calculate approximations to π: as a decimal it goes on and on for ever without going into an endlessly recurring cycle. The diagram here will help us with a way that we can do it using just Pythagoras' theorem. It shows an equilateral triangle OAB and an arc AB of a circle with centre O. If the radius is 3, what is the length of the arc?"

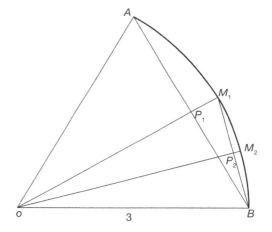

Qasim: "The angle AOB is 60° which is one sixth of 360°, so the arc length is $\frac{1}{6} \times 2\pi \times 3 \ldots$"

Paula: "That's π! But how are we going to calculate it?"

Teacher: "By a process of successive approximations. To start with, how long is AB, and what does that tell us about π?"

Ricky: "AB is 3, so π is greater than 3."

Teacher: "Right; so 3 is a rough approximation to π. To improve on it, we let $M_1$ be the midpoint of the arc, and we'll try to find $M_1B$ and double it. How can we find $M_1B$?"

Qasim: "From triangle $P_1M_1B$? $P_1B$ is 1.5, but what about $P_1M_1$?"

Paula: "You have to find $OP_1$ and take it away from $OM_1$."

Ricky: "And $OP_1$ is $\sqrt{3^2 - 1.5^2} = \sqrt{6.75} = 2.598$ to 3DP."

Teacher: "Good, but for this work you need to keep all answers to maximum accuracy."

Ricky: "OK, that's 2.598 076 211, so $P_1M_1 = 0.401\ 923\ 789$."

Qasim: "Then $M_1B$ is $\sqrt{1.5^2 + P_1M_1^2}$ which makes 1.552 914 271."

Paula: "Now double that and you get 3.105 828 541. Is that the next value for $\pi$?"

Teacher: "That's right, and next we bisect the arc $M_1B$ at $M_2$."

Ricky: "So start with $OP_2 = \sqrt{OB^2 - BP_2^2} = \sqrt{9 - 0.6028856833} = 2.897\,777\,479$."

Qasim: "Then $P_2M_2 = 3 - OP_2 = 0.102\ 222\ 521\ 2$ and
$BM_2 = \sqrt{0.1022225212^2 + 0.7764571355^2} = 0.7831571535$."

Paula: "And the next value for $\pi$ is $BM_2 \times 4 = 3.132\ 628\ 614$."

Teacher: "Good! You can carry on in the same way doing the steps with a calculator, or, as it's quite repetitive, you can set up a spreadsheet, like this:

| Pi calculation | | | | | | |
|---|---|---|---|---|---|---|
| | | | | | | |
| Stage | PB | OP | PM | MB | Powers of 2 | Pi approximation |
| 1 | 1.5 | 2.598076211 | 0.401923789 | 1.552914271 | 2 | 3.105828541 |
| 2 | 0.776457 | 2.897777479 | 0.102222521 | 0.783157153 | 4 | 3.132628613 |
| 3 | | | | | | |
| 4 | | | | | | |
| | | | | | | |

Each new $PB$ is just half of the previous $MB$. Then the new $OP$ is SQRT($3^2 - PB^2$)."

Qasim: "Then you take that away from 3 to make $PM$ and then $MB = $ SQRT($PB^2 + PM^2$)."

Teacher: "That's it; then you need a column with powers of 2, for which you simply tell it to double the number above."

Paula: "And that power of 2 times $MB$ gives the next approximation to $\pi$."

Ricky: "Once you've done the first couple of rows can you continue it by replication?"

Teacher: "Yes indeed, so the computer is doing all the repetitive work, but it isn't doing anything that you couldn't do yourself with a calculator. Try it and see what happens."

The class set to and produced the following:

**Pi calculation**

| Stage | PB | OP | PM | MB | Powers of 2 | Pi approximation |
|---|---|---|---|---|---|---|
| 1 | 1.5 | 2.598076211 | 0.401923789 | 1.552914271 | 2 | 3.105825841 |
| 2 | 0.776457 | 2.897777479 | 0.102222521 | 0.783157153 | 4 | 3.132628613 |
| 3 | 0.391579 | 2.974334584 | 0.025665416 | 0.392418775 | 8 | 3.139350203 |
| 4 | 0.196209 | 2.99357677 | 0.00642323 | 0.196314497 | 16 | 3.141031951 |
| 5 | 0.098157 | 2.998393762 | 0.001606238 | 0.09817039 | 32 | 3.141452472 |
| 6 | 0.049085 | 2.999598414 | 0.000401586 | 0.049086838 | 64 | 3.141557608 |
| 7 | 0.024543 | 2.999899602 | 0.000100398 | 0.024543624 | 128 | 3.141583892 |
| 8 | 0.012272 | 2.9999749 | 2.50997E-05 | 0.012271838 | 256 | 3.141590463 |
| 9 | 0.006136 | 2.999993725 | 6.27492E-06 | 0.006135922 | 512 | 3.141592106 |
| 10 | 0.003068 | 2.999998431 | 1.56873E-06 | 0.003067961 | 1024 | 3.141592517 |
| 11 | 0.001534 | 2.999999608 | 3.92183E-07 | 0.001533981 | 2048 | 3.141592619 |
| 12 | 0.000767 | 2.999999902 | 9.80457E-08 | 0.00076699 | 4096 | 3.141592645 |
| 13 | 0.000383 | 2.999999975 | 2.45114E-08 | 0.000383495 | 8192 | 3.141592651 |
| 14 | 0.000192 | 2.999999994 | 6.12786E-09 | 0.000191748 | 16384 | 3.141592653 |
| 15 | 9.59E-05 | 2.999999998 | 1.53196E-09 | 9.58738E-05 | 32768 | 3.141592653 |
| 16 | 4.79E-05 | 3 | 3.82991E-10 | 4.79369E-05 | 65536 | 3.141592654 |
| 17 | 2.4E-05 | 3 | 9.57479E-11 | 2.39684E-05 | 131072 | 3.141592654 |
| 18 | 1.2E-05 | 3 | 2.39369E-11 | 1.19842E-05 | 262144 | 3.141592654 |

(continued)

(continued)

**Pi calculation**

| Stage | PB | OP | PM | MB | Powers of 2 | Pi approximation |
|---|---|---|---|---|---|---|
| 19 | 5.99E-06 | 3 | 5.9841E-12 | 5.99211E-06 | 524288 | 3.141592654 |
| 20 | 3E-06 | 3 | 1.49614E-12 | 2.99606E-06 | 1048576 | 3.141592654 |
| 21 | 1.5E-06 | 3 | 3.73923E-13 | 1.49803E-06 | 2097152 | 3.141592654 |
| 22 | 7.49E-07 | 3 | 9.37028E-14 | 7.49014E-07 | 4194304 | 3.141592654 |
| 23 | 3.75E-07 | 3 | 2.35367E-14 | 3.74507E-07 | 8388608 | 3.141592654 |
| 24 | 1.87E-07 | 3 | 5.77316E-15 | 1.87254E-07 | 16777216 | 3.141592654 |
| 25 | 9.36E-08 | 3 | 0 | 9.36268E-08 | 33554432 | 3.141592654 |
| 26 | 4.68E-08 | 3 | 0 | 4.68134E-08 | 67108864 | 3.141592654 |
| 27 | 2.34E-08 | 3 | 0 | 2.34067E-08 | 1.34E+08 | 3.141592654 |

Paula:      "What would happen if you kept on and on?"

Teacher:    "Not much I guess; we've come to where *PM* registers as 0, which means that
            *MB* exactly halves each time while the power of 2 doubles, so there's no scope
            for more change. The value we've arrived at is correct to 9 DP, as $\pi$ is 3.14159
            26535 89793 to 15DP."

Qasim:      "Why does the value of *PM* suddenly drop to 0, when it has been roughly
            dividing by 4 from each stage to the next? The computer is quite capable of
            processing much smaller numbers than $10^{-15}$ isn't it?"

Teacher:    "Yes it is, and you are right about the roughly dividing by 4, but the next value
            of *P* is not found by dividing by 4; it is found by subtracting *OP* from 3. The
            computer can cope with numbers down to $10^{-99}$ or so as individual numbers,
            but it cannot distinguish $3 - 10^{-16}$ from 3; it would need to work to 16DP to
            do that. Once *OP* works out so near to 3 as to be indistinguishable from 3,
            then $3 - OP$ becomes 0, and from then on there is no point in continuing the
            calculation.

            It was quite smart of you, Qasim, to spot that *PM* divides by about 4 at each
            stage; in fact that ratio is soon pretty close. Have you any idea why that's so?"

That's for the reader to think about; it's beyond the class at this stage. As a hint: use a formula
for cos $2\theta$ in terms of cos $\theta$, plus the fact that cos $\theta$ is close to 1 when $\theta$ is small.

# Pyramids and cones

Teacher: "Do you know what a prism is, and how to find its volume?"

Paula: "It's a solid that has the same cross-section all the way up its height from the base, and you just multiply the base area by the height to get the volume."

Teacher: "Good. Now look at the diagram which shows a pyramid. That's a solid with a flat base, and each point on the base is joined by a straight line to a top point $T$. Here $B$ is the point in the base vertically below $T$."

Qasim: "So is the base horizontal?"

Teacher: "Yes, $TB$ gives the height $h$ of the pyramid, measured at right angles to the base. If the base area is $A$, we want to find the volume."

Ricky: "It's got to be less than $A \times h$ because the cross-section gets smaller as you go up from the base to the top."

Teacher: "That's right. Look at the cross-section that meets $TB$ in $P$, with $TP = xh$. What can you say about the shape and area of this cross-section?"

Paula: "If $x$ and $h$ are both lengths, doesn't that make $xh$ an area?"

Teacher: "You're right, it would be an area. But here $x$ is not itself a length, it is just a number to show what fraction of the height that cross-section is below the top; so $x$ is 0 at $T$ and increases to 1 as you go down towards the base."

Qasim:     "The cross-section is the same shape as the base, but scaled down by a factor $x$, so is the area $xA$?"

Teacher:   "No. Remember that an area always needs two lengths multiplied together, so if all lengths are scaled down by a factor $x$ then areas are multiplied by $x^2$. For instance, the cross-section half way up is a half scale copy of the base but has a quarter of the area of the base."

Paula:     "So the volume is some fraction of $Ah$ that depends on averaging $x^2$ for all values of $x$ from 0 to 1. Would the average of the numbers $0^2$, $0.1^2$, $0.2^2$ and so on up to $1^2$ give us some idea?"

Ricky:     "That makes $3.85 \div 11 = 0.35$."

Teacher:   "Good idea, and of course that approach can be pursued by taking smaller intervals; if you go up in steps of 0.01 you get about 0.335; (that's not as long-winded a calculation as it might seem, because there is a formula for adding up squares of consecutive numbers.)"

Qasim:     "So is the actual fraction $\frac{1}{3}$?"

Teacher:   "Yes, and there's an easy way to see that by looking at a special case. The diagram shows a cube whose centre $K$ has been joined by straight lines to the four corners of the base, making a pyramid. Can you see how many such pyramids would fit in the cube?"

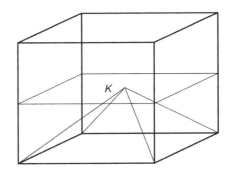

Ricky:     "You could join $K$ to the corners of any of the six faces and make a pyramid exactly like the one you've shown; so six of them would fill up the cube."

Teacher:   "That's right, and of course the pyramid has only half the height of the cube. I've shown the top face of a half cube that has the same height and same base as the pyramid."

Paula:     "And the pyramid is one sixth of the whole cube so it is one third of the half cube, making the volume equal to one third of the base area times the height."

Teacher:   "Good; and that also applies to any pyramid, which includes a pyramid on a circular base, called a cone. So what formula can you give for the volume of a cone with base radius $r$ and height $h$?"

Qasim:     "The base area is $\pi r^2$ so the volume is $\frac{1}{3}\pi r^2 h$."

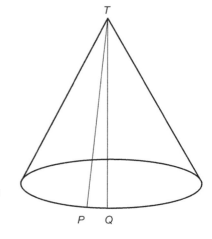

Teacher: "That's right. There's also a formula for the curved surface area. Look at *TPQ* in the diagram. What shape does it remind you of?"

Paula: "It's like a triangle, but not exactly. *TP* and *TQ* are straight lines, but *PQ* is a bit curved, and the inside is not flat as it's part of the curved surface."

Teacher: "That's true. But if you think of *PQ* getting very, very small, then the curvature matters less and less. What can you say about the area of *TPQ*, and how does that help you find the whole curved surface area?"

Qasim: "The base is *PQ* which is almost the same as a bit of the circumference, and the height is the same as *TP* or *TQ*."

Teacher: "Yes, that's called the slant height *l* of the cone. Carry on."

Qasim: "So the area is half times *l* times that bit of the circumference, so total area would be half times *l* times the whole of the circumference, that's $\frac{1}{2} \times l \times 2\pi r = \pi l r$."

Teacher: "Good; that formula is in fact exact; it's usually quoted as $\pi r l$.

Now, in the next diagram a cone has been cut off by a plane parallel to the base leaving a *frustum*. Can you find from the given dimensions (in mm) the volume of the frustum and its curved surface area?"

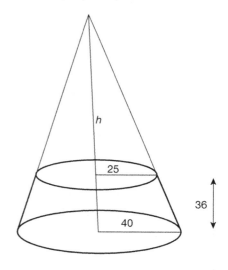

Ricky: "The two right-angled triangles are similar, so $\frac{h}{25} = \frac{h+36}{40}$. We can solve that and then get the volume of the original cone and of the cut off part and subtract."

Teacher: "Yes, that's fine; or you can reason this way without actually needing algebra: The top cone's base radius is $\frac{25}{40} = \frac{5}{8}$ of the whole cone's base radius, so the top cone's height is also $\frac{5}{8}$ of the whole cone's height, so what fraction of the whole height is the 36 mm?"

Paula: "That must be the other $\frac{3}{8}$. So then the whole height is $36 \div 3 \times 8 = 96$ mm."

Teacher: "Good. Now instead of working out two cones and subtracting, can you tell me what fraction of the whole volume was cut off and what was left? Remember that a volume always has three lengths multiplied together, and they are all scaled down the same way."

Qasim: "Then the cut off part is $\left(\frac{5}{8}\right)^3$, that's $\frac{125}{512}$ of the original volume, so the remainder, the frustum, is the other $\frac{387}{512}$. Then the frustum volume must be $\frac{387}{512} \times \frac{1}{3} \pi \times 40^2 \times 96$."

Ricky: "That comes to $38700\pi$ mm³."

Teacher: "Good. If you divide that by the height 36 of the frustum you get the average cross-section area."

Paula: "That's $1075\pi$ mm², but the average of the top and bottom areas, $625\pi$ and $1600\pi$, is $1112.5\pi$."

Teacher: "Yes, the average cross-section is a bit less than the arithmetic mean of the top and base areas. That fits with the fact that when the top is just a point (so you have a whole cone) the average cross-section is one third of the base rather than one half.

Now what about the curved surface?"

Qasim: "We need the slant height, don't we? The whole cone had height 96 and radius 40 mm so the whole slant height is $\sqrt{96^2 + 40^2} = 104$ mm."

Ricky: "That makes the whole curved surface $\pi \times 40 \times 104$, and the cut off part is $\frac{5}{8}$ of that."

Paula: "No, it's a scaled down area, so it's $\left(\frac{5}{8}\right)^2 = \frac{25}{64}$."

Ricky: "Yes, thanks for the reminder. So that leaves $\frac{39}{64}$ and makes the curved area $\frac{39}{64} \times \pi \times 40 \times 104 = 2535\pi$ mm²."

Teacher: "Well done. Now here's a challenge for you: If a frustum of any pyramid or cone has top and bottom areas $A$ and $B$, show that the overall average cross-section area is given by $\frac{1}{3}\left(A + B + \sqrt{AB}\right)$. The part $\sqrt{AB}$ is called the geometric mean of $A$ and $B$, and is known to be always less than the arithmetic mean (except when $A = B$), hence this overall average comes out less than the arithmetic mean, as we saw above."

The final challenge is included more for the reader's interest than for the pupils at this level. For why the geometric mean is less than the arithmetic mean see Chapter 14 on Another look at $(a-b)(a+b)$.

# 21 Volume and area of a sphere

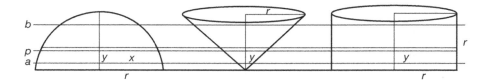

Teacher:    "Have a good look at the diagram, What do you see?"

Qasim:      "Is it a semicircle, cone and cylinder?"

Teacher:    "Yes, except that the semicircle represents a hemisphere, that's half a sphere.
            What about the dimensions of the three objects?"

Paula:      "They each have the same radius $r$."

Ricky:      "And it looks as if the cylinder and cone have height $r$ as well."

Teacher:    "That's right. That means that the cone would fit exactly inside the cylinder."

Qasim:      "It takes up one third; we saw that in the last lesson on pyramids. But what are
            the extra horizontal lines for?"

Teacher:    "They represent planes parallel to the base of the cylinder, $p$ at a height of $y$
            above the base, and another very close and parallel to it, plus two others called
            $a$ and $b$. The two that are very close together between them cut off a slice
            from each of the three solids. What shape are the slices, and what can you say
            about their sizes?"

Ricky:      "Each slice would be a circle, or a thin disc with circular top and bottom. The
            cylinder's slice obviously has radius $r$."

Paula:      "The whole cone has radius $r$ and also height $r$, so the slice cut by $p$ makes a
            smaller cone with height $y$ so its radius must be $y$ mustn't it?"

Teacher:    "Good. So what about the slice of the hemisphere? Its radius $x$ is one side of
            the right-angled triangle you can see; so what follows from that?"

Qasim: "Pythagoras' theorem: the other sides are $y$ and $r$, so $x^2 = r^2 - y^2$."

Teacher: "That's right. So now what are the areas of the three slices?"

Paula: "They're all circles. The cylinder's slice is $\pi r^2$ the cone's is $\pi y^2$ and the hemisphere's is $\pi\left(r^2 - y^2\right)$ or $\pi r^2 - \pi y^2$."

Ricky: "Hang on: that means that the hemisphere's and cone's slice areas add up to the cylinder's."

Teacher: "Good! And hence the volumes of the thin slices add up in the same way: hemisphere slice plus cone slice equals cylinder slice, since they all have the same thickness. So now what if you think of the whole of each solid between the planes $a$ and $b$ being cut up into a huge number of very thin slices?"

Paula: "The volume of hemisphere plus the volume of cone, each between $a$ and $b$, makes up the volume of cylinder between $a$ and $b$."

Teacher: "That's right, and can we say anything about total volumes?"

Qasim: "If we slice up the whole of each solid we get hemisphere plus cone equals cylinder, and since the cone takes up a third of the cylinder the hemisphere must take up two thirds of it."

Paula: "The cylinder volume is $\pi r^2 h = \pi r^3$, so the hemisphere's volume is $\frac{2}{3}\pi r^3$ and the whole sphere must be $\frac{4}{3}\pi r^3$."

Teacher: "Well done; that is the formula. And if you pack a whole sphere into a cylinder just big enough to hold it, the sphere takes up two thirds of the volume, which you can use in case you forget the formula. Remember (though you won't need this for exam purposes at this level) that the result we found gives the volume of parts of a sphere as well as the whole. For instance, what fraction of the hemisphere is more than $\frac{1}{2}r$ above the base?"

Ricky: "The cylinder volume above that level is $\frac{1}{2}\pi r^3$, and the part of the cone below $\frac{1}{2}r$ is a half scale version of the whole cone, so it's got $\frac{1}{8}$ of the volume, leaving $\frac{7}{8}$ above that level."

Paula: "That's $\frac{7}{8} \times \frac{1}{3}\pi r^3 = \frac{7}{24}\pi r^3$."

Ricky: "Yes, I was going to say that. So the top part of the hemisphere has volume $\frac{1}{2}\pi r^3 - \frac{7}{24}\pi r^3 = \frac{5}{24}\pi r^3$."

Qasim: "So that's $\dfrac{\frac{5}{24}\pi r^3}{\frac{2}{3}\pi r^3} = \frac{5}{16}$ of the hemisphere, and the other $\frac{11}{16}$ must be the part below the halfway level."

Teacher: "That's right, well done all of you. Now we want to look at surface areas. To do that let's imagine all three solids expanding very slightly, so that the radius and height of each becomes $r + \delta$, with the lowest central point of each being the centre of expansion – that's the vertex for the cone and the centre of the base for the other two solids. The two planes $a$ and $b$ do not move, and we are going to look at the extra volume between those planes on each solid. What can you say about the extra volume on the cylinder, between $a$ and $b$?"

Paula: "It's a layer of depth $\delta$ wrapped round the surface of the cylinder."

Ricky: "So that would be very nearly the curved surface area multiplied by $\delta$."

Teacher: "Good. What about the extra volume on the hemisphere?"

Qasim: "That's also a layer of depth $\delta$ covering that part of the surface, so again nearly the surface area times $\delta$."

Teacher: "Good. You're right to say 'nearly' because the layer of extra volume is not on a flat surface, so the surface area changes slightly as the expansion is happening, but by taking $\delta$ to be very small we can ignore that complication. What about the cone?"

Paula: "If that keeps the same shape and just gets a little bigger all the extra volume must be at the top, a layer of depth $\delta$ on top of the base."

Qasim: "So there's no extra volume between the two planes?"

Teacher: "That's right. The cone expands from the vertex keeping its original shape, so the extra volume is all at the top as Paula said. Now, what we found previously, that the volume between the planes on the hemisphere plus the same for the cone equals the volume of that part of the cylinder, that still holds good. What can you conclude about the extra volumes?"

Ricky: "The extra volume on the hemisphere between the planes must equal the extra volume on the cylinder between the planes."

Qasim: "And since those extra volumes are layers of the same depth $\delta$, they must be covering equal surface areas."

Teacher: "Good! And do you know how to find the curved surface area of a cylinder?"

Paula: "You can think of it as a rectangle that's been bent round. One side is the height of the cylinder and the other is the circumference of the base, so the whole area is $2\pi rh$."

Teacher: "Right; so now we can say that the surface area between two planes is the same on a sphere as on the cylinder that fits round the sphere. That was first found by the Greek mathematician Archimedes. What about the whole surface of the sphere?"

Ricky:     "Just put the planes $b$ and $a$ at the top and bottom; then the hemisphere curved surface equals the cylinder's which is $2\pi rr = 2\pi r^2$, so the whole surface is $4\pi r^2$."

Teacher:     "Good. Incidentally the hemisphere curved surface turns out to be exactly double the area of the flat circular base; that may be easier to remember than the formula itself. Here's a challenge to think about: What fraction of the earth's surface is north of the 30° parallel of latitude?"

# Straight line graphs and gradients

| | |
|---|---|
| Ricky: | "Sir, what does gradient of a line mean? It's something to do with how steep the line is; but is it like on the road you used to see a sign saying '1 in 4'?" |
| Teacher: | "Not exactly. What that road sign means is that you go up (or down) 1 metre for every 4 metres travelled along the road. In maths if we have a straight line graph drawn against $x$ and $y$ axes, then the gradient is the change in $y$ divided by the change in $x$; so we are dividing the amount risen by the amount travelled in the horizontal direction, not by the distance measured along the line." |
| Paula: | "What is the use of knowing the gradient?" |
| Teacher: | "If you have two varying quantities $x$ and $y$ it tells you how much $y$ increases per unit increase in $x$. For instance, suppose you want to hire a car for a day and that the company charges £12 for the day, plus 30p for every mile you travel. If you travel $x$ miles and are charged £$y$, how is $y$ related to $x$?" |
| Qasim: | "Does $y = 12 + 30x$ ?" |
| Ricky: | "That would make the mileage charge £30 per mile. It should be $y = 12 + 0.3x$, shouldn't it?" |
| Teacher: | "That's right. The diagram shows two graphs, one of which has the equation $y = 12 + 0.3x$. Can you see which one?" |
| Paula: | "It's the one sloping up, starting presumably at 12 on the $y$-axis." |
| Teacher: | "Yes; we say that the $y$-intercept is 12: in this context it's what you have to pay to hire the car even if you don't do any distance in it. What about the gradient?" |

| | |
|---|---|
| Qasim: | "Every extra mile; an extra 30p or £0.30, so the gradient is 0.3, isn't it?" |
| Teacher: | "Good, that's exactly what the gradient is telling us: the increase in $y$ per unit increase in $x$, which is 0.3 pounds per mile in this example." |
| Ricky: | "What is the other graph about?" |
| Teacher: | "That's a boy who has just had £5 pocket-money and wants to stock up on his favourite flapjack bars which he can get for 25p each. If he buys $x$ bars and has £$y$ left, what is $y$ in terms of $x$?" |
| Ricky: | "That would be $y = 5 - 0.25x$, would it?" |
| Teacher: | "That's right; and what are the $y$-intercept and the gradient?" |
| Qasim: | "The $y$-intercept is 5; that's what he has if he buys no flapjack at all; and the gradient looks like 0.25." |
| Paula: | "Isn't it $-0.25$? His money goes *down* by £0.25 for every further bar he buys." |
| Teacher: | "That's right, and that's why the graph slopes down from left right. Now in general a straight line graph will have an equation that can be written in the form $y = mx + c$. To find the $y$-intercept and the gradient let's look at a simple table of values:" |

| $x$ | 0 | 1 | 2 | 3 |
|---|---|---|---|---|
| $y$ | $c$ | $m+c$ | $2m+c$ | $3m+c$ |

| | |
|---|---|
| Ricky: | "The $y$-intercept must be $c$, because that's what $y$ is when $x = 0$." |
| Qasim: | "And every time $x$ increases by 1, $y$ increases by $m$, so the gradient is $m$." |
| Teacher: | "Good! So that's how you can find the gradient and intercept from the equation. This does not apply to lines that are parallel to the $y$-axis, however. Think of the $y$-axis itself, and take two points, say (0, 3) and (0, 8). What happens if you try to find its gradient?" |
| Qasim: | "That would be $\frac{5}{0}$ which is impossible, because no number multiplied by 0 can make 5." |
| Teacher: | "That's right; and if you think about it, the change in $y$ per unit change in $x$ can't exist when $x$ never changes as you move along the line." |
| Ricky: | "So does such a line have an equation at all?" |
| Teacher: | "Think of some points on the $y$-axis and tell me their coordinates." |
| Ricky: | "(0, 0), (0, 4), (0, −5), (0, 23). Oh, I suppose the equation is just $x = 0$ since that applies to all the points on the axis." |
| Paula: | "And would a vertical line through (7, 0) have equation $x = 7$?" |

Teacher: "That's right; all other lines have $x$ changing along them and so have gradients (including lines parallel to the $x$-axis: they have gradient 0 and equation $y = c$.) Using the gradient also enables you to find the equation of a line: what if a line passes through (3, 5) and (11, 37)?"

Paula: "The gradient must be $\frac{37-5}{11-3} = \frac{32}{8} = 4$. So the equation would be $y = 4x + c$; but how do we find $c$?"

Teacher: "Here's one way: if you change $x$ from 3 to 0, what is the change in $x$ and hence what is the change in $y$?"

Paula: "$x$ changes by $-3$, so $y$ changes by $-3 \times 4 = -12$; that would make $y = 5 - 12 = -7$ at $x = 0$, so the $y$-intercept is $-7$."

Ricky: "So the equation is $y = 4x - 7$; I suppose another way would be simply to put the values 3, 5 for $x$ and $y$ into the equation $y = 4x + c$, get $5 = 4 \times 3 + c$, from which $c = -7$."

Teacher: "That's right; and yet another way is to think of $(x, y)$ as a general point on the line, and (3, 5) as another point, and express the gradient as $\frac{y-5}{x-3}$, from which we can say $\frac{y-5}{x-3} = 4$, or $y - 5 = 4(x - 3)$, which again leads to $y = 4x - 7$. A good idea is to check the answer using the other point, in this case (11, 37). What is $4 \times 11 - 7$?"

Qasim: "That's 37, which is the $y$ value for that point."

Teacher: "That's right, and it checks the work. The use of equations for straight lines is often helpful in geometry. For instance, to find the side of a square that will just fit inside an isosceles triangle with corners $A$, $B$, $C$ at (0, 6), (−4, 0) and (4, 0): see the figure. To start with, can you find the equation for line $AC$?"

Qasim: "It joins (0, 6) to (4, 0) so the gradient is $-\frac{6}{4} = -\frac{3}{2}$."

Paula: "And the intercept is 6, so it's $y = -\frac{3}{2}x + 6$."

Teacher: "Good; and the coordinates of $P$ satisfy that equation, because $P$ is on that line. Can you see anything else about the coordinates of $P$?"

Ricky: "If $P$ is the corner of a square, then $MP = \frac{1}{2}QP$ because $MP$ is half the side of the square."

Teacher: "Right; so if we say $P$ is at $(x, y)$ then we have $y = 2x$ as well as $y = -\frac{3}{2}x + 6$."

Ricky: "Aha! So then we can say $2x = -\frac{3}{2}x + 6$."

Qasim: "That makes $4x = -3x + 12$, so $7x = 12$ and $x = \frac{12}{7}$."

Paula: "That makes the side of the square equal $\frac{24}{7}$ or $3\frac{3}{7}$."

Teacher: "Well done! Now suppose we want to find the centre of the circle that passes through $A$, $B$ and $C$. What would you do to find that by drawing?"

Paula: "The centre is equidistant from each corner, so you'd draw the perpendicular bisector of each side and find where they meet."

Ricky: "The perpendicular bisector of $BC$ is the $y$-axis, so we just need the perpendicular bisector of $AB$ or $AC$."

Teacher: "Right: we'll try and do it by calculation; so where is the midpoint of $AC$?"

Qasim: "You go halfway from 0 to 4 for $x$ and halfway from 6 to 0 for $y$: that makes it $(2, 3)$. But what about the gradient?"

Teacher: "Yes, we need a way to find that. Have a look at the diagram. What is the gradient of the line joining $O$ to $P$? And what about $OP'$, which is drawn at right angles to $OP$?"

Paula: "The gradient for $OP$ is $\frac{m}{1}$, that's just $m$."

Ricky: "And turning through a right angle means that from $O$ to $P'$ is 1 up and $-m$ along, which makes the gradient of $OP'$ $\frac{1}{-m}$ which is $-\frac{1}{m}$."

Teacher: "That's right; so if two lines are perpendicular the gradient of each is the negative of the reciprocal of the other. Now, in our triangle the gradient of $AC$ is $-\frac{3}{2}$. What does that make the gradient of the perpendicular bisector?"

Paula: "That's $-1 \div \left(-\frac{3}{2}\right) = \frac{2}{3}$. And the line goes through the midpoint $(2, 3)$ so its equation is . . . "

Ricky: "We don't really need the equation as a whole; we just want to know where it meets the $y$-axis; so from the midpoint $(2, 3)$ we want a change of $-2$ in $x$; that makes a change of $-2 \times \frac{2}{3} = -\frac{4}{3}$ in $y$; that takes $y$ from 3 to $3 - \frac{4}{3} = \frac{5}{3}$ or $1\frac{2}{3}$; the circle's centre is at $(0, 1\frac{2}{3})$."

Paula: "As I was saying before that interruption, the equation is
$$y - 3 = \frac{2}{3}(x - 2) = \frac{2}{3}x - \frac{4}{3} \text{ so } y = \frac{2}{3}x + 3 - \frac{4}{3} = \frac{2}{3}x + 1\frac{2}{3}, \text{ which makes the intercept}$$
$1\frac{2}{3}$ again."

Ricky: "Sorry, Paula!"

Teacher: "You're both right, and you can choose which method you prefer. To get your algebraic brains going, suppose the triangle had base *b* instead of 8 and height *h* instead of 6, and that the side of the square is then *s*. See if you can show that $\frac{1}{s} = \frac{1}{b} + \frac{1}{h}$."

# Percentage changes

| | |
|---|---|
| Teacher: | "Can you tell me what £2000 will grow to if it is increased by 3%" |
| Ricky: | "That's easy. 1% of £2000 is £20, so 3% is £60, so it makes £2060." |
| Teacher: | "Right. Now what if an amount $A$ is increased by 3%? What does it become?" |
| Qasim: | "I suppose 3% of $A$ is $\frac{3}{100} \times A$, so the new amount is $A + \frac{3}{100} \times A$." |
| Teacher: | "Yes. Can we make that simpler?" |
| Paula: | "It's $\frac{100A + 3A}{100} = \frac{103A}{100}$." |
| Qasim: | "Or you could call that $1.03A$; so the effect is to multiply $A$ by $1.03$." |
| Teacher: | "Good; that's a useful way to think of a percentage change. So if $A$ were decreased by 3%, what would that make?" |
| Ricky: | "It's $A - \frac{3}{100} \times A = \frac{97A}{100}$ or $0.97A$. So a 3% reduction is a multiplication by $0.97$." |
| Teacher: | "Yes. So what does a 15% increase or decrease do?" |
| Paula: | "Multiplies by $1.15$ or $0.85$?" |
| Teacher: | "OK. What about an increase of $x$%?" |
| Ricky: | "That would be multiplying by $1 + \frac{x}{100}$, would it?" |
| Teacher: | "Yes. Now, can you tell me the original price of an item if adding 20% brings it up to £6?" |
| Qasim: | "Just take 20% off? That's £1.20, so the original price was £4.80, was it?" |
| Teacher: | "Well, can you check that by increasing it by 20%?" |
| Qasim: | "20% of £4.80 is 96p; that brings it up to £5.76. Oh…" |
| Paula: | "The problem is that you did it by taking off 20% of the increased amount instead of 20% of the original amount." |

Ricky: "And you don't know the original amount; so how can you find 20% of it?"

Teacher: "That's right; you can't do it that way. Now think of the 20% increase as a multiplication. By how much? And how can you undo that?"

Qasim: "It's a multiplication by $1 + \frac{20}{100} = 1.2$. To undo it you divide by 1.2."

Ricky: "So you do £6 ÷ 1.2 which is £5."

Paula: "And that works, because 20% of £5 is £1 which brings it up to the given £6."

Teacher: "Right; so now, if a price was reduced by 30% to £14, what was it originally?"

Ricky: "The reduction means the price was multiplied by $1 - \frac{30}{100} = 0.7$, so the original price was £14 ÷ 0.7 = £20. "

Teacher: "Good; so now you can see how to undo a percentage increase or decrease. Using a multiplication also helps when you have a percentage change applied repeatedly. For instance, if a car is worth £25 000 to start with, but every year it loses 8% of its value at the start of that year, how much is it worth after 2 years? And how much after 6 years?"

Qasim: "It loses $\frac{8}{100}$ of £25 000, that's £2000, every year; so £4000 in 2 years and £12 000 in 6 years."

Ricky: "No, that's not right. It loses £2000 in the first year, which takes it down to £23 000, then the next year it loses 8% of £23 000; that's 8 × £230 = £1840, so after 2 years the value is down to £21 160. Then you go on like that for another 4 years."

Paula: "Is that the best you can do? Isn't there a quicker way?"

Ricky: "Can we do it by multiplying? The 8% decrease means multiplying by $1 - \frac{8}{100} = 0.92$, so we just keep multiplying by 0.92. After 2 years it's down to £25 000 × 0.92 × 0.92 = £21 160."

Qasim: "Aha; so to find the value after 6 years just do £25 000 × $0.92^6$ ; that's £15 158.87503."

Teacher: "Well done; that's £15 158.88 to the nearest penny. The same approach can help you with what is called compound interest. Suppose you put £15 000 in a savings account, and that each year the amount is increased by 4% of what was in the account at the beginning of that year; then how much is it after 5 years?"

Ricky: "That means the amount is multiplied by 1.04 each year, so it would grow to £15 000 × $1.04^5$, which is £18 249.79 to the nearest penny."

Teacher: "Good. How long would it take for the amount to increase by 50%?"

Qasim: "That means multiplying by 1.5, so if it takes $n$ years, $1.04^n = 1.5$."

Paula: "Do we know how to solve that for $n$?"

Teacher: "No; you can't do it properly till you learn about logarithms in the sixth form. Meanwhile you have to use trial."

Ricky: "I get $1.04^{10} = 1.480244\ldots$ and $1.04^{11} = 1.539454\ldots$"

Teacher: "Right; so 10 years is not quite enough, while 11 years gives you a bit more than 50% growth. Now can you tell me the percentage increase in the perimeter of a square when the length of each side increases by 30%?"

Qasim: "What was the length of each side to begin with?"

Teacher: "Do you really need to know that?"

Paula: "Is it just 4 times 30%, as the perimeter is 4 times the side?"

Teacher: "Well, try it with a side of 100 mm to start with."

Ricky: "The original perimeter is 400 mm. Each side changes to 130 mm, so the new perimeter is $4 \times 130 = 520$ mm, so the percent increase is $\frac{120}{400} \times 100\% = 30\%$. Oh!"

Teacher: Well, a 30% increase means that each side is multiplied by 1.3. So what does that do to the perimeter?"

Paula: "It gets multiplied by 1.3 as well; so that's why it increases by 30% too!"

Teacher: "Good; so what about the length of a diagonal; how much does that increase?"

Ricky: "Would that be 30% as well? The diagonal is just $\sqrt{2}$ times the side, so it also gets multiplied by 1.3."

Teacher: "Good. What are the percentage increases in the diameter and the circumference of a circle when the radius is increased by 45%?"

Qasim: "The diameter is just double the radius, so that increases by 45% too. Doesn't the circumference involve $\pi$?"

Ricky: "The circumference is $2\pi$ times the radius, but it doesn't matter what the multiplier is; when the radius is multiplied by 1.45 then the same happens to the circumference, so it's still a 45% change."

Teacher: "That's right."

Qasim: "What about the area? Does that change by 45% as well?"

Teacher: "Aha; that will have to wait till our next lesson."

# 24 Combining small percentage changes

| Teacher: | "How do you find the area of a rectangle given the length and width?" |
|---|---|
| Paula: | "Easy; just multiply them together." |
| Teacher: | "Right. Now what happens to the area if the length is increased by 12% and the width by 15%?" |
| Ricky: | "Would you have to know what the length and width were to start with?" |
| Qasim: | "Can we do the changes by multiplying? That's what we did last lesson. The length gets multiplied by 1.12 and the width by 1.15." |
| Teacher: | "Good. Now what does multiplying the length by 1.12 do to the area?" |
| Paula: | "It would multiply the area by 1.12, wouldn't it? Instead of $l \times w$ you've got $1.12l \times w$." |
| Ricky: | "Oh, and then multiplying the width by 1.15 multiplies the area by that as well." |
| Qasim: | "So altogether the area is multiplied by $1.12 \times 1.15 = 1.288$." |
| Teacher: | "Right; so what is the percentage increase?" |
| Ricky: | "An $x\%$ increase multiplies a number by $1 + \frac{x}{100}$ , so here $\frac{x}{100} = .288$ and $x = 28.8$ ; it's a 28.8% increase." |
| Paula: | "If you just add 12% and 15% you get 27%; but this is rather more." |
| Teacher: | "That's right. Now can you tell me what happens to the area when the length is increased by 1.2% and the width by 1.5%?" |
| Qasim: | "That multiplies the area by $1.012 \times 1.015 = 1.02718$; so it makes a 2.718% increase in the area." |
| Paula: | "That's closer to 1.2% + 1.5% this time." |

| Teacher: | "Yes; have a look at the diagram. The rectangle has had its length increased by 1.2%; that gives the extra tall thin rectangle on the right, which is 1.2% of the original, and the width has increased by 1.5%, giving an extra 1.5% on top of the original rectangle." | 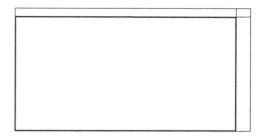 |

Qasim: "But when you do both changes there's also the little rectangle on the top right; is that why the total change is a bit more than the sum of the two changes?"

Teacher: "Yes; in fact that little rectangle is 1.5% of 1.2% of the original, which works out to 0.018%; that's how the total area change is 2.718%. Now can you tell me the percentage increase in the area of a circle if the radius is increased by 45%?"

Ricky: "The area is $\pi r^2$, which turns into $\pi(1.45r)^2 = \pi r^2 \times (1.45^2 = 2.1025)$."

Qasim: "So the area is multiplied by 2.1025, more than doubled."

Paula: "So it's more than 100% change; in fact if an $x$% change multiplies by $1+\frac{x}{100}$, we've got $\frac{x}{100} = 1.1025$ so $x = 110.25$, it's a 110.25% increase."

Teacher: "Good; now try it with 4.5% change and then with 0.45%."

Ricky: "With 4.5% the radius is multiplied by 1.045 and the area by $1.045^2 = 1.092025$, so that's a 9.2025% change."

Qasim: "And with 0.45% the area is multiplied by $1.0045^2 = 1.00902025$; so that's a 0.902025% change."

Paula: "That's just a little more than double the percentage change in the radius."

Teacher: "Yes; can you see how that connects with what we found about the area of a rectangle?"

Ricky: "With the rectangle we had two distances, length and width, that were multiplied and that increase by different percentage amounts. Here it's just one distance, the radius, multiplied by itself and then by $2\pi$, so the percentage change in the radius is added to itself; that's why it's doubled."

Teacher: "Good. Now let's consider this a bit more generally. Let $y = uv$ and let $u$ and $v$ increase by $p$% and $q$% respectively. What is the percentage increase in $y$?"

Qasim:  "$u$ gets multiplied by $1+\frac{p}{100}$ and $v$ by $1+\frac{q}{100}$ so $y$ is multiplied by $\left(1+\frac{p}{100}\right)\left(1+\frac{q}{100}\right)$."

Paula:  "That's $1+\frac{p}{100}+\frac{q}{100}+\frac{pq}{10000}$; so the increase is $\left(p+q+\frac{pq}{100}\right)\%$."

Teacher:  "Good. Now, can you see what happens to that when $p$ and $q$ are small?"

Paula:  "It's nearly $(p+q)\%$."

Note to the reader: The connection here between product and sum is reminiscent of logarithms and indices, and this is not a coincidence. If $A = lw$ then $\ln A = \ln l + \ln w$ so that $\Delta(\ln A) = \Delta(\ln l) + \Delta(\ln w)$; but since the derivative of $\ln x$ is $1/x$, we can express $\Delta(\ln A)$ approximately as $(1/A)\Delta A$ or $\Delta A/A$, with similar expressions involving $l$ and $w$, leading again to the basic principle.

Ricky:  "So if $u$ and $v$ are the same, so that $y = u^2$, then the percentage change in $y$ would be about double the percentage change in $u$."

Teacher:  "That's right. Can you use that to work out $5.02^2$ approximately?"

Qasim:  "$5^2$ is 25. The change from 5 to 5.02 is like from 500 to 502, so it's $\frac{2}{5}$ of 1%."

Teacher:  "Yes, that's a good way of getting the percentage change."

Qasim:  "Then the percentage change in the answer is double that, $\frac{4}{5}$ of 1%; so we have to add on $\frac{4}{5}$ of 1% of 25; that's $\frac{4}{5}\times 0.25 = 0.2$, so $5.02^2$ is about 25.2."

Teacher:  "Good. The exact answer is 25.2004. Now what about estimating the square root of 24.95?"

Paula:  "From 25 to 24.95 is a change of −0.05 in 25; that would be like −0.2 in 100, so it's a −0.2% change."

Ricky:  "And that has to be double the percentage change in the number being squared; so we have to go down by 0.1% from 5; that's a change of −0.005 from 5."

Qasim:  "So that's 4.995. My calculator gives $\sqrt{24.95} = 4.994997\ldots$ so that's pretty close."

Teacher:  "Well done all of you. Now what would happen if you had $y = uvw$ and if the three factors increase by small amounts $p$, $q$ and $r\%$ respectively?"

Ricky:  "You could say $y = uv \times w$ so the percentage change in $y$ approximately equals percentage change in $uv$ plus percentage change in $w$."

Paula:  "And the percentage change in $uv$ is approximately $(p + q)\%$; so overall you get $(p + q + r)\%$ change."

| Teacher: | "That's right, and the same applies to any number of factors; you just add the percentage changes, provided they are small. So can you see how $y$ would change if $y = kx^n$ where $k$ is a constant and $n$ is a positive integer, when $x$ changes by $p\%$?" |
|---|---|
| Qasim: | "You would just add $n$ changes of $p\%$ each – as $k$ doesn't change – so it's just $np\%$." |
| Teacher: | "Good; so if a balloon is being blown up and the volume increases by 1%, what is the increase in surface area? You know the formulae for volume and area of a sphere." |
| Ricky: | "The volume is proportional to the radius cubed, so to get a 1% increase in the volume there would have to be about $\frac{1}{3}$ of 1% increase in the radius." |
| Paula: | "And the area is $4\pi r^2$, so the percentage increase in that is about double the percentage increase in $r$, so about $\frac{2}{3}$ of 1%." |
| Teacher: | "Well done. Now what about division? What if $y = \frac{u}{v}$ and $u$ and $v$ change by small percentage amounts?" |
| Qasim: | "Would you subtract them instead of adding?" |
| Teacher: | "Good idea! Can anyone see why?" |
| Ricky: | "Well, if $y = \frac{u}{v}$ then $u = vy$ so percentage change in $u$ = percentage change in $v$ plus percentage change in $y$; it follows from that, doesn't it?" |
| Teacher: | "Yes indeed. So if a journey takes 4 hours at 30 mph, roughly how much time do you save by going at 31 mph?" |
| Paula: | "Time is distance over speed, and the distance is not changed but the speed is increased by $\frac{1}{30}$ of the original value, that's $\frac{1}{30} \times 100\% = 3\frac{1}{3}\%$ ." |
| Teacher: | "That's correct, but you don't need to express the relative change as a percentage. In this example it's simpler just to say that the speed increases by $\frac{1}{30}$ of its previous value." |
| Paula: | "OK; so that means that the time will reduce roughly by $\frac{1}{30}$ of its original value; that's $\frac{1}{30}$ of 4 hours or 240 minutes; so about 8 minutes is saved." |
| Teacher: | "Good. A direct calculation makes the time saved to be about 7.74 minutes or 7 minutes and 44.5 seconds. Now, what if the original speed was 60 mph, the time for the same distance 2 hours, and then the speed changed to 61 mph?" |
| Qasim: | "The change in speed is now $\frac{1}{60}$ of the original, so the time reduces by about $\frac{1}{60}$ of 2 hours, which is 2 minutes." |

Teacher:     "Good. Now see if you can calculate approximately the square root and the cube root of 65."

Note for the reader: Doubling the starting speed divides the time saving for a 1mph speed increase by 4 because the relative changes are now half of what they were, and the relative time change is applied to half the former time. This gives us a feeling for why the rate of change of $\frac{1}{x}$ is $-\frac{1}{x^2}$.

Further, the work above can be related to standard results in calculus, as follows.

## The product and quotient rules

If $y = uv$, then $\frac{\Delta y}{y} \approx \frac{\Delta u}{u} + \frac{\Delta v}{v}$ gives $\Delta y \approx v\Delta u + u\Delta v$, so that $\frac{\Delta y}{\Delta x} \approx v\frac{\Delta u}{\Delta x} + u\frac{\Delta v}{\Delta x}$, which gives the product rule for differentiation by letting $\Delta x$ tend to 0.

If instead $y = \frac{u}{v}$ then $\frac{\Delta y}{y} \approx \frac{\Delta u}{u} - \frac{\Delta v}{v}$ leads to $\Delta y \approx \frac{\Delta u}{v} - \frac{u\Delta v}{v^2} = \frac{v\Delta u - u\Delta v}{v^2}$. Dividing by $\Delta x$ and letting $\Delta x$ tend to 0 produces the quotient rule, which is thus seen as a rather disguised version of the simpler principle that small percentage changes subtract when applied to the top and bottom of a fraction.

## The derivative of $x^n$

Let $y = x^n$. Then, for small changes, $\frac{\Delta y}{y} \approx n\frac{\Delta x}{x}$, so $\frac{\Delta y}{\Delta x} \approx \frac{ny}{x} = \frac{nx^n}{x} = nx^{n-1}$. That's it, apart from the important matter of showing the conceptual difference between $\frac{\Delta y}{\Delta x}$ and $\frac{dy}{dx}$, and making it plausible that for the latter the $nx^{n-1}$ is exact.

## Area under $y = x^n$

The diagram shows the graph of $y = x^n$. Let $Q$ be the point $(X, X^n)$. We are looking for the area $A$ bounded by $OP$, $PQ$ and part of the curve. Let $B$ be the area above the curve bounded by $OR$ and $RQ$. Then $A + B$ is a rectangle with area $XX^n = X^{n+1}$. Divide the areas $A$, $B$ into thin vertical and horizontal strips as shown. The vertical strip $\Delta A$ has area approximately $y\Delta x$, where $(x, y)$ is the point at the top of the left edge of the strip. Similarly $\Delta B$ is approximately $x\Delta y$. The ratio $\Delta A : \Delta B \approx y\Delta x : x\Delta y = \frac{\Delta x}{x} : \frac{\Delta y}{y} \approx 1 : n$, because $y = x^n$. The same ratio applies to all similar pairs of strips, (and the approximation tends to exactitude when the widths of the strips tend to 0), from

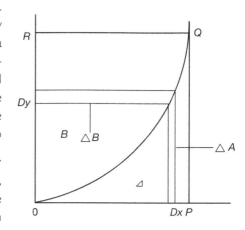

which we can conclude that the whole areas $A$ and $B$ are in the same ratio $1:n$. This makes $B = nA$ so that $X^{n+1} = A + B = A(1 + n)$ and hence $A = \dfrac{X^{n+1}}{n+1}$, the familiar integration formula. This analysis assumes $n > 0$. The case $n < 0$ is messier, but can be done.

## Conclusion

Percentage changes are very much part of everyday mathematics. Whether one hears about changes in the cost of living, in house prices or in the number of asylum seekers, those changes are likely to be reported as percentages of a previous value. For a maths student to be able to see clearly and easily that a 1% increase in the radius of a sphere results in approximately 2% increase in the surface area and approximately 3% increase in the volume, or that a 3% drop in mains voltage will result in an electric fire's power output (given by voltage squared divided by resistance) reducing by about 6%, is to my mind a worthwhile accomplishment. It's also handy to be able to approximate some powers and roots easily using this approach.

I realise that the A-level syllabus is crowded as it is, and teaching time short in these exam-driven days. Perhaps the best place for this topic is in the GCSE or Additional Maths course; then the 6th form teacher could use the small change power law to derive the basic differentiation formula, while driving home the important difference between relative and absolute changes. At the very least, the surprisingly simple and useful relationships explored here should be known by mathematics teachers!

# Angle properties of circles

Ricky:     "Sir, what does angle subtended mean?"

Teacher:   "It's an angle that measures how long something looks from a point. The sun and moon give us an example. Which of them looks bigger from the earth?"

Paula:     "Neither; they look the same size, but the sun is much bigger, isn't it?"

Teacher:   "Yes indeed, very much bigger. But it is also much further away, about 93 million miles, while the moon is a little under a quarter of a million miles away. The sketch, which is not to scale, gives you the idea. An observer A on the earth sees them nearly the same size. The angle A is the angle subtended by the moon's diameter, and also the angle subtended by the sun's diameter, at the observer's eye."

Qasim:     "Is that why we get eclipses with the moon just obscuring the sun?"

Teacher:   "Yes, that's part of how God created the universe; it has enabled us to learn things about the sun from the corona that surrounds it when the body of the sun is obscured by the moon. But now I want you to copy the next diagram, in which the arc AB is occupied by enemy troops in a war game, and you are watching them from O. You have to turn your line of sight from OA all the way to OB and back; the angle between, angle AOB, is the angle subtended by the enemy arc at O. Some other members of your team are in places like P and Q, on the other arc, the rest of the circumference. They are also watching the enemy along arc AB, but the angle subtended at their positions is smaller. I want you to draw this, with various sizes of the arc AB and various positions of P and Q, and measure the angles subtended by the enemy arc at O, P and Q and tell me what you notice."

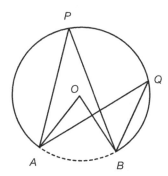

After some drawing and measuring:

Paula:       "I've got 64° subtended at *O* and 32° at *P* and at *Q*."

Qasim:       "I did a big arc; it subtends 142° at *O* and 72° at *P* and *Q*."

Ricky:       "Shouldn't that have been 71°? It looks as if the angle subtended at *O* is twice as big as the angle subtended at any point on the rest of the circumference."

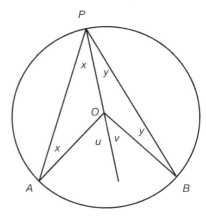

Teacher:     "Yes, good; that was what I expected you to find. Measurement isn't always exactly accurate. It looks as if when you watch arc *AB* from *O* it looks twice as big as if you watch it from somewhere like *P* or *Q*. But now we want to look at *why* there is this relationship we seem to be seeing. In the new diagram, why have I marked two angles both with *x*?"

Qasim:       "That means they're equal; but why? Oh, *OPA* is an isosceles triangle, because *OA* and *OP* are both radii."

Paula:       "And the angles marked *y* are equal for the same reason, with *OP = OB*."

Teacher:     "Right. Now what about angle *u*?"

Ricky:       "It's an exterior angle of triangle *APO*, so it equals $x + x = 2x$."

Note: most pupils will more likely work out $\angle AOP$ as $180° - 2x$ and then subtract this from 180° to get $u = 2x$. They can then be reminded of the exterior angle property which gets there in one step.

Qasim:       "So then likewise. $v = y + y = 2y$. Aha, that's how $\angle AOB = 2\angle APB$, because it's $2x + 2y$ and $\angle APB = x + y$."

Teacher:     "That's right; and did *P* need to be in any special place?"

Paula:       "No, it just had to be on the circle to make *OP* a radius."

Teacher:     "Yes, so we have shown that the angle subtended by an arc at the centre of the circle is twice as big as the angle subtended by that arc at any point on the rest of the circumference."

Ricky:       "Is that still true when *P* is quite far over, near *A* or *B*, so that *O* is not inside triangle *APB*?"

Teacher:     "Good question! The result is still true: the arc looks twice as big from the centre as it does from anywhere else on the circle, but the proof is a little different. You still have pairs of equal angles from two isosceles triangles, and exterior angles equal to double those angles, but you have to subtract angles instead of adding them to go from there. Now we want to look at some consequences of this important result. What if AB is a diameter of the circle, so that each of the arcs joining A to B is a semi-circle?"

Qasim:     "Then the angle AOB is 180° so APB = 90°."

Paula:     "We saw that before when we did rectangles, didn't we?"

Teacher:   "Yes, indeed: angle in a semi-circle is a right-angle can be proved on its own as we saw, but it also follows from the angle at centre theorem. Now look at the next diagram. If angle P is 48°, can you tell me the angles at Q and R?"

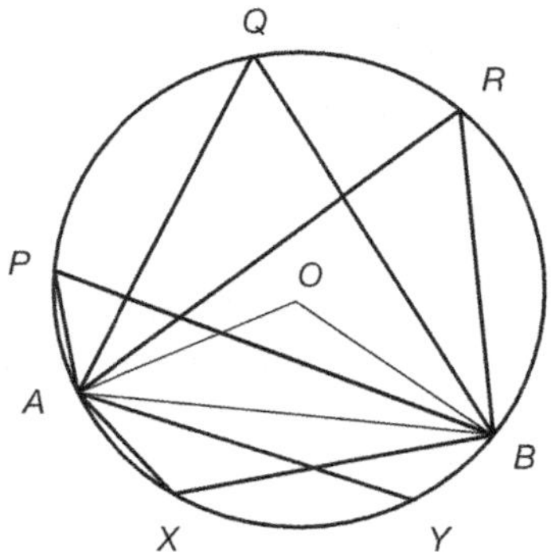

Ricky:     "They have to be 48° too, don't they? Because the angle at the centre O is double each of the angles at P, Q and R."

Teacher:   "Good! And we express that by saying either that angles standing on the same arc are equal, or that angles in the same segment are equal."

Qasim:     "Are we supposed to think of the lines PA, PB as a pair of legs, with feet at A and B?"

Teacher:   "That's right; and QA, QB are another pair of legs with feet at A and B, so the angles at P, Q and R all stand on the arc AXB and thus are equal. I've also drawn the line AB, which is called a *chord*. It divides the circle into two *segments* which can be called APB and AXB."

Paula:     "That's not like segments of an orange, is it?"

Teacher:   "You're right, it isn't. Segments of an orange look more like what you get when you draw two radii of a circle; the part between them is called a *sector*. So here is a case where technical language differs from everyday language in the use of the same word. But to come back to our subject: The angles at P, Q, R are *angles in the same segment*, which is the segment above AB, segment APB (or AQB or ARB). Angles in the same segment are equal. Now what about the angles in segment AXB?"

Ricky:     "They are equal to each other, but do they relate to the ones in the upper segment?"

Teacher:   "Imagine viewing the major arc APB from X or from O. What angles are involved?"

Ricky:     "The angle at X is just AXB, but at O, to view the whole of the major arc you have to turn through the reflex angle AOB, more than 180°."

Qasim: "And the two viewing angles at $O$ for the two arcs add up to 360°; then the angles at the circumference have to add up to half that, 180°; that makes $\angle X = 180° - 48° = 132°$."

Paula: "Hey! Isn't that what we found when we drew cyclic quadrilaterals in the lesson on special quadrilaterals: their opposite angles added up to 180°."

Teacher: "Yes indeed; opposite angles of a cyclic quadrilateral are *supplementary*, meaning they supplement each other to make a total of 180°. That is something you found before, but now it again comes out of the result about the angle at the centre. But now, to get practice using especially angles standing on the same arc, see if you can find the lettered angles in the diagram."

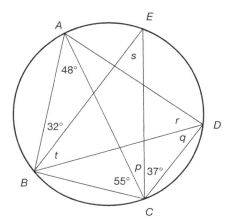

Ricky: "Is $p$ standing on an arc? It's more like hanging from arc $AE$."

Qasim: "If you turned the figure round you could see $p$ standing on arc $AE$, and the other angle that's doing that is the 32° angle at $B$. So that makes $p = 32°$."

Paula: "You can see $q$ standing on arc $BC$, as does the 48° angle at $A$; so that makes them equal."

Teacher: "Good; you're getting it. For $r$, see the two legs $DA$ and $DB$ that make the angle, then the feet are $A$ and $B$, the angle is standing on arc $AB$. Two other legs with feet at $A$ and $B$ are $CA$ and $CB$, and the angle between them is 55°, so that is the size of $r$ as well. I'll leave you to find $s$ and $t$, and also see if you can find a quick way to calculate the angle $ABC$."

# Trigonometry with general triangles

Paula: "Sir, how can you have the sine of an angle like 120°? You have to be in a right-angled triangle to do trigonometry, don't you?"

Teacher: "Well, that's how we started. But have a look at the triangle $OPM$ in the diagram. Can you tell me the sine, cosine and tangent of $\theta$ in terms of $x$, $y$ and $r$?"

Ricky: "That's easy. $\sin \theta = \frac{y}{r}$, $\cos \theta = \frac{x}{r}$ and $\tan \theta = \frac{y}{x}$."

Teacher: "That's right, they just follow from the way sine, cos and tan are defined in a right-angled triangle. But now suppose that $\theta$ increases beyond 90°."

Qasim: "Then you can't have a right-angled triangle with $\theta$ in it."

Teacher: "That's true; but $\frac{y}{r}$, $\frac{x}{r}$ and $\frac{y}{x}$ can still be worked out (except $\frac{y}{x}$ when $x = 0$), and these are now used as definitions for sine, cosine and tangent of $\theta$. In fact if you take $r$ to be 1, and plot graphs of $y$, $x$ and $\frac{y}{x}$ against $\theta$ those give you graphs of $\sin \theta$, $\cos \theta$, and $\tan \theta$ against $\theta$, for all values up to 360°."

Paula: "What about beyond 360°?"

Teacher: "No problem; but of course you're then back at and past $A$, so you're just repeating values you had at the start: $\sin(\theta + 360°) = \sin\theta$, and the same applies for cos and tan. Now suppose you are told that $\sin\theta = \sin 20°$. Can you find all possible values of $\theta$ ?"

Qasim: "$\theta$ has to be 20°, doesn't it?"

Teacher: "Well, that's the first and most obvious answer. But are there others?"

| | |
|---|---|
| Ricky: | "You'd have to look for places on the circle where $\frac{y}{r}$ is the same as it is at 20°." |
| Paula: | "Would that be at $Q$ on the diagram? That's where $y$ is the same as it is at $P$." |
| Teacher: | "Yes, that's right. And if $\theta$ is 20°, what is the angle $AOQ$?" |
| Ricky: | "It's $180° - 20° = 160°$. So does that mean that $\sin(180° - \theta)$ is always the same as $\sin\theta$ ?" |
| Teacher: | "Right. Now, what if we are given that $\cos\theta = \cos 20°$ What can $\theta$ be apart from 20°?" |
| Qasim: | "The cosine is $\frac{x}{r}$, so we need somewhere on the circle where $x$ is the same as at $P$." |
| Paula: | "That must be at $S$, which makes the angle $360° - 20° = 340°$." |
| Teacher: | "Good, or it could be $-20°$, meaning 20° in the clockwise direction. The general result is that $\cos(360° - \theta) = \cos(-\theta)$ is the same as $\cos\theta$." |
| Ricky: | "And if you have $\tan\theta = \tan 20°$ you have to find where $\frac{y}{x}$ is the same as it is at $P$." |
| Paula: | "$\frac{y}{x}$ is the gradient of $OP$, so we want to keep on that gradient; that takes us to $R$, making the angle 200°." |
| Ricky: | "That means $\tan(\theta + 180°) = \tan\theta$, doesn't it?" |
| Teacher: | "Yes, that's right. Now look at the diagram with triangle $ABC$ whose side lengths are called $a$, $b$, $c$. In $\triangle BCD$ can you express the height $h$ in terms of $a$ and angle $B$?" |
| Qasim: | "That's easy; $h$ is the opposite and $a$ the hypotenuse, so $h = a\sin B$." |
| Teacher: | "Right, and what about $h$ as a side of $\triangle ACD$ ?" |
| Paula: | "That's $h = b\sin\angle CAD$." |
| Teacher: | "Yes, so we have $a\sin B = b\sin\angle CAD$. If we divide both sides by $\sin B$ and $\sin\angle CAD$, what do we get?" |
| Paula: | "$\dfrac{a}{\sin CAD} = \dfrac{b}{\sin B}$. That's like the sine rule, but it should be $\dfrac{a}{\sin A} = \dfrac{b}{\sin B}$, shouldn't it?" |
| Ricky: | "But wait a minute. Angle $CAD$ is next to angle $CAB$ which is what we call angle $A$, so it's $180° - A$." |

Qasim: "And sin$(180° − A)$ = sin $A$, so we do get the same sine rule even with angle $A$ being obtuse."

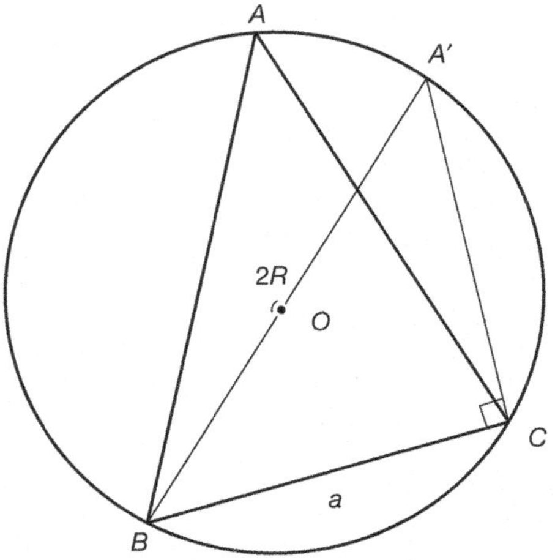

Teacher: "That's right. Incidentally there is another way to the sine rule using angle properties of circles. In the diagram the circle $ABC$ with centre $O$ and diameter $2R$ has been drawn."

Ricky: "So the right angle at $C$ is angle in a semi-circle?"

Qasim: "And the angles at $A$ and $A'$ are equal because they are on the same arc $BC$."

Teacher: "Yes; so now can you relate the side $a$ to the diameter $2R$ ?"

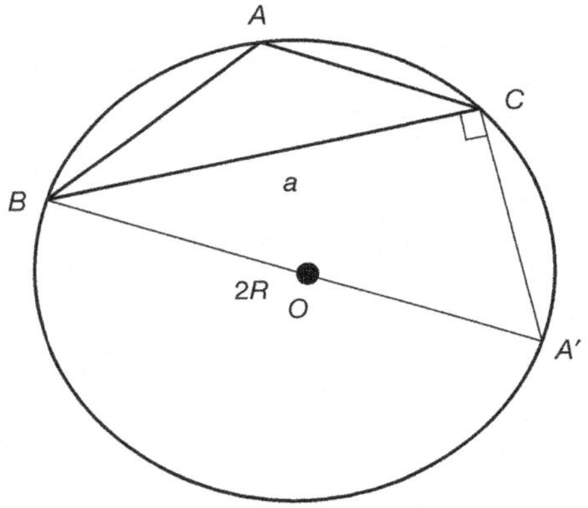

Paula: "$a = 2R$ sin $A'$ and that's $2R$ sin $A$."

Teacher: "Good; and now look at the next diagram in which the angle $A$ is obtuse."

Ricky: "This time $\angle A' = 180° − \angle A$ because of opposite angles of a cyclic quadrilateral, and $a$ is still $2R\sin A'$ ."

Qasim: "So now $a = 2R\sin(180° − A)$ and that's $2R\sin A$ . It doesn't matter whether $A$ is acute or obtuse."

Paula: "So then we must also have b = $2R\sin B$ and c = $2R\sin C$ , which is why $\dfrac{a}{\sin A} = \dfrac{b}{\sin B} = \dfrac{c}{\sin C}$ , because they are each equal to 2R."

Teacher: "Well done all of you! Now, if you use the sine rule to find an angle, that needs some care. Suppose you are given triangle $ABC$ with $BC = 10$ cm, $AC = 7$ cm and $\angle B = 35°$ and you are to find $\angle A$."

Qasim: "No problem. Use the angle on top form of the sine rule: $\dfrac{\sin A}{a} = \dfrac{\sin B}{b}$ , so $\dfrac{\sin A}{10} = \dfrac{\sin 35°}{7}$ ; that makes sin $A$ = 0.81939…so $A$ = 55.0° to 1DP."

Ricky: "But is that the only possible value for $\angle A$? What about $180° − 55.0 = 125.0°$ ? "

Teacher:    "Well spotted, Ricky. There are in fact two possible answers, and the diagram shows that. Imagine you were solving the problem by accurate drawing rather than calculation. What would you do?"

Paula:      "Start with $BC$, then draw angle $B$, then to make $AC = 7$ cm you have to draw an arc with centre $C$ and radius 7 cm and see where that meets the line from $B$ at $35°$ to $BC$."

Ricky:      "And the arc meets the line in two places $A_1$ and $A_2$."

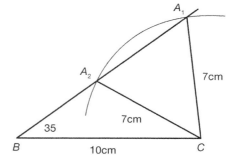

Teacher:    "That's right; and since triangle $CA_1A_2$ has equal 7cm sides the angles at $A_1$ and $A_2$ are equal, which makes $\angle BA_2C = 180° - \angle BA_1C$, just as we found when doing the calculation."

Qasim:      "Is this the reason why the congruence test with two sides and an angle requires the angle to be included rather than opposite one of the sides?"

Teacher:    "Yes, exactly! If the given angle is opposite one of the given sides, there are liable to be two different possible versions of the triangle. There are exceptions, including the case where the equal angles are right angles, since then the two possible triangles are mirror images of each other."

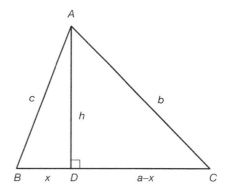

Paula:      "Does the sine rule mean we can now solve any triangle problem?"

Teacher:    "No; you can only use it when at least one of the three equal fractions is completely known; that means you have to know a side and the angle opposite to that side. If instead you only know two sides and the angle between them, or only know the three sides, you need another piece of equipment. Suppose in the diagram we know the sides $a$ and $c$ and the angle $B$ and we want to find the opposite side $b$. Any ideas? The altitude $AD = h$. has been drawn in."

Ricky:      "Well, $b^2 = h^2 + (a - x)^2 = h^2 + a^2 - 2ax + x^2$."

Qasim:      "And also $h^2 + x^2 = c^2$, so that $b^2 = c^2 + a^2 - 2ax$. But we don't know $x$, do we?"

Paula:        "Yes, we can find it: it's $c\cos B$ from triangle $ABD$. That makes $b^2 = c^2 + a^2 - 2ac \cos B$."

Teacher:      "That's right! It's called the cosine rule, usually stated as $a^2 = b^2 + c^2 - 2bc \cos A$ by just changing the letters round. Can you see how to use it to find an angle from the three sides?"

Ricky:        "If you solve for A you get $2bc \cos A = b^2 + c^2 - a^2$ that $\cos A = \dfrac{b^2 + c^2 - a^2}{2bc}$. Is the cosine rule affected by possible obtuse angles?"

Teacher:      "Yes; we have $a^2 = b^2 + c^2 - 2bc \cos A$. What happens if $A = 90°$?"

Paula:        "$\cos 90° = 0$, so you just come back to Pythagoras' theorem."

Ricky:        "And if $A < 90°$ the side $a$ is reduced, but if $A > 90°$ does that make cos A negative?"

Teacher:      "Yes, if you look back at the first diagram, obtuse angles are in the second quadrant, where $Q$ is, and in that quadrant $x$ is negative and thus so is the cosine. The diagram we just used for the cosine rule then has $D$ to the left of $B$, so that the length $DB = x$ is now given by $c\cos(180° - B)$ and is added to $a$ to make $b^2 = h^2 + (a + x)^2$ which comes to $a^2 + c^2 + 2ac \cos(180° - B)$ and that's the same as $c^2 + a^2 - 2ac \cos B$."

Paula:        "So in the formula, subtracting $2ac \cos B$ is actually adding something, making $b$ bigger than it would be in a right-angled triangle."

Teacher:      "That's it; and if you use the cosine formula to find an angle from knowing the three sides, when the cosine comes out negative then the inverse cosine of that number will be an obtuse angle. Now you can try the following problem: If the *Victory* is 75 miles from port on a bearing of 324° while the *Golden Hind* is 38 miles from port on a bearing of 039°, what is the distance and bearing of the *Golden Hind* from the *Victory*? You will only need to use the cosine rule once; after that use the sine rule which is less work."

# Irrational numbers

Ricky: "Sir, what are irrational numbers?"

Paula: "They're numbers that go on and on for ever, aren't they?"

Qasim: "Is there something unreasonable about them?"

Teacher: "Possibly; the Greek word 'alogos' or 'no word' suggests the fact that there is no way of expressing them; but it's probably more helpful for you to think not so much of Latin 'ratio' meaning reason, but of ratio in the mathematical sense, meaning how many times one number is bigger than another. The ancient Greeks, who had great mathematicians, at first considered all numbers to be either whole numbers like 7 or 18, or ratios of whole numbers like $\frac{7}{18}$ or $\frac{18}{7}$. At some stage they made an embarrassing discovery. Have a look at the diagram. The main square has side of length 2, so its area is 4 square units. It's divided into four smaller squares, and their diagonals have been drawn. What shape do they make? And how big is it?"

Ricky: "It's a square too; all the sides are equal and the angles are twice 45°."

Qasim: "And each diagonal halves its square, so they make a square of area 2."

Teacher: "So then how long is each diagonal?"

Paula: "It must be the square root of 2; that follows anyway from Pythagoras' theorem."

Teacher: "Indeed; so how big is √2?"

Qasim: "My calculator says 1.414213562."

Teacher: "OK; but if you squared that number would you get 2?"

Qasim: "According to the calculator you do."

Ricky: "But that can't be exactly right; if you did the squaring by hand the last digit would have to be $2 \times 2 = 4$. So you'd get a long decimal nearly equal to 2 but ending in 4."

Teacher: "Well spotted. Could the exact root end in some other digit?"

Paula: "If it ended in 1, so would the square; if in 3, the square would end in 9."

Qasim: "It doesn't work with any digits; none of their squares end in 0."

Ricky: "So it must be a never ending decimal. Is that why it's irrational?"

Teacher: "Not exactly. If you work out $\frac{18}{7}$ as a decimal, you get 2.428571428571 ... going on forever; the division never stops. Yet $\frac{18}{7}$ is rational; it's a ratio of two whole numbers."

Paula: "So could $\sqrt{2}$ be expressed in that way even though the decimal goes on for ever?"

Teacher: "Try $\frac{17}{12}$. What do you get squaring that?"

Qasim: "That's $\frac{289}{144}$, which is $2\frac{1}{144}$; fairly close."

Teacher: "Or $\frac{99}{70}$."

Ricky: "That squared makes $\frac{9801}{4900}$ or $2\frac{1}{4900}$, very close; but still not exact."

Teacher: "That's right; and you can get better and better approximations. But could a fraction multiplied by itself actually give a whole number?"

Paula: "There'd have to be some cancelling; but then, if you could cancel in a sum like $\frac{99}{70} \times \frac{99}{70}$, you'd have to be able to divide 99 and 70 by a common factor, and if you could do that, you could simplify the original fraction by cancelling."

Teacher: "Exactly; so then the square root would have to be a whole number. If it's not, and you try a fraction, that squared may be close to $\sqrt{2}$, but will always be a more complicated fraction than the one you started with. That was the embarrassing discovery made by followers of Pythagoras, one of whom is supposed to have been thrown overboard at sea to punish him for having made this scandal public."

Qasim: "Does that apply just to $\sqrt{2}$, or to roots of other numbers as well?"

Teacher: "It does, and it doesn't only apply to square roots. If you raise any fraction that is not a whole number to any power, the answer will always be a more complicated fraction, never a whole number; so every root of a whole number is either a whole number or is irrational."

Ricky: "What about the decimal expansion? Is that different for rational and irrational numbers?"

| Teacher: | "Yes; in the example I gave, $\frac{18}{7}$, the decimal expansion went on for ever, but it was simply repeating the sequence 428157 over and over again. Does that always happen when you express a fraction as a decimal?" |
|---|---|
| Paula: | "No, it might terminate, like 0.5 for a half." |
| Qasim: | "Yes, but what if it doesn't? Then you're doing a division sum that goes on for ever without coming out." |
| Teacher: | "Yes. Try $\frac{64}{35}$ by dividing 64 by 35. The calculator says 1.8285714... but you try it by hand." |
| Paula: | "It goes 1 with remainder 29, bring down the first 0 after the decimal point to make 290; then it goes 8 with remainder 10; make that 100." |
| Qasim: | "Then $100 \div 35$ makes 2, with remainder 30; $300 \div 35 = 8$, with remainder 20; $200 \div 35$ goes 5, remainder 25..." |
| Teacher: | "And so on and so on. Now, how many possible remainders are there when you divide by 35?" |
| Ricky: | "Just 35; from 0 up to 34." |
| Teacher: | "Right; and what happens if at some stage you get a remainder you've had before?" |
| Paula: | "Then the calculation must repeat what happened previously." |
| Ricky: | "That's provided by now the only new figure being brought down is 0." |
| Teacher: | "Good point, Ricky. Initially you may be bringing down other figures, but eventually only 0s are left to bring down if you are dividing one whole number by another. And so what is bound to happen eventually?" |
| Qasim: | "Eventually you must repeat a remainder you've had previously, and that must happen at some stage after you've only got 0s to bring down, so then the calculation repeats a previous cycle and goes on doing that for ever." |
| Teacher: | "Good. That shows that a rational number, when expressed as a decimal, either terminates or goes into an endlessly repeated cycle at some stage. Now, does every terminating decimal give a rational number?" |
| Paula: | "Yes, it must do, mustn't it? Because if you multiply it by 10 enough times you get a whole number; so the original decimal is a whole number divided by a power of 10." |
| Teacher: | "Well expressed, Paula. Now what about a decimal that goes into an endlessly recurring cycle?" |
| Qasim: | "Haven't we been shown that that comes from dividing one whole number by another?" |

Ricky: "We've been shown that doing that division can lead to a recurring decimal, but is that the same as saying every recurring decimal comes from such a division?"

Teacher: "No, it's not; well spotted again. We've seen that if a number is rational then its decimal expansion terminates or recurs; but have not yet shown that if a number has a recurring decimal expansion then it's rational."

Paula: "Isn't that just splitting hairs?"

Teacher: "No, but I'm glad you asked that. It's an important distinction between a statement and its converse. Let me give you first a trivial example: If any number is a multiple of 9, then it is a multiple of 3. Agreed?"

Paula: "Yes of course. And would the converse be: If any number is a multiple of 3, then it is a multiple of 9?"

Teacher: Yes indeed, and that's obviously false. To take a less trivial example: if any number is a sum of two odd primes, then it is an even number greater than 4. That is obviously true. What about the converse?"

Qasim: "That would be: if any number is an even number greater than 4, then it is the sum of two odd primes."

Teacher: "Yes; and no one knows whether that is true or not; it's known as the Goldbach Conjecture, and has still not been proved, nor has anyone found a counterexample. So now let's come back to a decimal that goes into an endlessly recurring cycle. I'll start with an example: look at $1.8\dot{2}8571\dot{4}$, in which the dots over the 2 and the 4 indicate the beginning and end of a cycle that repeats for ever."

Ricky: "That's what we got from $64 \div 35$ isn't it?"

Teacher: "Yes; but what if you didn't know that? What would you do starting with the decimal?"

Qasim: "Call it $x$ and multiply by 10, so $10x = 18.\dot{2}8571\dot{4}$."

Ricky: "Oh, then you could multiply by 10 enough times to make a whole cycle of digits come left of the decimal point."

Paula: "You need to do it 6 times, so then $10x \times 10^6 = 18285714.\dot{2}8571\dot{4}$."

Ricky: "Aha; the decimal part is still the same as it was before, because of the way the cycle goes on for ever."

Qasim: "So now you can subtract and say $10^7 x - 10x = 18285714 - 18$ or $9999990x = 18285696$, so we get $x = \dfrac{18285696}{9999990}$."

| | |
|---|---|
| Teacher: | "Well done all of you! That's certainly a rational number. Try putting it in your calculator." |
| Paula: | "It comes out as $\frac{64}{35}$ !" |
| Teacher: | "Good; as the Queen once said when a passer-by saw her, didn't think it could really be the Queen, and told her that she looked just like the Queen: 'How very reassuring!' It's not surprising though, seeing as we started with the decimal expansion of $\frac{64}{35}$. Now we have just done a single example. Does this give us a general strategy for showing that a recurring decimal always represents a rational number?" |
| Ricky: | "I think it does. First, multiply by whatever power of 10 it takes to make the part after the decimal point be only the endlessly repeated cycle. Then multiply by 10 the same number of times that there are digits in the cycle to get a new number whose fractional part is exactly the same, then subtract and you have an integer times the original decimal equals another integer." |
| Teacher: | "Good; that's exactly it. So what does that tell us about the decimal expansion of an irrational number?" |
| Qasim: | "It must go on for ever without recurring." |
| Teacher: | "Yes; that doesn't mean that a cycle can't be repeated a number of times, even ten million times perhaps, but it never becomes an endlessly recurring cycle. Because irrational roots can't be expressed exactly either as fractions or as decimals, it's often useful to leave them as roots. If you have one of the latest calculators, try working out $\sqrt{98} - \sqrt{32}$." |
| Paula: | "Mine says it's $3\sqrt{2}$ ! How does it get that?" |
| Teacher: | "OK. To start with, what would you get if you squared $\sqrt{a} \times \sqrt{b}$, where $a$ and $b$ are positive numbers?" |
| Qasim: | "That would be $\sqrt{a} \times \sqrt{b} \times \sqrt{a} \times \sqrt{b}$ . That makes $ab$, doesn't it?" |
| Teacher: | "Yes it does, since of course $\sqrt{a} \times \sqrt{a} = a$, because that's what being a square root is all about. So then what does that tell us about $\sqrt{ab}$ ?" |
| Ricky: | "It must be the same as $\sqrt{a} \times \sqrt{b}$ . And does $\sqrt{\frac{a}{b}} = \frac{\sqrt{a}}{\sqrt{b}}$ ?" |
| Teacher: | "Yes indeed, and you can prove that in exactly the same way." |
| Paula: | "What about $\sqrt{a+b}$? Is that the same as $\sqrt{a} + \sqrt{b}$ ?" |
| Teacher: | "If it did, what would happen to Pythagoras' theorem?" |
| Qasim: | "Instead of working out $\sqrt{a^2 + b^2}$ to get the hypotenuse, you could short-circuit that to $a + b$." |

| | |
|---|---|
| Paula: | "Oh, and that can't be right, because the hypotenuse must be less than the other two sides added. It looks as if $\sqrt{a+b}$ has to be less than $\sqrt{a}+\sqrt{b}$ ." |
| Teacher: | "That's right; and you've seen previously that the square of the sum of two numbers is more than the sum of their squares; since taking a square root is just inverse to squaring, we don't expect the sum of square roots to be the same as the square root of the sum." |
| Ricky: | "What about that $\sqrt{98}-\sqrt{32}$ calculation? Does it help to express 98 as a product?" |
| Qasim: | "It's 2 × 49 so $\sqrt{98}=\sqrt{2}\times\sqrt{49}$ ; that's $7\sqrt{2}$ since 49 is the square of 7." |
| Paula: | "And $\sqrt{32}=\sqrt{2}\times\sqrt{16}$ , which is $4\sqrt{2}$ , so then we've got $7\sqrt{2}-4\sqrt{2}=3\sqrt{2}$ ; so that's how the calculator got that answer!" |
| Teacher: | "Good! Now try it on $6\div\sqrt{2}$ ." |
| Qasim: | "It gives $3\sqrt{2}$ . Why is that?" |
| Teacher: | "Try writing it as a fraction and then multiplying by $\frac{\sqrt{2}}{\sqrt{2}}$ . " |
| Qasim: | "That's $\frac{6}{\sqrt{2}}\times\frac{\sqrt{2}}{\sqrt{2}}=\frac{6\sqrt{2}}{2}$ ; so that's how it makes $3\sqrt{2}$ ." |
| Teacher: | "Yes, this process is called rationalising the denominator; we are no longer dividing by an irrational square root. A more subtle version of this will help you with an expression like $\dfrac{1}{\sqrt{5}+2}$ . Try that." |
| Paula: | "The calculator says $-2+\sqrt{5}$. How?" |
| Ricky: | "If that is right, then $(\sqrt{5}-2)\times(\sqrt{5}+2)$ must be 1. Oh, I can see why; it's a case of $(a-b)(a+b)=a^2-b^2$ ; it makes $5-2^2$ which is 1." |
| Teacher: | "Well done. So what you would do starting with $\dfrac{1}{\sqrt{5}+2}$ is to multiply by $\dfrac{\sqrt{5}-2}{\sqrt{5}-2}$ which gives the result. Just remember to leave square roots as they are when possible, rather than going into messy decimal approximations; though of course sometimes you do need those as well. Take for example calculating the dimensions of a sheet of A4 paper." |
| Paula: | "Why do you need to calculate that? Didn't someone just decide how big to make it?" |
| Teacher: | "No; there was thinking and calculating involved. The A series of paper sizes has a particular feature: if you cut an A4 sheet in two so as to halve its length, the two cut pieces are the same shape as the original sheet, and are called A5." |
| Qasim: | "Aren't all rectangles similar anyway?" |
| Ricky: | "No way! Think of a square compared with a long thin rectangle." |

| | |
|---|---|
| Teacher: | "That's right. Two rectangles are similar if the ratio of length to width is the same for both." |
| Qasim: | "So here $l:w = w:\frac{1}{2}l$, is that right?" |
| Teacher: | "Yes, because the width of A4 becomes the length of A5, and half the length of A4 is the width of A5." |
| Ricky: | "So $\frac{l}{w} = \frac{w}{\frac{1}{2}l}$ which is the same as $\frac{2w}{l}$, so then what?" |
| Teacher: | "Now multiply both sides by $wl$; that's often called cross-multiplying." |
| Qasim: | "Then $l^2 = 2w^2$ ?" |
| Teacher: | "Yes; so what does that give for the ratio $l:w$?" |
| Paula: | "$l = \sqrt{2w^2} = \sqrt{2}w$, so the ratio is $\sqrt{2}:1$. But we still don't know how big they are." |
| Teacher: | "That's right. The extra information is that the biggest sheet in the range, A0, has an area of 1 square metre. You cut that in two to make A1 with area half a square metre." |
| Qasim: | "So A2 is a quarter, A3 an eighth and A4 a sixteenth of a square metre." |
| Ricky: | "One square metre is 1000 mm by 1000 mm which is a million $mm^2$." |
| Paula: | "So A4's area is $1000000 \div 16 = 62500 \, mm^2$." |
| Ricky: | "That makes $lw = \sqrt{2} \, w^2 = 62500$. so $w = \sqrt{\frac{62500}{\sqrt{2}}} = 210.2241038$." |
| Qasim: | "Then $l = \sqrt{2} \times w = 297.3017788$." |
| Teacher: | "Good! The measurements are rounded to the nearest mm, so A4 is defined as 297 by 210 mm, though you may find the actual measurements vary a little from that." |
| Paula: | "The ratio 297:210 equals 99:70, like the fraction $\frac{99}{70}$ you gave us as a close approximation to $\sqrt{2}$." |
| Ricky: | "Sir, my friend told me there are lots more irrational than rational numbers. Is that true?" |
| Paula: | "That can't make sense; there are obviously infinitely many of both." |
| Teacher: | "Indeed there are, and it would look as if there can't be any way of saying that one infinity is bigger than another. But a 19th-century mathematician called Cantor had insights that changed that. To start with, think of a room with lots of chairs and lots of people. Can you think of a quick way of finding out whether there are more chairs or more people?" |
| Qasim: | "You could invite everybody to sit down." |

Ricky: "And then, if there are people left standing there are more people than chairs; if there are chairs left unoccupied there are more chairs than people."

Paula: "And if neither of those happens there are the same number of chairs and people."

Teacher: "That's right. Cantor used that idea of matching the members of two sets to decide whether they had the same size or cardinality. He used the set of natural numbers 1, 2, 3... like the set of chairs in the example. Suppose you have chairs numbered 1, 2, 3,... but going on for ever. Now let's think of a set of people called squares, labelled 1, 4, 9, 16 and so on. If you asked them all to sit down, would there be chairs or people left over?"

Ricky: "So 1 sits on 1, 4 on 2, 9 on 3, 16 on 4 and so on? That would use all the chairs and seat all the people."

Teacher: "Yes; so the set of squares, despite being what seems a small subset of all the natural numbers has the same cardinality as the set of all natural numbers. Now let's think of a people labelled as fractions: $\frac{1}{2}, \frac{1}{3}, \frac{2}{3}, \frac{1}{4}, \frac{3}{4}, \frac{1}{5}, \frac{2}{5}$ and so on."

Qasim: "For each denominator there are finitely many fractions so you can seat the rest of the fractions with denominator 5, then the two with denominator 6, then all with denominator 7 and so on. You'd never run out of chairs, nor of people."

Teacher: "That's right; so the set of fractions also has the same cardinality as the natural numbers: we say that it is a *countable* set. What about the set of all rational numbers, not just the ones between 0 and 1?"

Paula: "You can't list them by denominator because there are infinitely many with each denominator."

Teacher: "That's right; so instead we will add the numerator and denominator of each rational number (cancelled down to lowest terms) and call that the complexity of the number: so for complexity 9 for instance, what numbers would we have?"

Qasim: "You have $\frac{1}{8}, \frac{2}{7}$, not $\frac{3}{6}$ because that cancels down, then $\frac{4}{5}, \frac{5}{4}, \frac{7}{2}$ and $\frac{8}{1} = 8$."

Ricky: "So you just list all the numbers with complexity 1, then with complexity 2 and so on, because there is only a finite number with each complexity, so there's no rational number left out; but what about the negative numbers? They've not been included."

Teacher: "Quite right; but to include those, just list each negative number after the corresponding positive number."

Paula: "So for complexity 9 you have $\frac{1}{8}, -\frac{1}{8}, \frac{2}{7}, -\frac{2}{7}, \frac{4}{5}, -\frac{4}{5}$ and so on."

| Teacher: | "That's right; there are still finitely many for each complexity, so no rational number is missed; quite a surprising result really, considering that every pair of rational numbers, no matter how close together, has infinitely many other rational numbers in between them." |
|---|---|
| Qasim: | "What about the irrationals then?" |
| Teacher: | "Well, let's suppose for the moment that the set of irrational numbers is countable. What can you deduce about the set of *all* real numbers, rational and irrational?" |
| Ricky: | "That would be countable too, wouldn't it? Couldn't you just accommodate all the rational numbers on the even numbered chairs and all the irrationals on the odd numbered chairs?" |
| Teacher: | "Yes indeed; any union of two (or more) countable sets is countable. But now let's suppose that we have any countable set of real numbers: that we have a list something like this: |

1st no: 783.086945 ...

2nd no: 28.820458 ...

3rd no: −3579.3084625 ...

4th no: 0.978956 ...

...

And so on; each number goes on forever (so a number like 1.5 would appear on the list as 1.500000 ... going on forever.) The list goes on forever as well."

| Qasim: | "So could a list like that include every number there is?" |
|---|---|
| Teacher: | "Well, that's the point we're after. If it does then the set of all numbers is countable like the set of rational numbers. However, we're going to find that, however the list is made, we can always find a number that is missing from the list. The number I'm making starts 0.1398 ..." |
| Paula: | "Why those digits?" |
| Teacher: | "Right: I just start with 0 before the decimal point. Then the first digit after the point is $0 + 1 = 1$, because the first number in the list had first decimal digit 0. The second digit is $2 + 1 = 3$ because the second digit in the second number in the list was 2. Likewise the third digit is $8 + 1 = 9$ to make the new number different in the third place from the third number in the list. For the fourth digit I did $9 - 1 = 8$, again making the new number different from the fourth number in the list. I could have made it 0, but I didn't because, for instance, the number 1.499999 ... on forever is the same as 1.50000 ... on forever, so I don't want to replace 9 with 0." |

Ricky: "What if the new number you're making agrees completely with the 569th number in the list?"

Qasim: "You just have to wait till you get to the 569th digit and then add 1 or take away 1 from the 569th digit in the 569th number."

Teacher: "That's right. The list goes on for ever, but so do the digits of the number I'm making, so the new number will disagree with every number in the list in at least one digit."

Ricky: "So the set of all numbers is uncountable, and that makes the set of irrational numbers uncountable, so there are lots more of them than rationals, like my friend said."

# Minimising via reflection

Teacher: "In the diagram a kingfisher is at *A*, 60 m above the ground in a tree beside a stream. The stream is teeming with fish, and the kingfisher can go anywhere between *G* and *H* to get a fish and then fly up to its nest at *B*, 90 m above the ground. The distance *GH* is 200 m. At what point *P* on *GH* should the kingfisher catch a fish so as to make its total flight distance $AP + PB$ be as short as possible? Try this first just by calculation."

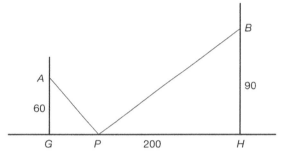

Some work using a spreadsheet gave the following results:

| GP | AP | PB | AP+PB |
|---|---|---|---|
| 10 | 60.82763 | 210.238 | 271.0656 |
| 20 | 63.24555 | 201.2461 | 264.4917 |
| 30 | 67.08204 | 192.3538 | 259.4359 |
| 40 | 72.11103 | 183.5756 | 255.6866 |
| 50 | 78.1025 | 174.9286 | 253.0311 |
| 60 | 84.85281 | 166.4332 | 251.286 |
| 70 | 92.19544 | 158.1139 | 250.3093 |
| 80 | 100 | 150 | 250 |
| 90 | 108.1665 | 142.1267 | 250.2932 |
| 100 | 116.619 | 134.5362 | 251.1553 |
| 110 | 125.2996 | 127.2792 | 252.5789 |

*(continued)*

(continued)

| GP | AP | PB | AP+PB |
|---|---|---|---|
| 120 | 134.1641 | 120.4159 | 254.58 |
| 130 | 143.1782 | 114.0175 | 257.1958 |
| 140 | 152.3155 | 108.1665 | 260.482 |
| 78 | 98.40732 | 151.6047 | 250.0121 |
| 79 | 99.20181 | 150.8012 | 250.003 |
| 80 | 100 | 150 | 250 |
| 81 | 100.8018 | 149.2012 | 250.003 |
| 82 | 101.6071 | 148.4049 | 250.0119 |
| 79.8 | 99.84007 | 150.16 | 250.0001 |
| 79.9 | 99.92002 | 150.08 | 250 |
| 80 | 100 | 150 | 250 |
| 80.1 | 100.08 | 149.92 | 250 |
| 80.2 | 100.1601 | 149.84 | 250.0001 |

Qasim: "It looks as if the shortest total distance is 250 m, achieved when $GP = 80$ m."

Paula: "Then $P$ is 80 m from $G$ and 120 m from $H$."

Ricky: "And the two parts of the journey have length 100 and 150 m. The ratio 80:120 is 2:3, and so is 100:150."

Qasim: "And that's also the ratio of the two heights, 60:90."

Ricky: "So the least distance occurs when the triangles $AGP$, $BHP$ are similar. But is that just a coincidence, or is it generally true?"

Interlude for the reader: If the class were able to differentiate and use the chain rule, and if we let $AG = a$, $BN = b$, $GH = l$, $GP = x$ and $AP + PB = s$, then $s = \sqrt{x^2 + a^2} + \sqrt{(l-x)^2 + b^2}$,

so $\dfrac{ds}{dx} = \dfrac{x}{\sqrt{x^2+a^2}} - \dfrac{l-x}{\sqrt{(l-x)^2+b^2}} = \dfrac{GP}{AP} - \dfrac{PH}{PB}$. For a minimum total distance we need $\dfrac{GP}{AP} = \dfrac{PH}{PB}$, or $\cos APG = \cos BPH$, so that triangles $AGP$, $BHP$ are similar as Ricky observes in the special case above.

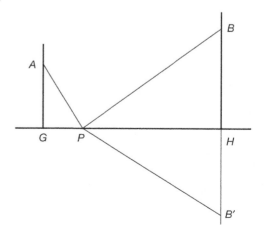

Teacher: "Well, let's look at the next diagram, in which $HB'$ is the reflection of $HB$ in the stream."

Paula: "So the triangles $BPH$ and $B'PH$ are congruent, aren't they? Then $AP + PB$ is the same as $AP + PB'$."

| Teacher: | "Yes. Carry on." |
|---|---|
| Qasim: | "That means that to make $AP + PB$ as short as possible is the same as making $AP + PB'$ as short as possible." |
| Ricky: | "Then $P$ has to be placed to make $APB'$ be a straight line. Then of course angles $APG$ and $B'PH$ will be vertically opposite and hence equal, so that's why the triangles $AGP$, $BHP$ are similar!" |
| Teacher: | "Good! And so of course the two parts of the journey will make equal angles with the stream." |
| Paula: | "That's like a ray of light hitting a mirror and reflecting off at the same angle as the angle of incidence; we've been doing that in physics." |
| Teacher: | "Yes indeed. In fact the reflection law is related to the fact that light takes the path of least time in going through any optical system, which in turn comes from the wave properties of light. Now I want to look at another minimising problem. An island is in the shape of an acute-angled triangle $ABC$. Lookout stations are to be placed at $U$, $V$, $W$ on the coasts $BC$, $CA$ and $AB$. They will be connected to each other by cables. Where should the lookout stations be placed so as to minimise the total length of cable? Have a look at the diagram, in which $U'$ and $U''$ are the reflections of $U$ in $AB$ and $AC$." |

| Qasim: | "The total length of cable is the same as $U'W + WV + VU''$. Could we make those three line segments into one straight line?" |
| Ricky: | "Just draw a straight line from $U'$ to $U''$ and put $W$ and $V$ where that line meets the coasts?" |
| Teacher: | "Yes, indeed. That does give the minimum length of cable for a given choice of where $U$ should be, because the positions of $U'$ and $U''$ are determined by the position of $U$. The next figure shows that done." |
| Paula: | "So $U'U''$ is the total length of cable, is it?" |
| Teacher: | "Yes, and now we just have to decide where to put $U$. I've also drawn in lines from $A$ to $U$, $U'$ and $U''$." |

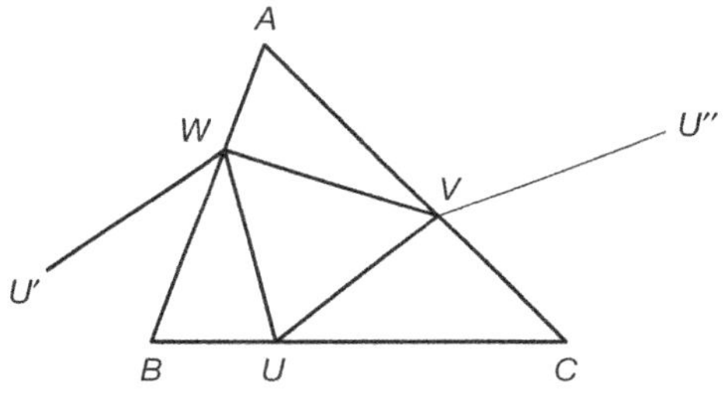

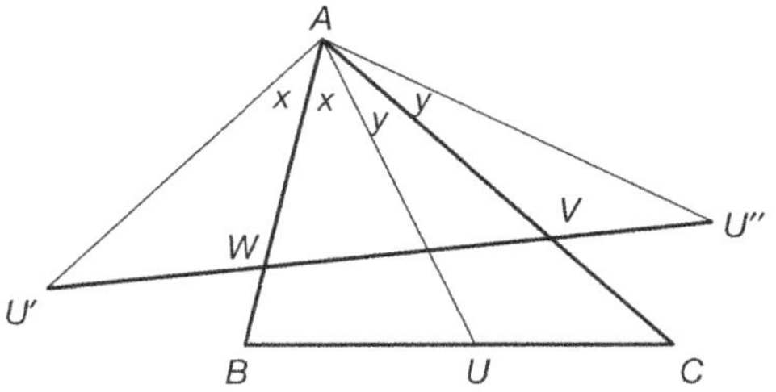

Ricky: "Those three lines from A are all equal because of AU' and AU" being the reflections of AU in AB and AC. So that makes triangle U' AU" isosceles."

Qasim: "The angles marked $x$ are equal because of the reflection, and so are the angles marked $y$."

Paula: "And $x + y = \angle BAC$. That means $\angle U'AU''$ is twice $\angle BAC$."

Ricky: "So that isosceles triangle U' AU" always has the same angle at A, wherever you put U. All the versions of the triangle are similar to each other."

Teacher: "That's right; and we want the version that is smallest, to make U' U" as small as possible."

Ricky: "Then we've got to make AU as small as possible."

Paula: "That means AU has to be perpendicular to BC; it can't get shorter than that."

Qasim: "So presumably BV will be perpendicular to CA and CW perpendicular to AB."

Teacher: "That's right: the best places to put the lookout stations are at the feet of the altitudes from the corners. That triangle of cables is called the pedal triangle for triangle ABC and has the shortest perimeter of any triangle with corners on the three island coasts. Now try the following: find the length of the shortest journey from the point S (40, 103) via a point P on the y-axis and a point Q on the x-axis to the point T (116, 30)."

# Maximum area with given perimeter

Teacher: "If a farmer wants to make a rectangular paddock using 400 m of fencing, what should be the lengths of the sides?"

Paula: "A square would have side 100 m and area 10 000 m². But is that the best?"

Ricky: "He could do 150 m by 50 m, but that's only 7500 m²."

Qasim: "What about 101 by 99? That comes to 9999 m²."

Ricky: "It looks as if the square gives the biggest area, and the more oblong we make it the smaller the area will be; but how can we prove that?"

Teacher: "Let's call the perimeter $4a$ instead of 400 m. That makes it more general. So if it was a square the side would be $a$. What if instead the length was $a + x$?"

Paula: "The width would have to be $a - x$ to keep the perimeter at $4a$."

Qasim: "Then the area is $(a + x) \times (a - x)$; that makes $a^2 - x^2$."

Ricky: "Aha; that means it has to be less than $a^2$ except when $x = 0$, and as $x$ gets bigger the area gets smaller."

Paula: "Even if $x$ is negative? Although it doesn't make sense for $x$ to be negative if we're calling $a + x$ the *length* of the rectangle."

Teacher: "Yes; and in any case with $x$ negative $x^2$ would still be positive. The square is the rectangle that has biggest area for a given perimeter. Arithmetically stated, if two variable numbers have a fixed sum, their product is greatest when they are equal."

Ricky: "Does that work with more than two numbers?"

Teacher: "Yes, provided the numbers are all positive. Suppose you have $n$ numbers with total $na$ so that $a$ is the average of them all. If they are equal, what is their product?"

Qasim: "They must all be $a$, so that their product is $a^n$."

| | |
|---|---|
| Teacher: | "Right. Now, if they are not equal, there must be at least one above $a$ and at least one below $a$ if $a$ is to be their average. Let the lowest number be $l$ and highest be $h$. What happens to the product $lh$ if we move $l$ up and $h$ down by equal amounts?" |
| Paula: | "That would be like making a rectangle with fixed perimeter more nearly square, so the product would increase." |
| Teacher: | "Right; and if $lh$ increases, what happens to the product of all the numbers?" |
| Ricky: | "It would also increase, provided the other numbers have a positive product." |
| Teacher: | "That's right; that is why we specify that the numbers concerned are all positive. So, we move the extreme numbers $l$ and $h$ together by equal amounts until one of them reaches $a$, and then stop." |
| Qasim: | "So now there is one less number that is different from $a$ than there was before." |
| Ricky: | "So now they might all be equal to $a$; or if not, do you just repeat the process with the new lowest and highest numbers?" |
| Teacher: | "Exactly; so long as they are not all the same there must be at least one below and at least one above $a$. Each stage increases the product of all the numbers and ends with one more number being equal to $a$." |
| Paula: | "So eventually they must all be equal to $a$ and then have product $a^n$, which has to be greater than the original product. So that proves it." |
| Teacher: | "Yes; the proof we have done comes from Professor Polya, and can be used to solve lots of maximisation problems. For instance, suppose you want to design a cuboid box to have maximum volume for a given surface area. What shape should it be?" |
| Qasim: | "I guess it would be a cube; but how to prove that?" |
| Teacher: | "OK; let's call the dimensions $l$, $w$, $h$. Then what are the surface area and volume?" |
| Ricky: | "The volume is $lwh$ and surface area is $2lw + 2lh + 2wh$." |
| Teacher: | "Right: and because the surface area is fixed, so is the sum $lw + lh + wh$. Now what do you get if you multiply the three terms $lw$, $lh$ and $wh$ instead of adding them?" |
| Paula: | "That makes $l^2 w^2 h^2$, which is the square of the volume." |
| Ricky: | "Oh, so if you make $lw$, $lh$ and $wh$ all equal, the square of the volume will be made as big as possible, hence so will the volume." |
| Teacher: | "Right; and to make those three products $lh$, etc. equal you have to make the length, width and height all equal, so that does make a cube." |

| Qasim: | "Back in two dimensions with the farmer's paddock, what if it can be any shape, not just a rectangle? Could another shape make a bigger area than a square?" |
|---|---|
| Paula: | "I think I'd go for a circle; but I guess that would be pretty hard to prove." |
| Teacher: | "In fact, with what you've done before it's not so hard, at least to show that any shape that is not a circle can be changed to give more area with the same perimeter. Suppose the whole length of fencing is called $L$. Start at any point $A$ and walk round a distance $\frac{1}{2}L$ to a point $B$. Now imagine a straight line $AB$ and consider the two sides of the paddock, left and right of $AB$. Choose whichever side has the greater area and change the fencing on the other side to be the mirror image in $AB$ of the side that had the greater area." |
| Paula: | "What if both sides had the same area anyway?" |
| Teacher: | "Then just reflect either side of fencing in $AB$ to replace the other. What we now have is a closed curve of fencing that is symmetrical about $AB$. Let $P$ be any point on one side and $P'$ its mirror image in $AB$. If the angle $APB$ is a right angle, what can you conclude about the circle on $AB$ as diameter?" |
| Ricky: | "It must go through $P$; we learned that from the fact that a rectangle has equal diagonals that bisect each other." |
| Teacher: | "Right. That circle goes through all the points $P$ for which $\angle APB$ is a right angle. If that applies to all the points on the fence, then the fence is already made into a circle." |
| Qasim: | "So if it's not a circle there must be a point where $\angle APB$ is not a right angle." |
| Teacher: | "Correct. Now imagine the scene in the diagram with the shaded pieces made of plywood and jointed freely at $A$, $P$, $B$ and $P'$, with the inside of $APBP'$ being empty space, so that you could push $A$ and $B$ together or pull them apart." |
| Ricky: | "Then the plywood area would stay fixed, but the inside area would change." |
| Teacher: | "Yes, and the inside area is two congruent triangles, $APB$ and $APB'$." |
| Linda: | "In each triangle two sides are fixed but the angle between them, at $P$ and at $P'$, can vary." |
| Teacher: | "Right. Now how do you work out area of a triangle?" |
| Qasim: | "Half base times height. If you take $AP$ as base, the height is the perpendicular from $B$ to $AP$." |

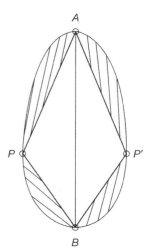

Ricky:      "That height will always be less than *BP* except when the angle at *P* is a right
            angle. Ah, so that means that since the angle is not a right angle to begin with
            we can move *AP* together or apart until the angle at *P* is a right angle, and this
            movement will increase the area of each triangle."

Teacher:    "Exactly; and that means the total area inside the curve will increase
            without changing the perimeter. That shows that a non-circular curve never
            has maximum possible area for a given perimeter. Now see what is the
            maximum area the farmer could enclose with a 400 m length of fencing."

Note: The above proof is due to Steiner and was first published in 1842.

# Farey sequences

## Fractions in order of size

Teacher: "We're going to look at arranging fractions between 0 and 1 in order of size."

Qasim: "Is that possible? Is there a smallest fraction greater than 0?"

Teacher: "No, there is no smallest fraction. And in between any two fractions, no matter how close to each other they are, say $\frac{1}{1000000}$ and $\frac{1}{1000001}$, there are infinitely many other fractions; you can keep subdividing any interval, no matter how small."

Paula: "So how can we arrange fractions in order of size?"

Teacher: "We have to limit ourselves to fractions with denominators up to some given value. For instance, what about all the fractions with denominator up to 4: can you arrange those in order of size?"

Ricky: "That's easy: $\frac{1}{4}, \frac{1}{3}, \frac{1}{2}, \frac{2}{3}, \frac{3}{4}$."

Paula: "Should we have included $\frac{2}{4}$?"

Teacher: "No, because that's equal to $\frac{1}{2}$ which we have already. What Ricky has given us is called the *Farey sequence* of order 4, or $F_4$. The name comes from a geologist, John Farey, who wrote about them in the *Philsophical Magazine* in 1816; but Charles Haros, a mathematician, had studied them and written an article in 1802. Now what about the next sequence, of order 5?"

Qasim: "Is that $\frac{1}{5}, \frac{1}{4}, \frac{1}{3}, \frac{2}{5}, \frac{1}{2}, \frac{3}{5}, \frac{2}{3}, \frac{3}{4}, \frac{4}{5}$?"

Teacher: "That's right; and the next one is easy; why?"

Paula: "Because the only new fractions are $\frac{1}{6}$ at the start and $\frac{5}{6}$ at the end. But after that the next one with sevenths is different. How do we tell where to put all those?"

Ricky: "To compare two fractions you express them with common denominator, is that right?"

Teacher:   "Yes, just as you do to add or subtract fractions. In fact I also want you to look at the differences between neighbouring fractions: for instance, what is $\frac{2}{5}-\frac{1}{3}$ in $F_5$ ?"

Paula:   "That's $\frac{6}{15}-\frac{5}{15}=\frac{1}{15}$."

Teacher:   "Yes. Now find the right order for fractions in $F_7$, see if you notice a possible quicker way to place the new fractions, and also find all the differences between neighbours; you should notice something."

The class found that $F_7$ was $\frac{1}{7},\frac{1}{6},\frac{1}{5},\frac{1}{4},\frac{2}{7},\frac{1}{3},\frac{2}{5},\frac{3}{7},\frac{1}{2},\frac{4}{7},\frac{3}{5},\frac{2}{3},\frac{5}{7},\frac{3}{4},\frac{4}{5},\frac{5}{6},\frac{6}{7}$.

The differences were $\frac{1}{42},\frac{1}{30},\frac{1}{20},\frac{1}{28},\frac{1}{21},\frac{1}{15},\frac{1}{35},\frac{1}{14}$ and then the same again in reverse order.

Qasim:   "The differences all have a numerator of 1, and the denominator is just the two neighbouring denominators multiplied."

Paula:   "And I noticed that the new fractions seem to be simply formed from the ones on either side of them. For instance $\frac{2}{7}=\frac{1+1}{4+3}$ and $\frac{4}{7}=\frac{1+3}{2+5}$; you just add the numerators and add the denominators of the two neighbours to get the new fraction. That's apart from the first and last ones, $\frac{1}{7}$ and $\frac{6}{7}$ which don't have two neighbours."

Teacher:   "You're right; but if we start and finish each sequence with $\frac{0}{1}$ and $\frac{1}{1}$ that provides neighbours on both sides for every new fraction, and that's commonly done."

Ricky:   "The denominators have to add up to 7 when you're doing the new fractions in $F_7$. If that works generally, it saves a lot of effort placing new fractions. But does it go on working in $F_8$ and so on? And do the differences still keep having numerator 1?"

Teacher:   "Good questions. To address those, let's start by checking whether adding numerators and adding denominators always gives a fraction in between the two you start with. Let's suppose we have two positive fractions, that $\frac{a}{b}<\frac{c}{d}$ and that we form $\frac{p}{q}=\frac{a+c}{b+d}$. Let's now look at $\frac{p}{q}-\frac{a}{b}$."

Ricky:   "That's $\frac{a+c}{b+d}-\frac{a}{b}=\frac{b(a+c)-a(b+d)}{b(b+d)}=\frac{bc-ad}{b(b+d)}$. How do we know whether that's positive or negative?"

Qasim:   "If we know $\frac{a}{b}<\frac{c}{d}$ then $\frac{c}{d}-\frac{a}{b}$ is positive, and that's $\frac{bc-ad}{bd}$; so $bc-ad$ is positive, which makes $\frac{bc-ad}{b(b+d)}$ positive."

Teacher: "That's right, given of course that the letters all stand for positive numbers, which they do. You can check similarly that $\frac{c}{d} - \frac{p}{q}$ is also positive; I'll leave that as an exercise. In fact the result is rather obvious if you think of an exam in two parts. Suppose you get a low mark 9/20 in the first part and a better mark 22/30 in the second part; your overall mark is 31/50, which is somewhere in between the two."

Paula: "So does that prove that every new fraction in going from one sequence to the next is always formed by adding numerators and denominators of its neighbours?"

Teacher: "No, we have not proved that yet; nor have we proved that the difference between neighbours always has numerator 1. We have established those facts for $F_7$, and it's fairly easy to check that they're still true in $F_8$. What we are going to do is to show that if they're true in a particular Farey sequence, then they continue to be true in the next one. So let's suppose we are going from $F_{n-1}$ to $F_n$, and that a new fraction $\frac{m}{n}$ is between $\frac{a}{b}$ and $\frac{c}{d}$ which are in $F_{n-1}$. Now let's look at the differences between the new fraction and its neighbours."

Ricky: "So you want $\frac{m}{n} - \frac{a}{b}$ ? That makes $\frac{bm-an}{bn}$. And $\frac{c}{d} - \frac{m}{n} = \frac{cn-dm}{dn}$ ."

Teacher: "Yes, and I'm now going to call those differences $\frac{r}{bn}$ and $\frac{s}{dn}$ ."

Qasim: "So $bm - an = r$ and $cn - dm = s$, is that right?"

Teacher: "That's right, and we're going to treat those as simultaneous equations in $m$ and $n$ to be solved in terms of the other letters. You know how to do that, don't you?"

Paula: "We multiply the first equation by $c$ and the second by $a$ to make $bcm - acn = cr$ and $acn - adm = as$. Then add to get $bcm - adm = cr + as$ ."

Ricky: "That's $(bc - ad)m = as + cr$ so $m = \frac{as + cr}{bc - ad}$ ."

Qasim: "And if you eliminate $m$ from both equations you get $n = \frac{bs + dr}{bc - ad}$. But now what?"

Teacher: "Well, at this point we are going to use the fact that the two things we have noticed so far about Farey sequences are true in $F_{n-1}$. That means that the difference between $\frac{c}{d}$ and $\frac{a}{b}$, which were neighbours in $F_{n-1}$, has numerator 1 and denominator equal to the product of the two fractions' denominators."

Paula: "Oh, that means $\frac{c}{d} - \frac{a}{b} = \frac{bc - ad}{bd} = \frac{1}{bd}$, so $bc - ad = 1$ ."

Qasim: "So that makes $m = as + cr$ and $n = bs + dr$ ."

| Teacher: | "Yes, so the new fraction $\frac{m}{n}$ can be written as $\frac{as+cr}{bs+dr}$ ." |
|---|---|
| Ricky: | "Is there any possibility of that cancelling down? Could $r$ and $s$ have a common factor apart from 1? |
| Teacher: | "Good question! But no, just as $\frac{2}{4}$ is not allowed in $F_4$ because it cancels down, so $\frac{m}{n}$ can't cancel down, which means $s$ and $r$ have no common factor greater than 1; if they did, that would be a common factor for $m$ and $n$. Can we say anything about the values of $r$ and $s$?" |
| Ricky: | "Could they be both 1? That would make $\frac{m}{n} = \frac{a+c}{b+d}$, which we know is between $\frac{a}{b}$ and $\frac{c}{d}$ ." |
| Qasim: | "Yes, in fact that's the only possibility! Because if either $s$ or $r$ were more than 1, then with $bs+dr = n$, $b+d$ would have to be less than $n$, which means that $\frac{a+c}{b+d}$ would be there already in between $\frac{a}{b}$ and $\frac{c}{d}$, in which case they couldn't be neighbours to a new fraction in $F_n$." |
| Teacher: | "Well done! And of course $r$ and $s$ were the numerators in the differences between the new fraction and its neighbours; so the two features we noticed in $F_7$ persist to $F_n$ whenever they are true in $F_{n-1}$ and hence they work in every Farey sequence. Now, can we find the neighbours of $\frac{3}{8}$ in $F_{10}$ and in $F_{50}$ ?" |
| Paula: | "We can easily work up to $F_{10}$, but $F_{50}$ is a long way to go!" |
| Teacher: | "Yes, I wasn't expecting you to list the sequences up to $F_{50}$! We can do it by using what we have discovered about differences between neighbours. Let's start with $\frac{a}{b}$ and $\frac{c}{d}$ being just below and just above $\frac{3}{8}$ in some Farey sequence. What do we know about $\frac{3}{8} - \frac{a}{b}$ ?" |
| Ricky: | "It has to be $\frac{1}{8b}$, so $\frac{3b-8a}{8b} = \frac{1}{8b}$, that makes $3b-8a = 1$. But that's only one equation for two unknowns." |
| Teacher: | "Indeed, but there will be different solutions for different Farey sequences. Can you find any solution in whole numbers?" |
| Qasim: | "How about $b = 3$, $a = 1$ ?" |
| Teacher: | "OK. Now if we let $a = 1+x$ and $b = 3+y$, what can we say about $x$ and $y$?" |
| Ricky: | "We get $3(3+y) - 8(1+x) = 1$, that makes $3y - 8x = 0$. So $8x = 3y$." |

Teacher: "And so $x$ must be a multiple of 3 and $y$ must be a multiple of 8. Let's say $x = 3k$, $y = 8k$, which makes $8x$ and $3y$ both equal $24k$. We then have $\dfrac{a}{b} = \dfrac{1+3k}{3+8k}$. If we now let $k = 0, 1, 2, 3\ldots$ we get $\dfrac{a}{b} = \dfrac{1}{3}, \dfrac{4}{11}, \dfrac{7}{19}, \dfrac{10}{27}$ and so on. Can you see which is the neighbour in $F_{10}$ ?"

Qasim: "It must be $\dfrac{1}{3}$: the next one doesn't appear till $F_{11}$."

Paula: "So for the neighbour in $F_{50}$ we need $3 + 8k$ to be not more than 50 but as near 50 as possible; that makes $8k \leq 47$; the highest value of $k$ is 5."

Qasim: "That makes the neighbour $\dfrac{1+15}{3+40} = \dfrac{16}{43}$."

Teacher: "Well done; and you can check that $\dfrac{3}{8} - \dfrac{16}{43}$ equals $\dfrac{1}{8 \times 43} = \dfrac{1}{344}$. I'll leave you to check that the neighbours on the other side of $\dfrac{3}{8}$ are $\dfrac{2}{5}$ in $F_{10}$ and $\dfrac{17}{45}$ in $F_{50}$. And you can also try to find the neighbours of $\dfrac{2}{3}$ in $F_{1000}$."

# 31 Touching circles and Farey sequences again

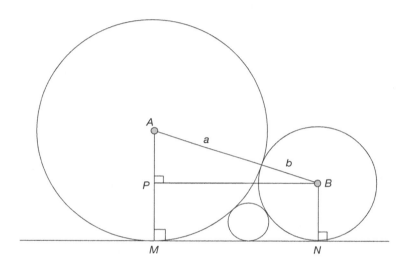

Teacher: "In the diagram three circles are touching each other and also touching a straight line. The two big circles have radii $a$ and $b$. We are going to find first the length of the common tangent $MN$ and then the radius of the small third circle."

Qasim: "It looks as if $MN = PB$."

Teacher: "Yes, because the tangent $MN$ is perpendicular to both radii, and the line $BP$ has been drawn at right angles to $AM$."

Paula: "Then $PM = BN = b$ so $AP = a - b$."

Ricky: "And $AP = a + b$, so $PB^2 = (a+b)^2 - (a-b)^2$."

Qasim: "That comes to $4ab$, so $MN = PB = \sqrt{4ab} = 2\sqrt{ab}$. But how are we going to find that small radius? Don't we need extra lines in the diagram?"

Tch: "No, as it happens we don't. Just think of the point where the small circle touches the line, let's call that $X$, and let's call the radius which we want to find $r$. Then what would $MX$ and $XN$ be?"

Paula: "From what we did that's easy: $MX = 2\sqrt{ar}$ and $XN = 2\sqrt{rb}$ ."

Ricky: "Aha! But $MX + XN = MN$ so $2\sqrt{ar} + 2\sqrt{rb} = 2\sqrt{ab}$ . We should be able to solve that for $r$."

Teacher: "Yes indeed; that illustrates the beautiful way in which algebra can work in geometry. It will help to use the fact that $\sqrt{ar} = \sqrt{a} \times \sqrt{r}$ ."

Ricky: "So we've got $\sqrt{a}\sqrt{r} + \sqrt{b}\sqrt{r} = \sqrt{ab}$."

Qasim: "Then $\left(\sqrt{a} + \sqrt{b}\right)\sqrt{r} = \sqrt{ab}$ so $\sqrt{r} = \dfrac{\sqrt{ab}}{\sqrt{a} + \sqrt{b}}$ ."

Teacher: "Yes. So what can you say about $\dfrac{1}{\sqrt{r}}$ ?"

Qasim: "That's $\dfrac{\sqrt{a} + \sqrt{b}}{\sqrt{ab}} = \dfrac{1}{\sqrt{b}} + \dfrac{1}{\sqrt{a}}$ ."

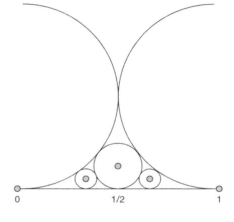

Teacher: "Yes, $\dfrac{1}{\sqrt{r}} = \dfrac{1}{\sqrt{a}} + \dfrac{1}{\sqrt{b}}$ is a neat way of expressing the relationship, and we're going to use that result as well as the length of the common tangent. The next diagram shows a number axis from 0 to 1. The two big semicircles are touching the axis at 0 and at 1. What is their radius?"

Paula: "They're touching in the middle so the radius must be $\dfrac{1}{2}$ ."

Teacher: "That's right. In between is a smaller circle touching the axis at $\dfrac{1}{2}$ . What radius does it have?"

Ricky: "If we call it $r$ we have $\dfrac{1}{\sqrt{r}} = \dfrac{1}{\sqrt{\frac{1}{2}}} + \dfrac{1}{\sqrt{\frac{1}{2}}} = 2\sqrt{2}$, so $r = \dfrac{1}{\left(2\sqrt{2}\right)^2} = \dfrac{1}{8}$ ."

Teacher: "Good. Now what about the smaller circle on the left of that?"

Qasim: "For that we get $\dfrac{1}{\sqrt{r}} = \dfrac{1}{\sqrt{\frac{1}{2}}} + \dfrac{1}{\sqrt{\frac{1}{8}}} = \sqrt{2} + \sqrt{8} = 3\sqrt{2}$, so $r = \dfrac{1}{\left(3\sqrt{2}\right)^2} = \dfrac{1}{18}$ ."

Teacher: "Right; and where does it touch the number axis?"

Paula: "We have to use $2\sqrt{ab}$ with $a = \dfrac{1}{2}, b = \dfrac{1}{18}$ . That gives $2 \times \sqrt{\dfrac{1}{36}} = \dfrac{1}{3}$. So the other circle with the same radius touches at $\dfrac{2}{3}$ , does it?"

Teacher: "Yes, well done. Let's call those the $\dfrac{1}{3}$ circle and the $\dfrac{2}{3}$ circle. What about in between the 0 semicircle (the big one on the left) and the $\dfrac{1}{3}$ circle? And between the $\dfrac{1}{3}$ circle and the $\dfrac{1}{2}$ circle in the middle?"

Similar calculations showed that between the 0 and the $\frac{1}{3}$ circle is one of radius $\frac{1}{32}$ that touches the axis at $\frac{1}{4}$, while between the $\frac{1}{3}$ and $\frac{1}{2}$ circles is one of radius $\frac{1}{50}$ that touches the axis at $\frac{2}{5}$ (which is $\frac{1}{3} + 2\sqrt{\frac{1}{18} \times \frac{1}{50}} = \frac{1}{3} + \frac{1}{15}$).

Ricky: "This is looking like the Farey sequence again: the circle between the $\frac{1}{3}$ and $\frac{1}{2}$ circles touches at $\frac{2}{5}$ which is the fraction between $\frac{1}{3}$ and $\frac{1}{2}$ in $F_5$. But I don't know about the radii."

Teacher: "See if you can find other circles that touch at fractions with denominator 5, and what their radii are."

This yielded circles touching at $\frac{1}{5}, \frac{3}{5}$ and $\frac{4}{5}$, all with the same radius of $\frac{1}{50}$ as the one that touches at $\frac{2}{5}$.

Ricky: "Aha! It looks as if the radius depends on the denominator of the fraction where the circle touches the axis. That would mean that the new fractions in any Farey sequence all have circles of the same radius touching the axis where they are."

Qasim: "And when the denominator is 2, the radius is $\frac{1}{8}$, for denominator 3 it's $\frac{1}{18}$ and for denominator 4 it's $\frac{1}{32}$. Each radius is a fraction with numerator 1, and its denominator seems to be twice a square number."

Paula: "Yes, if the fraction touches at $\frac{m}{n}$ the radius looks like it's $\frac{1}{2n^2}$."

Teacher: "Well done! But now, does that pattern persist?"

Ricky: "We'll need to start with two neighbouring fractions $\frac{a}{b}$ and $\frac{c}{d}$ in some Farey sequence, that are going to have a new neighbour $\frac{m}{n} = \frac{a+c}{b+d}$ in the next Farey sequence."

Paula: "And $bc - ad$ has to be 1 if those fractions are neighbours."

Qasim: "So we assume that there is an $\frac{a}{b}$ circle with radius $\frac{1}{2b^2}$, and a $\frac{c}{d}$ circle with radius $\frac{1}{2d^2}$ and we have to locate another circle in between them; we need to show that it touches the axis at $\frac{a+c}{b+d}$ and that its radius is $\frac{1}{2(b+d)^2}$."

Ricky: "We have to get the radius first, using $\frac{1}{\sqrt{r}} = \frac{1}{\sqrt{\frac{1}{2b^2}}} + \frac{1}{\sqrt{\frac{1}{2d^2}}} = b\sqrt{2} + d\sqrt{2}$, so that $\sqrt{r} = \frac{1}{(b+d)\sqrt{2}}$, and that makes $r = \frac{1}{2(b+d)^2}$, which is what we wanted to show!"

Teacher: "That's right; now what about where it touches the axis?"

Qasim:
"If we use the $\frac{a}{b}$ circle with radius $p$ together with this new circle – let's call its radius $r$ – then the new circle touches the axis at a distance $2\sqrt{pr}$ past $\frac{a}{b}$.

That's $2\sqrt{pr} = 2\sqrt{\dfrac{1}{2b^2} \times \dfrac{1}{2(b+d)^2}} = \dfrac{1}{b(b+d)}$ past $\frac{a}{b}$, so where it touches the axis

is at $\dfrac{a}{b} + \dfrac{1}{b(b+d)} = \dfrac{a(b+d)+1}{b(b+d)} = \dfrac{ab+ad+1}{b(b+d)}$."

Paula:
"That was supposed to be at $\dfrac{a+c}{b+d}$. What's gone wrong?"

Teacher:
"Well, we've got the $b + d$ in the denominator, but multiplied by $b$; so we would like the numerator to be $b(a+c) = ab + bc$, while what we have is $ab + ad + 1$."

Paula:
"Instead of $bc$ we've got $ad + 1$."

Ricky:
"And remember, $bc - ad = 1$ for neighbouring fractions; that makes $bc = ad + 1$, so we have got $ab + bc$ on the top. That means that the new

circle does touch the axis at, $\dfrac{a+c}{b+d}$ as well as having radius $\dfrac{1}{2(b+d)^2}$; so the

pattern does continue after all!"

Teacher:
"Well done! The circles are called Ford circles, after the American mathematician Lester R. Ford Sr, who wrote about them in 1938.

The picture below, from pqrtheory.wordpress.com, shows them for $F_{12}$."

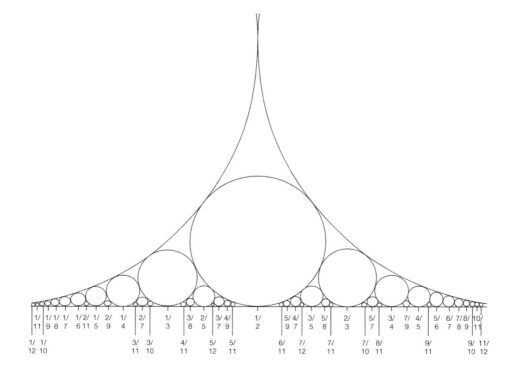

# Part III
## 16–18 years old

# Remainder theorem and factorising polynomials

Teacher:    "Suppose you have 16 marbles to divide equally among 5 children. How many does each get?"

Carol:      "That's easy: 17 divided by 5 equals 3, remainder 2."

Bilal:      "Or it could be $17 \div 5 = 3.4$."

Alan:       "Not with marbles! Who would want 0.4 of a marble?"

Teacher:    "That's right. If we had been talking about chocolate bars then 3.4 bars each would make sense, but I deliberately made it marbles so that the number each child gets is a whole number, and there may be some left over that can't be shared out. What we are doing is expressing 17 as the biggest possible multiple of 5 plus a number less than 5: $17 = 3 \times 5 + 2$. We call 17 the *dividend*."

Alan:       "Is that like a dividend in business?"

Teacher:    "Yes, the idea there is that people have bought shares to help a company get going, and then some of the profit is to be divided out among the shareholders; that's the dividend (though in fact it's usually expressed as so much per share, so in effect the arithmetic division has already been done.) The number 5 we are dividing by is called the *divisor*, the share per child is the *quotient* and the number left over is the *remainder*."

Bilal:      "So dividend = quotient × divisor + remainder."

Teacher:    "Exactly; and this applies too when we divide a polynomial by another polynomial. In this process we allow number coefficients to be fractions, and we continue the division until the degree of the remainder is less than the degree of the divisor. The important special case we are going to look at is when the divisor is a linear polynomial, we'll call it $x - a$ and call the dividend $f(x)$, the quotient $Q$ and the remainder $r$."

Carol:      "Are $Q$ and $r$ just numbers?"

Teacher:   "Q is usually not just a number but a polynomial with degree one lower than that of $f(x)$. But, since we are dividing by a linear polynomial the remainder is just a number. We then have, as Bilal said

dividend = quotient × divisor + remainder, which means that
$$f(x) \equiv Q \times (x - a) + r."$$

Bilal:   "What are the three lines for, instead of just = ?"

Teacher:   "I could have put just =, but the three lines draw attention to the fact that what I've written is not an equation to be solved to find a value of $x$: it's just a way of rewriting the dividend $f(x)$ and is true whatever value $x$ has. Can you see how we can use this to find the value of $r$?"

Alan:   "You'd have to get rid of the term $Q \times (x - a)$; I guess you could take $x = a$."

Bilal:   "So then you get $f(a) = 0 + r = r$, do you?"

Teacher:   "That's right; and we've now proved the remainder theorem: The remainder when a polynomial $f(x)$ is divided by $x - a$ equals $f(a)$."

Carol:   "What if you were dividing by, say $2x + 3$ ?"

Alan:   "You'd have $f(x) = Q \times (2x + 3) + r$, so take $x = -\frac{3}{2}$ and get $f\left(-\frac{3}{2}\right) = r$."

Teacher:   "Yes; and if you divide by $ax + b$ the remainder is $f(-\frac{b}{a})$. A special case of the remainder theorem is when the remainder is 0."

Carol:   "That means $x - a$ or whatever is a factor of the polynomial."

Teacher:   "Yes, and that's useful when we try to factorise, say, a cubic polynomial. We'll try this on $f(x) = 6x^3 - 31x^2 + 34x + 15$. Could $x - 1$ be a factor?"

Bilal:   "$f(1) = 6 - 31 + 44 + 15$; that's not 0, so there'll be a remainder; don't need to work out what it is."

Carol:   "And $f(-1) = -6 - 31 - 34 + 15$. That's not 0 either, so $x + 1$ can't be a factor. Should we try f(2)?"

Teacher:   "No, because that makes all the terms with $x$ in them even, while the 15 at the end is odd, so you can't get 0. If there is a factor of the form $x - a$ and the other factor is $px^2 + qx + r$, then when you multiply out $(x - a)(px^2 + qx + r)$ then the constant term is $-ar$ which has to match 15, so only try numbers which are factors of the constant term in $f(x)$."

Alan:   "We try $f(3) = 6 \times 3^3 - 31 \times 3^2 + 34 \times 3 + 15 = 162 - 279 + 102 + 15 = 0$. So $x - 3$ is a factor."

Bilal:   "Now to find the other factors should we use long division?"

Teacher:    "You can do; but there's a quicker way. Write it as
$$6x^3 - 31x^2 + 34x + 15 = (x - 3)(6x^2 + qx - 5).$$"

Carol:      "Is that $6x^2$ because you have to multiply $x$ by something to make $6x^3$?"

Bilal:      "And the $-5$ to make $+15$ when multiplied by $-3$?"

Teacher:    "That's right; and now there's still $qx$ to find. When you multiply out, what term will you get in $x^2$?"

Alan:       "It'll be $qx^2 - 18x^2$; so $q - 18$ has to match $-31$ That makes
$$q = 18 - 31 = -13.$$"

Teacher:    "Good; and to be sure we've not gone wrong, what is the term in $x$ when you multiply out the right hand side?"

Carol:      "It's $-5x - 3qx$; that's $-5x + 39x = 34x$."

Bilal:      "That matches the $34x$ in $f(x)$ so we're on track."

Alan:       "And now we just have to factorise $6x^2 - 13x - 5$; I think that's
$(2x - 5)(3x + 1)$."

Teacher:    "Well done all! But be aware that sometimes the quadratic factor won't factorise further into linear factors. If that's the case you won't be expected to go that far."

 # Adding arithmetic series

| | |
|---|---|
| Teacher: | "How would you tackle adding up $13 + 20 + 27 + 34 \ldots + 706 + 713$?" |
| Carol: | "It looks like the terms are increasing by 7 from each to the next. Does that continue all the way?" |
| Teacher: | "Yes, that's what is intended. That kind of series is called an *arithmetic* series, also known as an arithmetic progression. Now what is the average of the first and last terms?" |
| Bilal: | "That's $726 \div 2 = 363$." |
| Teacher: | "Right; and what about the second and last but one; what is their average?" |
| Bilal: | "$20 + 706 = 726$, same as before, so it's still 363." |
| Alan: | "That's going to continue, because at the front end you keep adding 7 to get the next term, and at the far end you keep taking away 7." |
| Teacher: | "That's right; so what can you say about the average of all the numbers?" |
| Carol: | "It must be 363 as well. So if we knew how many terms there are we could find out the sum easily." |
| Alan: | "To go from 13 to 713 in steps of 7 needs 100 steps, so are there 100 terms?" |
| Teacher: | "No, be careful; if you had just two terms there'd be one step between them, and for three terms there are two steps, and so on." |
| Alan: | "Oh, so it's 101 terms, and the total is $363 \times 101 = 36663$." |
| Teacher: | "Good; and you can use this approach with any arithmetic series. We started by averaging the first and last terms. If you think of this in terms of statistics, what do you call the average of the highest and lowest of a set of data?" |
| Bilal: | "It's the mid-range, isn't it?" |

Teacher: "That's right; and we've seen that for an arithmetic series the mid-range equals the mean of the whole set."

Bilal: "What about the median?"

Alan: "In 101 terms that would be the 51st, which is 50 steps from the first term, so it's $13 + 50 \times 7 = 363$. Oh, that's the same again!"

Bilal: "I suppose that's really to be expected: you start with the very lowest and very highest numbers, then the next lowest and next highest, and so on, always with the same average, so ultimately there's either just one number left between the numbers in the last pair, or else there is just a last closest pair whose average is the median."

Teacher: "That's right; so for an arithmetic series the mean, median and mid-range are all equal."

Carol: "And the mode?"

Alan: "There isn't a mode when all the numbers are different, silly!"

Teacher: "All right, no need to be rude to Carol; but of course there isn't a mode. Now can you use what you know to tell me the sum of all the integers from 1 up to $n$?"

Carol: "The mean equals the midrange, which is $\frac{1}{2}(1+n)$ and there are $n$ numbers, so the total is $\frac{1}{2}n(n+1)$; that's the formula for $T_n$, the $n$th triangular number too, isn't it?"

Teacher: "Yes, that's how the triangular numbers are defined: $1, 1 + 2, 1 + 2 + 3$ and so on. Now what about the sum of the first $n$ odd numbers?"

Alan: "They start with 1 and go up in steps of 2, so the $n$th is $1 + 2(n-1) = 2n - 1$."

Bilal: "So the mean equals the midrange $= \frac{1}{2}(1 + 2n - 1) = n$."

Carol: "So the total must be $n \times n = n^2$."

Teacher: "Well done all of you! Can you see that illustrated by the dots in the diagram?"

Bilal: "There's one black dot in the bottom left hand corner, then three hollow ones above and to the right, then five black ones, and so on."

Alan: "Each L-shaped layer of dots has two more than the one before, always the next odd number."

Carol: "And each time you add a new L-shaped layer you complete another square array: $1+3 = 2^2, 1+3+5 = 3^2, 1+3+5+7 = 4^2$, and so on."

Teacher: "Good; you've grasped it. Now what about the sum

$$1+2+3+\ldots(n-1)+n+(n-1)+(n-2)+\ldots+3+2+1?"$$

Bilal: "$1+2+1 = 4$, $1+2+3+2+1 = 9$, $1+2+3+4+3+2+1 = 16\ldots$"

Carol: "They're all square numbers. Does that mean the answer is $n^2$?"

Alan: "It's all the numbers up to $n$ and then all the numbers up to $n-1$, in reverse order, which doesn't matter. So that's $T_n + T_{n-1} = \frac{1}{2}n(n+1) + \frac{1}{2}(n-1)n = \frac{1}{2}n \times 2n$."

Carol: "So it is $n^2$."

Teacher: "Yes, well done; that's sometimes called the Duke of York's theorem."

Alan: "The grand old Duke of York, he had ten thousand men; he marched them up to the top of the hill and he marched them down again – just like the numbers going up from 1 to $n$ and then going down to 1 again."

Teacher: "Exactly: and can you see how that is illustrated in the next diagram?"

Bilal: "There's one black dot in the bottom left hand corner, then two hollow ones making a sloping row, then three black ones in the next row."

Carol: "Then four, then five, then four, three, two, one again, and it all adds up to five squared."

Teacher: "That's right. You can also see it as two triangular arrays, the bigger one from the bottom left up to the main diagonal with five black dots, and the rest of the square made by the smaller triangle, so it shows $T_5 + T_4 = 5^2$."

Alan: "What about sums of non-arithmetic series, say $1^2 + 2^2 + 3^2$ and so on?"

Teacher: "It's actually easier to look at the sum of cubes, $1^3 + 2^3 + 3^3 + \ldots + n^3$. Try that."

Bilal: "The first few sums are $1, 9, 36, 100, 225\ldots$"

Carol: "Those are all squares: $1^2, 3^2, 6^2, 10^2, 15^2,\ldots$"

Alan:    "Those are the squares of the triangular numbers! It looks as if the sum of the first $n$ cubes is the squares of the sum of the first $n$ numbers, that makes $\frac{1}{4}n^2(n+1)^2$. But how do we know that it's correct for all $n$ and not just for the first few?"

Teacher:    "Good question Alan. The formula is in fact correct, but the simple way to prove that will have to wait for another lesson. Meanwhile you could try the exercise below."

## Exercise

The multiplication table up to $n \times n$ is shown below

| 1 | 2 | 3 | 4 | 5 | . . . | $n$ |
|---|---|---|---|---|-------|-----|
| 2 | 4 | 6 | 8 | 10 | . . . | $2n$ |
| 3 | 6 | 9 | 12 | 15 | . . . | $3n$ |
| . . . | | | | | | |
| . . . | | | | | | |
| $n$ | $2n$ | $3n$ | $4n$ | $5n$ | . . . | $n^2$ |

Find (a) the total of all the numbers, (b) the total of all the numbers that are in the "outer layer" of the table, i.e. those that are in the last row or the last column.

(c) Use your answers to show that the sum of cubes is indeed the square of the sum of the numbers from 1 to $n$.

# d why? by dx

## Or what is differentiation for?

After a year of learning additional maths I could differentiate any power of $x$, but I no longer knew what it was all about. I suspect that I'm not alone in this.

Teacher: "So what do we differentiate a function for?"

Alan: "To find the gradient."

Teacher: "And what is that for?"

Bilal: "It tells you how steep the graph is, and you can work out the equation of a tangent or normal."

Teacher: "Yes; anything else?"

Silence.

Teacher: "OK; think of the equation that gives Fahrenheit equivalents to Celsius temperatures: $F = 1.8C + 32$. What is $F$ when $C = 10$, and what is $\frac{dF}{dC}$?"

Carol: "$1.8 \times 10 + 32 = 50$, and the gradient is just 1.8."

Teacher: "Good; now can you use Carol's answers, not the original formula, to give $F$ when $C = 15$?"

Alan: "The value of $C$ has increased by 5, from 10 to 15, so the value of $F$ increases by $1.8 \times 5 = 9$, so that makes $F = 59$ when $C = 15$."

Teacher: "Good; you can do easy conversion by remembering that 10 °C = 50 °F and that $F$ increases by 9 when $C$ increases by 5. Can you use this to convert 86 °F to °C?"

Bilal: "Yes, that means $F$ has increased from 50 by 36, which is $4 \times 9$, so $C$ has increased from 10 by $4 \times 5 = 20$, making 30 °C."

Teacher: "Good. Now what is the gradient of $y = x^2$ at $x = 10$?"

Carol:     "Easy; it's 2*x* which is 20."

Teacher:   "So can you use that to estimate $10.04^2$?"

Carol:     "$10^2 + 0.04^2$ makes 100.0016, but is that the right way? I haven't used the gradient."

Teacher:   "No, you haven't, and 100.0016 is not a good estimate. Have a look at this diagram. A square of side $x = 10$ and area $x^2$ is enlarged a bit by making the side $x + a = 10.04$ instead of *x*. Now look at the extra area; it's in three parts."

$a = 0.04$

$x = 10$

Alan:      "Two of them are the thin rectangles *xa* each, and there's the little square $a^2$ in the corner. So the total area now is $x^2 + 2xa + a^2$."

Bilal:     "We know that anyway from multiplying out $(x + a)(x + a)$."

Teacher:   "Good; but which bits of the extra area are important when *a* is small, and how does that relate to the gradient of $x^2$?"

Carol:     "The two thin rectangles are much more than the little corner square, so the extra area is close to 2*xa* which is 2*x* times the change in *x*."

Teacher:   "That's right, and so the change in $x^2$ divided by the change in *x* makes $2x + a$, and that tends to 2*x* when the change in *x* tends to 0, and can be approximated by 2*x* when *a* is small. So what about $10.04^2$?"

Alan:      "The gradient at *x* = 10 is 20, so the change in $x^2$ is close to $0.04 \times 20 = 0.8$, making $10.04^2$ about 100.8."

Teacher:   "Good; the exact value, which includes the little square in the corner, is 100.8016. Can anyone use the same ideas to estimate $\sqrt{99.4}$?"

Bilal:     "Do you start with $10^2 = 100$, and see what change in *x* would give a change of −0.6 in $x^2$?"

Teacher:   "That's good. Carry on."

Bilal:     "The change in *x* gets multiplied by 20 to make the change in $x^2$, so to go the other way you have to divide the change in $x^2$ by 20, that's $-0.6 \div 20 = -0.03$, making the answer 9.97."

Teacher: "Good. The answer from a calculator is $\sqrt{99.4} = 9.96995\ldots$. Now can you estimate $13.5^2$ starting from $10^2$?"

Carol: "Using the same gradient of 20 the change in $x^2$ would be $3.5 \times 20 = 70$; that makes 170."

Alan: "But the actual answer is 182.25, so 170 is not a good approximation."

Carol: "I guess the little square in the corner is not so little anymore. In fact it's $3.5^2 = 12.25$, quite a sizeable part of the whole change."

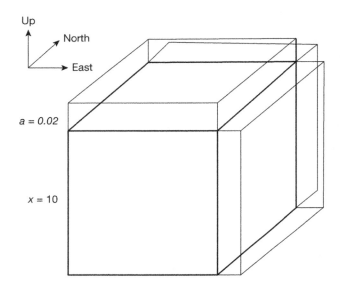

Teacher: "Yes, that's because we were trying to use the gradient at $x = 10$ as an approximation for the overall rate of change when making quite a big change in $x$. With a straight line graph that's no problem, because the gradient is the same between any two points; but with a curved graph the gradient changes so you can only get a good approximation using the gradient when you stick to small changes. Now can you estimate $10.02^3$ and $\sqrt[3]{994}$?"

Bilal: "$10^3$ is 1000 and the gradient is $3x^2 = 300$ at $x = 10\ldots$"

Carol: "Sir, is there a diagram to show why the gradient is $3x^2$, like the one you did with the square being enlarged?"

Teacher: "Yes, have a look at this, which is not to scale of course; the change in $x$ is much smaller than I can show it. There is a cube with side $x$ and volume $x^3$. Then $x$ is increased by $a$, and I've fixed the bottom SW (left front) corner of the cube, so that the increase is all in the east, north and upward directions. You can see that part of the increase consists of three slabs of new volume, on the east face, the north face and the top face. How much do those slabs contribute to the extra volume?"

Alan: "$x^2a$ each, so that's $3x^2a$. Ah, that's $3x^2$ times the change in $x$; is that why the gradient is $3x^2$? But what about the rest of the increase in volume?"

Teacher: "You're right about $3x^2a$ being the reason why the gradient is $3x^2$. Now what extra bits of volume can you see?"

Bilal: "Where the top slab meets the east slab there's space for a rod, $a \times a \times x$ making $xa^2$."

Carol: "And there are two more where the east and north slabs meet and where the top and north slabs meet, so that makes $3xa^2$."

Alan: "And then where the three rods meet, at the top north-east corner, should be a cube of side $a$, volume $a^3$. So we've got a total volume of $x^3 + 3x^2a + 3xa^2 + a^3$; oh, that is what you get when you expand $(x+a)^3$."

Teacher: "Well done. So you've got the original volume and then three terms giving the change. Now, if $a$ is small, which part of the extra volume is biggest?"

Alan: "The slabs, making $3x^2a$ which is $3x^2$ times the change in $x$. The rods are much smaller when $a$ is small, and the little cube is smallest of all."

Carol: "But what if $a$ was big?"

Teacher: "Then, if $a$ is big compared to $x$, the cube $a^3$ is the biggest part, and the rods too will be bigger than the slabs. That's why we can only use the gradient to relate small changes in $x$ and $x^3$. So what about $10.02^3$?"

Bilal: "The change in $x$ is 0.02. Multiply that by the gradient $3x^2 = 300$ to give $0.02 \times 300$ which is $2 \times 3 = 6$, so the new volume is about 1006."

Carol: "On the calculator I get 1006.012008."

Teacher: "Good; the 6 is the three slabs, the 0.012 is the rods and the last 0.000 008 is the cube in the corner. Now what about $\sqrt[3]{991}$?"

Alan: "This time we want the change in volume to be −9, so we divide that by the gradient: $-9 \div 300 = -0.03$, which gives the change in $x$, so that makes $10 - 0.03 = 9.97$."

Teacher: "Well done; and the actual answer is 9.969 91 correct to 5DP. So now what else can you tell me about what the gradient is for?"

Bilal: "If $y$ is a function of $x$ and you know what $y$ is and what the gradient is at say $x = 10$, then if you make a small change in $x$ the resulting change in $y$ is nearly proportional to the change in $x$, and the gradient is the constant that relates the two; Change in y approximately equals change in x times the gradient."

Carol: "But it isn't really a constant is it? It would have a different value at x = 20, unless the graph is a straight line."

Teacher: "That's true; the gradient only acts as a constant while you consider small changes from one value of x. The same approach can be used to solve equations that are difficult to solve exactly, for instance, to find a positive root of $x^3 = 50x + 90$. Can you see what whole number x is near?"

Alan: "How about 8? $8^3 = 512$ and $50 \times 8 + 90 = 490$."

Teacher: "Good. Now let's rewrite the equation as $x^3 - 50x - 90 = 0$ and call the left hand side $f(x)$ for short."

Carol: "So $f(8) = 512 - 400 - 90 = 22$."

Teacher: "Right; and what about $f'(8)$?"

Bilal: "$f'(x) = 3x^2 - 50$ so $f'(8) = 3 \times 64 - 50 = 142$. But how does that help?"

Teacher: "Well, we are trying to solve $f(x) = 0$ and we have $f(8) = 22$; so we want to change x in such a way that $f(x)$ becomes 0; so if we let $f(x) = y$ we are looking to change y by −22. What change in x is needed?"

Carol: "The change in y is approximately 142 times the change in x; so change in x should be $-22 \div 142$ which is about −0.155 to 3DP."

Bilal: "That change makes x become $8 - 0.155 = 7.845$."

Carol: "Yes, and $f(7.845) = 0.563$, a lot nearer to 0 than 22!"

Teacher: "Right; and of course you can repeat the process after working out the gradient at x = 7.845, which comes to 134.632; the next change in y is to be −0.563."

Alan: "That needs the change in x to be $-0.563 \div 134.632 = -0.00418$, or just −0.004 to 3DP, making the new x = 7.841."

Bilal: "And I make $f(7.841)$ to be 0.025 to 3DP."

Teacher: "That's good. The next change will be very small indeed; in fact, if you want the solution correct to 3DP, we know it is a little less than 7.841, so try 7.8405."

Alan: "Why not just 7.840?"

Teacher: "Well, if that gives a negative value of y, we then know that the root is between 7.840 and 7.841, but we would not know yet whether the root is nearer to 7.840 or 7.841."

Bilal:  "$f(7.8405)$ comes to $-0.042$,"

Teacher:  "Yes, and as that is negative while $f(7.841)$ is positive, the root is between 7.8405 and 7.841, which makes it 7.841 correct to 3DP. The method, which is simply using our knowledge of the gradient to work out what change in $x$ will give a desired change in $f(x)$, is known as Newton's method or as the Newton-Raphson method: to solve $f(x) = 0$, starting at $x = x_0$, let $x_1 = x_0 - \dfrac{f(x_0)}{f'(x_0)}$."

Alan:  "I've noticed that if you differentiate the area $\pi r^2$ of a circle with respect to $r$ you get the circumference $2\pi r$. Is that just a coincidence?"

Bilal:  "And if you differentiate the volume of a sphere you get the surface area."

Carol:  "But it doesn't work for a square or a cube; if you differentiate the volume you get only half the surface area. So what's going on?"

Teacher:  "OK, let's think of a planet that's a perfect sphere with radius $r$, surface area $S$ and volume $V$. Suppose there's a fall of snow of depth $a$ over the whole planet. How much snow is that?"

Alan:  "It's a depth $a$ covering area $S$, so that should be $Sa$ shouldn't it? That means the change in volume of the whole planet equals the surface area times the increase in radius, or $\delta V = S \times \delta r$, making $\dfrac{dV}{dr} = S$."

Teacher:  "Good; that's essentially it; but remember that, because the snow is falling on a sphere, the surface area increases as more snow falls, so original surface $S$ times the depth $a$ is only an approximate answer, but it's a good approximation when $a$ is small compared to $r$, and that does lead to the volume differentiated giving the surface area."

Carol:  "Does that work the same way for the area of a circle when differentiated giving the circumference?"

Teacher:  "Yes, just think of a circle's radius being increased slightly by $a$, making an extra area that is a thin ribbon of width $a$ whose length is $2\pi r$ on the inside and $2\pi(r + a)$ on the outside; that's an area of $2\pi ra$ plus a little bit that can be ignored when $a$ is small."

Bilal:  "And why doesn't it work for a square or a cube?"

Teacher:  "That's not so much because of a different shape, but because of the different length we use to specify the size of the square or cube, namely the whole length of one side. If instead we let $x$ be the distance from the centre of the square to each side, like a kind of radius, then the side of the square would be $2x$ and its area $4x^2$. What do you get when you differentiate that, and how does that relate to the perimeter?"

Bila:     "You get 8x, and the perimeter is 4 × 2x, that's 8x too!"

Teacher:   "Yes, because this time the extra area is mostly 4 thin rectangles of length 2x and width $a$. And likewise with the cube, if we measure from the centre to each face and then increase that, the extra volume is mostly six slabs, one on each face of the cube, instead of three. If on the other hand you let x be the diameter of a circle, what is the area in terms of x? And what happens when you differentiate that?"

Carol:     "The area would be $\pi\left(\dfrac{x}{2}\right)^2 = \dfrac{1}{4}\pi x^2$, which differentiates to $\dfrac{1}{2}\pi x$, but the circumference is $\pi x$."

Teacher:   "Yes, can you see why the two are different this time?"

Alan:      "I guess the width of the extra ribbon of area is half the increase of the diameter, so the extra area is about half $a$ times the circumference, making the gradient half the circumference."

Teacher:   "Yes, that's right. Now, if you had an equilateral triangle of side x, and you differentiated the area with respect to x, how would the result compare with the perimeter? Secondly, what measurement of an equilateral triangle's size would you use so that differentiating the area gave the perimeter? I'll leave you to think about that."

The answer to the last question actually applies to any regular polygon, not just a triangle.

# Integration without calculus

Alan: "Whatever can that mean? Integration is part of calculus, isn't it?"

Teacher: "It is now, but hasn't always been. The connection with differentiation, which we will look at soon, was a momentous discovery. But that's not how integration began. You think of integration as anti-

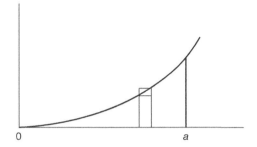

differentiation, but that is not the original meaning of the term. We're going to look at finding the area under the graph of $y = x^3$ between 0 and $a$, as in the diagram. The problem is that the top boundary is a curve and we don't have an elementary way to deal with that. So we divide the area up into lots of thin strips, just one of which I have shown. Let's take it that there are $n$ strips all of the same width."

Carol: "So each strip has width $\frac{a}{n}$."

Bilal: "The first strip goes from 0 to $\frac{a}{n}$, the second from $\frac{a}{n}$ to $\frac{2a}{n}$ and so on?"

Teacher: "Yes; so the $r$th strip is from $x = \frac{(r-1)a}{n}$ to $x = \frac{ra}{n}$."

Alan: "But even within that strip the height is varying, so how do we get its area?"

Teacher: "We can't get the exact area yet, but we can give lower and upper limits. In the diagram there is a lower rectangle whose height is the lowest height that occurs in the strip."

Bilal: "So that is $\left( \frac{(r-1)a}{n} \right)^3$, is it?"

Teacher:  "Yes, because the graph we're working with is of $y = x^3$. Then there is also an upper rectangle whose height is the highest that occurs in the strip."

Carol:  "That's $\left(\dfrac{ra}{n}\right)^3$."

Teacher:  "Yes. Now if we add up all the lower rectangles we'll get a lower bound for the area, and adding up all the upper rectangles will give us an upper bound. Do you remember the formula for the sum of the cubes of the first $n$ natural numbers?"

Carol:  "We found it's the square of the sum of the numbers; that's $\dfrac{1}{4}n^2(n+1)^2$."

Teacher:  "Right; so we'll start with the upper rectangles sum. What will that be?"

Bilal:  "It's the sum of $\left(\dfrac{ra}{n}\right)^3 \times \dfrac{a}{n}$ with $r$ going from 1 to $n$; that will be $\left(\dfrac{a}{n}\right)^4 \sum\limits_{r=1}^{n} r^3$."

Alan:  "That makes $\left(\dfrac{a}{n}\right)^4 \times \dfrac{1}{4}n^2(n+1)^2$."

Teacher:  "That's right; it can also be written as $\dfrac{1}{4}a^4 \dfrac{(n+1)^2}{n^2}$. Now what about the lower sum?"

Bilal:  "Start with the sum of $\left(\dfrac{(r-1)a}{n}\right)^3 \times \dfrac{a}{n}$; that's $\left(\dfrac{a}{n}\right)^4 \sum\limits_{r=1}^{n}(r-1)^3$. Do I need to expand out $(r-1)^3$?"

Teacher:  "No. Think of $\sum\limits_{r=1}^{n} r^3$ as $1^3 + 2^3 + 3^3 + \ldots + n^3$. Now do the same with $\sum\limits_{r=1}^{n}(r-1)^3$."

Bilal:  "Aha! It's $0^3 + 1^3 + 2^3 + \ldots + (n-1)^3$."

Alan:  "So that's the same as $\sum\limits_{r=1}^{n} r^3$ but with $n$ replaced by $n-1$, which makes $\dfrac{1}{4}(n-1)^2 n^2$. Then the lower sum comes to . . . $\dfrac{1}{4}a^4 \dfrac{(n-1)^2}{n^2}$ after tidying up."

Carol:  "So now what? We still don't have the area under the curve."

Teacher:  "Not yet, but we know that it is between $\dfrac{1}{4}a^4 \dfrac{(n-1)^2}{n^2}$ and $\dfrac{1}{4}a^4 \dfrac{(n+1)^2}{n^2}$. And that is true whatever the value of $n$ is. What happens to the two sums when $n$ is made bigger and bigger without limit?"

Carol:  "Oh! If you write $\dfrac{(n-1)^2}{n^2}$ as $\left(1-\dfrac{1}{n}\right)^2$ you can see that it is less than 1 but approaches 1 as $n$ gets bigger and bigger."

Bilal:  "And $\dfrac{(n+1)^2}{n^2} = \left(1+\dfrac{1}{n}\right)^2$ is more than 1 but tends to 1 as $n$ tends to infinity."

Teacher:  "Good. What can you conclude about the actual area under the curve?"

Alan:   "It must be exactly $\frac{1}{4}a^4$ , as it's always between two bounds which both approach that value as *n* increases."

Teacher:   "Good. So now we know the area. We have found it by *integrating*, putting together into a whole, a number of strips, for each of which we had lower and upper bounds. This is how integration was done by the ancient mathematicians such as Eudoxus and Archimedes."

Carol:   "Do we have to be able to do this with lots of other graphs? That summation could be quite hard to do."

Teacher:   "Yes indeed it could! But no, we don't need to go on using this method, because of the ground-breaking discovery made in the 17th century that integration is closely related to differentiation, as we shall see shortly."

# 36 Integration using calculus

Teacher: "We're now going to look at an area under the graph of $y = f(x)$ between $x = a$ and $x = b$, as in the diagram. As before, we think of it as divided up into lots of thin strips. One those, going from $x$ to $x + \delta x$, is shown. What can we say about its area?"

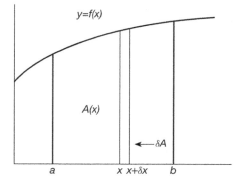

Carol: "The height is $f(x)$ at one end and $f(x + \delta x)$ at the other end; I suppose you multiply one of those by $\delta x$ and get either an underestimate or an overestimate."

Teacher: "Yes, and you saw last time that when the number of strips increases without limit then both underestimates and overestimates get closer and closer to the actual area; so let's just take $f(x)\delta x$ as our estimate for $\delta A$, the area of a strip. If we then add up these estimates we get $\sum_{x=a}^{b} f(x)\delta x$ as our estimate of the area from $a$ to $b$ under the graph."

Alan: "So then what?"

Teacher: "Well, we need to get the limit of that sum as the width $\delta x$ of each strip tends to 0; we can write that as

$$\lim_{\delta x \to 0} \sum_{x=a}^{b} f(x)\delta x$$

but a special notation was introduced by the German philosopher and mathematician Gottfried Leibnitz, who discovered calculus at the same time in the 17th century as Sir Isaac Newton did in England. The Greek capital S, $\Sigma$, turns into an old English long S, $\int$, and $\delta x$ is replaced by $dx$."

Bilal: "Is that like replacing $\frac{\delta y}{\delta x}$ by $\frac{dy}{dx}$ when you let $\delta x$ tend to 0 to get the gradient at a point instead of an average gradient?"

Teacher: "Yes; that's right; it was Leibnitz too who introduced the $\frac{dy}{dx}$ notation. So then the limit of the sum is written as $\int_a^b f(x)dx$, read as the integral from $a$ to $b$ of $f(x)dx$, or of $f(x)$ with respect to $x$."

Alan: "But how do we find it; do we have to go through all that summation of series again?"

Teacher: "No; we can capitalise on the great discovery made by those 17th-century pioneers. Let's let $A(x)$ stand for the area under the graph from $a$ up to $x$, as in the diagram. Then look at $\delta A$, the extra bit of area when you go from $x$ to $x + \delta x$. What do we know about that?"

Bilal: "It's about $f(x)\delta x$; a bit more than that, at least it's between that and $f(x+\delta x)\delta x$."

Teacher: "Good. So what if we divide $\delta A$ by $\delta x$? What can we say about $\frac{\delta A}{\delta x}$?"

Carol: "It must be between $f(x)$ and $f(x+\delta x)$."

Teacher: "Right; so now what do we do to go from $\frac{\delta A}{\delta x}$ to $\frac{dA}{dx}$?"

Alan: "Don't you just let $\delta x$ tend to 0?"

Bilal: "And then $f(x+\delta x)$ just tends to $f(x)$, doesn't it?"

Teacher: "Yes, we're assuming $f$ is a continuous function, which means just what you said."

Carol: "So then $\frac{dA}{dx} = f(x)$. Does that mean you can find $A(x)$ by finding a function which differentiated makes $f(x)$?"

Teacher: "Yes indeed; that is what is now known as the Fundamental Theorem of Calculus. And that is why we now call anti-differentiation integration. So now let's go back to the problem we did without calculus last time: finding the area under $y = x^3$ between 0 and $a$. What function differentiates to give $x^3$?"

Alan: "It's $\frac{x^4}{4}$, or maybe I should say $\frac{x^4}{4} + c$."

Teacher: "That's right; there is always an unknown constant, as every constant when differentiated gives 0. But if we are considering an area starting at $x = 0$, we can say what $c$ has to be in that case."

Carol: "It must be 0, otherwise there would be non-zero area between 0 and 0. So then the area up to $a$ is $\frac{a^4}{4}$."

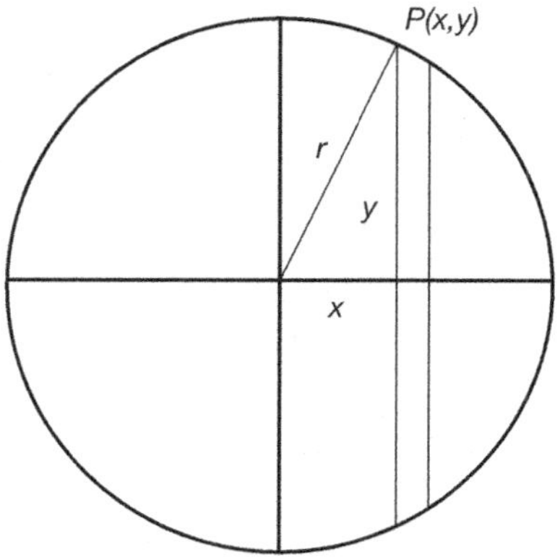

Bilal: "That's just what we got last time using the series, but this is a lot easier."

Teacher: "Yes! And we can also use this approach to find volumes. Let's look at finding the volume of a sphere of radius $r$. The volume can be cut up into discs, one of which is shown in the diagram at $P$."

Alan: "It's like a cylinder but with a bevelled edge, so we can't get its volume exactly."

Carol: "But it was the same with the strips that made up the area we found before. We don't have to have it exact, because we'll make the thickness of the disc tend to 0."

Bilal: "If we treat it as a cylinder of radius $y$ and thickness $\delta x$ that makes its volume $\pi y^2 \delta x$."

Teacher: "Good; and now we need to make the sum of all such cylinders and then get the limit of that sum as $\delta x \to 0$."

Alan: "Do we take $x$ from $-r$ to $r$, or from 0 to $r$?"

Teacher: "You can do either. I think it is slightly less effort to go from 0 to $r$ and then double to get the full sphere."

Bilal: "So we have to work out $\int_0^r \pi y^2 dx$. But what differentiated with respect to $x$ will make $y^2$?"

Teacher: "Can you see how $x$, $y$ and $r$ are related in the diagram?"

Bilal: "Oh yes; they're sides of a right-angled triangle. That makes $x^2 + y^2 = r^2$."

Carol: "So $y^2 = r^2 - x^2$, and we are doing $\int_0^r \pi (r^2 - x^2) dx$. That's $\pi \left( r^2 x - \frac{1}{3} x^3 \right)$."

Alan: "You have to take $x = r$ and then $x = 0$ and subtract; it gives $\pi \left( r^3 - \frac{1}{3} r^3 \right) - 0 = \frac{2}{3} \pi r^3$."

Teacher: "Good; and then you double that to get $\frac{4}{3} \pi r^3$ for the volume of the whole sphere. It's a formula you have already known and used, and perhaps have seen a different way to get it [see Chapter 21]. But integration by anti-differentiation gives you a quick way to derive the formula. It can also be used to find the volume of other solids of revolution."

# Summing series

## Using differencing instead of induction

**Teacher:** "At New Year my electricity meter showed 32161 kWh. I read it again after a week, then after two weeks, and so on. Here are the readings: 32236, 32319, 32396, 32483, 32561. What can I do with them?"

**Carol:** "You can work out how much electricity you've used each week."

**Teacher:** "That's right. Let's use $r_n$ to stand for the reading after $n$ weeks, and $u_n$ to stand for the amount used in week $n$. Make a table of $r_n$ and $u_n$ against $n$."

The class produced the following table:

| $n$ | $r_n$ | $u_n$ |
|---|---|---|
| 0 | 32161 | |
| 1 | 32236 | 75 |
| 2 | 32319 | 83 |
| 3 | 32396 | 77 |
| 4 | 32483 | 87 |
| 5 | 32561 | 78 |

**Teacher:** "Now how would you say $u_n$ can be obtained from $r_n$ in general?"

**Bilal:** "Well, $u_1 = r_1 - r_0$, $u_2 = r_2 - r_1$, and so on."

**Alan:** "So $u_n = r_n - r_{n-1}$ is the general rule."

**Teacher:** "That's right; and we call $r_n - r_{n-1}$ the *backward difference* of $r_n$, written $\nabla r_n$ for short." ($\nabla$ is pronounced "del.")

**Carol:** "Why backward? Is there a forward difference too?"

**Teacher:** "There is: that is $\Delta r_n = r_{n+1} - r_n$; but we are going to focus on the backward difference; you'll see why shortly. Suppose I wanted to work out how much electricity I had used in the first four weeks of the year, how could I do that?"

Alan: "You could just add up the first four numbers in the $u_n$ column; but there's probably a quicker way."

Bilal: "Can't you just do the reading after four weeks minus the reading at the start?"

Teacher: "You can indeed, and if I was asking for the total used in the first 40 weeks that method would save a lot of time! In general we can say that, if we have any sequence of numbers $r_1, r_2, r_3, \ldots$ and if we form the backward differences $u_n = \nabla r_n$, then the sum $\sum_{i=1}^{n} u_i = r_n - r_0$. Can you see why that is?"

Alan: "The sum is just $r_1 - r_0 + r_2 - r_1 + r_3 - r_2 + \ldots + r_n - r_{n-1}$, and all the terms from $r_1$ up to $r_{n-1}$ are both added and subtracted, so they all cancel leaving just $r_n - r_0$ exactly like with the electricity readings."

Teacher: "Good. So you can see that the differencing and the summing operations are in a way inverse to each other. Another way to see it is to let $s_n$ be the sum to $n$ terms of a series $u_1 + u_2 + u_3 + \ldots$. What can you say about $\nabla s_n$?"

Carol: "That's the sum to $n$ terms minus the sum to $n-1$ terms of the same series, so it must be just the $n$th term of the series."

Teacher: "Right; so if you sum a series and difference the answer you get back to the general term in the series, while if you difference a sequence and sum the differences you get back, not quite to the general term of the original sequence, but to the general term minus the starting term. For instance, recently we looked at the sum of the numbers from 1 to $n$ and got the answer $T_n = \frac{1}{2}n(n+1)$. What do you get if you do the backward difference of $\frac{1}{2}n(n+1)$?"

Bilal: "That's $\frac{1}{2}n(n+1) - \frac{1}{2}(n-1)(n-1+1)$ which is $\frac{1}{2}n(n+1-n+1) = n$."

Carol: "And that's what it should be: the $n$th term of the series $1 + 2 + 3 + \ldots$"

Alan: "Is that enough to prove that the formula $\frac{1}{2}n(n+1)$ is correct?"

Teacher: "Not quite, but nearly. For instance, if I proposed the formula $\frac{1}{2}n(n+1)+12$ for the sum of the numbers up to $n$, and if we did $\nabla\left(\frac{1}{2}n(n+1)+12\right)$ that would also come to $n$; the extra constant 12 would just be cancelled. Remember that the sum of the first $n$ differences of a sequence equals the $n$th term of the sequence minus the start value, that is the 0th term. With the formula $\frac{1}{2}n(n+1)$ that's fine, because that formula does give 0 when $n = 0$. If we used the wrong formula $\frac{1}{2}n(n+1)+12$ we would then subtract $\frac{1}{2} \times 0 \times 1 + 12 = 12$ and thus get back to the correct formula."

Alan: "We tried to add up the cubes of numbers from 1 to $n$ and found the answers were the squares of triangular numbers, suggesting $1^3 + 2^3 + 3^3 + \ldots + n^3 = T_n^2$. Can that be proved?"

Bilal: "We can try $\nabla T_n^2 = \frac{1}{4}n^2(n+1)^2 - \frac{1}{4}(n-1)^2 n^2 = \frac{1}{4}n^2\{n^2 + 2n + 1 - (n^2 - 2n + 1)\} = n^3$. Aha, that worked! Also $T_0^2 = 0$, so there is nothing to subtract."

Teacher: "That's right. You can do it a bit more neatly by factorising the difference of two squares: $T_n^2 - T_{n-1}^2 = (T_n - T_{n-1})(T_n + T_{n-1})$. What do we know about $T_n - T_{n-1}$?"

Carol: "That was $n$. And also $T_n + T_{n-1}$ comes to $n^2$ we saw that before."

Bilal: "So that makes $T_n^2 - T_{n-1}^2 = n^3$, so the sum of cubes must be $T_n^2 - T_0^2 = T_n^2$."

Alan: "Isn't there another way, using induction?"

Teacher: "Yes, carry on."

Alan: "You first show it's true for $n = 1$, which it is, then assume that it is true for $n = k$ and try to deduce that it then must be true for $n = k + 1$."

Bilal: "So you have to add $(k+1)^3$ onto $T_k^2$ and show that makes $T_{k+1}^2$?"

Alan: "Yes; so do $\frac{1}{4}k^2(k+1)^2 + (k+1)^3 = \frac{1}{4}(k+1)^2(k^2 + 4(k+1))$."

Carol: "As $k^2 + 4k + 4 = (k+2)^2$, that does make $\frac{1}{4}(k+1)^2(k+2)^2$ which is $T_{k+1}^2$; so it works; but I think the other way is easier."

Teacher: "Yes, for checking the formula for a sum the difference method is more straightforward; induction has its uses too. Differencing can also help with finding formulae for sums."

Alan: "What about adding up the squares of numbers from 1 to $n$? That doesn't seem to give such a simple formula."

Teacher: "Right. Do you know what $\nabla n(n+1)$ is?"

Carol: "That's $n(n+1) - (n-1)n$; comes to $2n$."

Teacher: "OK, now try $\nabla n(n+1)(n+2)$."

Bilal: "It's $n(n+1)(n+2) - (n-1)n(n+1) = n(n+1)(n+2 - (n-1))$."

Alan: "That's $3n(n+1)$, so $\nabla \frac{1}{3}n(n+1)(n+2) = n^2 + n$, which means we can sum to $n$ terms the series with $n$th term $n^2 + n$; that makes $\sum_{r=1}^{n}(r^2 + r) = \frac{1}{3}n(n+1)(n+2) - 0$."

Carol: "And we know $\sum_{r=1}^{n} r = \frac{1}{2}n(n+1)$, so then $\sum_{r=1}^{n} r^2$ must be $\frac{1}{3}n(n+1)(n+2) - \frac{1}{2}n(n+1)$, that's $\frac{1}{6}n(n+1)[2(n+2) - 3] = \frac{1}{6}n(n+1)(2n+1)$."

Teacher: "That's right; and you can check the result using backward difference."

Alan: "Is there a pattern that goes further? We've got $\nabla n(n+1) = 2n$ and $\nabla n(n+1)(n+2) = 3n(n+1)$. Does $\nabla n(n+1)(n+2)(n+3) = 4n(n+1)(n+2)$?"

Bilal: "And $\nabla n(n+1)(n+2)(n+3)(n+4) = 5n(n+1)(n+2)(n+3)$?"

Teacher: "Yes, that pattern continues, as you can easily verify by doing the $\nabla$. The general result is $\nabla n(n+1)(n+2)\ldots(n+k-1) = kn(n+1)\ldots(n+k-2)$, again easy to verify. Does this remind you of anything we did in calculus?"

Alan: "Is it like differentiating $x^k$ and getting $kx^{k-1}$?"

Teacher: "Yes, that's it. I'm glad you used $x^k$ rather than $x^n$ because in our difference work we are using $n$ for the variable, not for the power to which it is raised. If you think of plotting say $u_n = n(n+1)(n+2)$ against $n$ with just integer values of $n$, then you get a series of points for $n = 0,1,2,3$ and so on, and $\nabla n(n+1)(n+2)$ gives you the difference $u_n - u_{n-1}$ which is also the gradient of the straight line joining the points $(n-1, u_{n-1})$ and $(n, u_n)$, since the difference between $n-1$ and $n$ is just 1. That gradient works out as $3n(n+1)$. If instead you think of the continuous function $y = x^3$ you get the gradient at a point $(x, y)$ by working out the difference $(x + \delta x)^3 - x^3$, dividing this by $\delta x$ to give the gradient of the chord joining $(x, y)$ to $(x + \delta x, y + \delta y)$ and then taking the limit of this as $\delta x$ tends to 0, which comes to $3x^2$."

Bilal: "If you decided to plot points for some function at $x = 0, a, 2a, 3a$ etc for some number $a$, would there be a function with a simple gradient using that interval $a$?"

Alan: "How about $x(x + a)$ or $x(x + a)(x + 2a)$ etc.?"

Carol: "If you find the gradient of $x(x+a)(x+2a)$ from $x - a$ to $x$, it's
$$\frac{x(x+a)(x+2a)-(x-a)x(x+a)}{a} = \frac{x(x+a)3a}{a} = 3x(x+a)."$$

Teacher: "Well done! And in calculus we have the special case where $a$ tends to 0, making the gradient of $x^3$ equal to $3x^2$, while now we have been looking at the case where $a = 1$, using the letter $n$ instead of $x$. And just as differentiation provides an approach to finding areas under a graph (which are sums of many small strips, with the width of strips tending to 0) so differencing can help with finding sums of series. For instance, a greengrocer makes a pyramid of oranges with one fruit at the top, $1 + 2 = 3$ in the next layer down, then $1 + 2 + 3 + 4$ in the layer below that, and so on. How many oranges are there in $n$ layers?"

Bilal: "That means we have to add up $T_1 + T_2 + T_3 + \ldots + T_n$."

Carol: "So we need a formula whose backward difference is $\frac{1}{2}n(n+1)$."

Alan: "That's easy; it's $\frac{1}{6}n(n+1)(n+2)$, isn't it? And that gives 0 when $n = 0$ so there is nothing to subtract."

Teacher: "That's right. Now try the exercise below."

## Exercise

**1** Find:

(a) the sum to $n$ terms of $1^3 + 3^3 + 5^3 + \ldots$

(b) $\displaystyle\sum_{r=1}^{n} r(r-1)(r-2)$

(c) $\displaystyle\sum_{r=1}^{n} \frac{1}{r(r+1)}$

(d) the sum to $n$ terms of $1^2 - 2^2 + 3^2 - 4^2 + \ldots$.

**2** Prove that $\displaystyle\sum_{r=1}^{n} r^5 + \sum_{r=1}^{n} r^7 = \frac{1}{8}n^4(n+1)^4$.

**3** Given that $a_n = \dfrac{1}{n+1} + \dfrac{1}{n+2} + \ldots + \dfrac{1}{2n}$, $b_n = 1 - \dfrac{1}{2} + \dfrac{1}{3} - \dfrac{1}{4} + \ldots - \dfrac{1}{2n}$, find $\nabla a_n$ and $\nabla b_n$ and show that $a_n = b_n$.

**4** Let $s_n$ be the sum to $n$ terms of the series $1 \times 1 + 3 \times 2 + 5 \times 4 + 7 \times 8 + \ldots$. The formula $f_n = 2^n(an+b) + c$ is proposed for $S_n$, with $a, b, c$ being constants to be found. By comparing $\nabla s_n$ and $\nabla f_n$ show that this formula works with the right values of $a$, $b$ and $c$, and find these values.

**5** Verify that:

(a) $3^2 + 4^2 = 5^2$

(b) $10^2 + 11^2 + 12^2 = 13^2 + 14^2$

(c) $21^2 + 22^2 + 23^2 + 24^2 = 25^2 + 26^2 + 27^2$.

Write down (d), given that the left hand side ends with $40^2$. Try to find the $n$th term in the sequence 4, 12, 24, 40 ... and hence write down and prove the statement in line ($n$).

# 38 GPs, perfect numbers and loan repayment

Teacher: "What formula produces the numbers 1, 2, 4, 8, 16 . . . ? And what do you get if you sum them?"

Bilal: "You keep doubling, so that looks like $2^n$. But that would start 2, 4, 8.. instead of 1, 2, 4, . . ."

Carol: "We could make it $2^{n-1}$; that starts off with $2^0 = 1$, then 2 and so on."

Alan: "When you sum them you get 1, 3, 7, 15, 31 . . . They seem to be one less than a power of 2; is the $n$th sum $2^n - 1$?"

Teacher: "Yes; the $n$th term is $2^{n-1}$ and the sum to $n$ terms appears to be $2^n - 1$. Can we prove that?"

Carol: What about doing $\nabla\left(2^n - 1\right)$? That's $2^n - 1 - \left(2^{n-1} - 1\right) = 2^n - 2^{n-1}$."

Bilal: "You can factorise that: it's $2^{n-1}\left(2 - 1\right)$; that makes $2^{n-1}$ which is the formula for the $n$th term."

Teacher: "Good; and there's no need to think about subtracting $2^0 - 1$, which is 0 anyway, because we know the formula $2^n - 1$ works for early values of $n$. Now what about summing powers of 3, starting with 1?"

Carol: "That's 1, then $1 + 3 = 4$, then $1 + 3 + 9 = 13$, then $1 + 3 + 9 + 27 = 40 \ldots$"

Bilal: "If you do $3^n - 1$ you get 2, then 8, then 26, then 80 . . ."

Alan: "Those numbers are twice as big as the sums! So the sum looks as if it's $\dfrac{3^n - 1}{2}$; and the backward difference of that is $\dfrac{3^n - 1}{2} - \dfrac{3^{n-1} - 1}{2} = \dfrac{3^{n-1}(3 - 1)}{2}$. That makes $3^n$ so the formula goes on working!"

Teacher: "Good, that's correct. What about the sequence 1, 10, 100 . . . ?"

Carol: "The $n$th term is $10^{n-1}$ and the sums are 1, 11, 111, 1111 . . ."

Bilal: "But the formula $10^n - 1$ makes 9, 99, 999 and so on. So we need to divide that by 9 and get $\frac{10^n - 1}{9}$ as the right formula, do we?"

Alan: "Yes, and do you know what? Each time we are dividing by the number one less than the base that's being raised to different powers. So maybe

$$1 + x + x^2 + x^3 + \ldots + x^{n-1} = \frac{x^n - 1}{x - 1}!"$$

Teacher: "That's right; well done! And you can check that by differencing or derive it directly: let the sum be called $S$, then $xS = x + x^2 + x^3 + \ldots + x^n$. So what happens when you subtract $S$ from $xS$?"

Bilal: "It almost all cancels; all that's left is $x^n - 1$."

Carol: "So then $(x - 1)S = x^n - 1$, making $S = \frac{x^n - 1}{x - 1}$."

Teacher: "Yes. A series in which the ratio of successive terms is constant is called a *geometric* series (because the ancient Greek mathematicians didn't have a good way of writing numbers and therefore preferred to think of ratios in terms of geometry rather than arithmetic). We can use what we've found to look at the topic of perfect numbers, which goes back to the ancient mathematician Euclid."

Bilal: "Are those numbers whose factors less than the number add up to the number itself: like 6 which equals $1 + 2 + 3$?"

Alan: "And $28 = 1 + 2 + 4 + 7 + 14$."

Teacher: "That's right. The next one is 496. When you factorise these numbers into primes, you get $6 = 2 \times 3$, $28 = 2^2 \times 7$ and $496 = 2^4 \times 31$."

Carol: "They're all even, just a power of 2 times a prime number."

Alan: "And the prime number is just under double the power of 2: like 7 is $2^3 - 1$ and $31 = 2^5 - 1$."

Teacher: "Well spotted. We're going to look at that now. Suppose the number $n = 2^k \times m$ is perfect, where $m$ is some odd number. How would we express that?"

Bilal: "Some of the factors are $m$, $2m$, $4m$... up to $2^k \times m$, adding up to $(2^{k+1} - 1)m$. But the last term was $n$ itself, so if we include that the total becomes $2n$; then there are also $1, 2, 4 \ldots 2^k$, adding up to $2^{k+1} - 1$."

Alan: "Also we have to include each of those powers of 2 multiplied by any factor of $m$."

Carol: "But if $m$ is prime there won't be any factors other than 1 and $m$."

Teacher: "That's true; but we're not going to assume yet that $m$ has to be prime. Any factor $f$ of $m$ gets multiplied by all those powers of 2. If the sum of those other factors of $m$ is called s, then we have a total of $\left(2^{k+1}-1\right)(m+1+s)$ for all the factors, including $n$ itself."

Alan: "So then $2n = 2^{k+1}m = \left(2^{k+1}-1\right)(m+1+s)$. That makes $m = \left(2^{k+1}-1\right)(1+s)$."

Bilal: "We still don't know about s, do we?"

Teacher: "Well, let's think about that. If s is not 0, so that $m$ is not prime, then, from what Alan just said, $m$ has a factor $1+s$ which is greater than 1 but less than $m$. But this factor is then one of several such factors whose sum is s."

Carol: "But that's impossible. How can s be a sum of positive numbers that include $1+s$?"

Teacher: "That's right, it's impossible. That shows us that s must be 0 and $m$ must be prime."

Alan: "So $n = 2^k \left(2^{k+1}-1\right)$, with $2^{k+1}-1$ having to be prime, in order for $n$ to be a perfect even number."

Bilal: "What about perfect odd numbers?"

Teacher: "Aha, that's still an open problem. No odd perfect number has yet been found, nor has anyone proved that they don't exist. We also don't know whether there is a finite number of even perfect numbers, because $2^{k+1}-1$ doesn't have to be prime. There are still discoveries out there waiting to be made! But now let's do a couple of practical examples using geometric series. First, suppose you put £1000 into a savings account that pays 4% p.a. interest, compounded every year, and you keep adding £1000 yourself on each anniversary of the date you started, till you have paid in £10 000 altogether, and then wait another year. How much is the investment worth then, ten years after the start?"

Alan: "Is the interest paid into the same account to earn more interest? If so the first instalment has been multiplied by 1.04 ten times over, making $£1000 \times 1.04^{10}$."

Teacher: "That's right; that's what compounding means."

Carol: "So the second instalment grows to $£1000 \times 1.04^9$, the third to $£1000 \times 1.04^8$ and so on."

Bilal: "The total is $£1000 \times \left(1.04^{10} + 1.04^9 + \ldots + 1.04\right)$."

Alan: "That's the same as $£1040(1 + 1.04 + 1.04^2 + \ldots + 1.04^9)$, which makes $£1040 \times \dfrac{1.04^{10}-1}{1.04-1}$."

Carol: "That works out to £12 486.35 to the nearest penny."

| Teacher: | "Good. And what would the total have been if the interest for each year had been paid out to you and not earned extra interest?" |
|---|---|
| Bilal: | "You'd have got $10 \times £40 + 9 \times £40 + 8 \times £40 + \ldots + £40$ interest." |
| Carol: | "That's $55 \times £40 = £2200$, so at the end you'd have £12200; that's £286.35 less." |
| Teacher: | "Right. Next, suppose you want to borrow £1000 and repay by monthly instalments, with an interest rate of 2% per month." |
| Bilal: | "Is that the same as 24% per year? That seems quite steep." |
| Teacher: | "It is steep, in fact it's more than 24% per annum. Can you work out how much it is?" |
| Alan: | "If you paid nothing for a whole year the debt would increase by 2% each month, so it gets multiplied 12 times over by 1.02." |
| Carol: | "So it grows to $£1000 \times 1.02^{12} = £1268.24$; that makes the annual rate 26.824%." |
| Teacher: | "Yes, and that's not untypical of the rate a credit card company might charge. But now what if you don't wait a whole year but pay every month; how much each month?" |
| Bilal: | "Could we do a spreadsheet and use trial? We multiply the amount by 1.02 each month and take away the instalment we've guessed so far, and see how much is left after 12 months." |
| Teacher: | "Yes, that's one way of doing it." |

So the class make a simple spreadsheet and find that, with an instalment of £90 per month there is £61.15 left at the end, while with £100 per month the final debt is −£72.97, meaning that nearly £73 too much has been paid over the year. Further trial gives the following results:

| Monthly payment, £ | 95 | 94 | 94.5 | 94.6 | 94.57 | 94.56 |
|---|---|---|---|---|---|---|
| Final amount owing, £ | −5.91 | 7.57 | 0.80 | −0.54 | −0.14 | −0.01 |

| Carol: | "So the right amount to pay is £94.56 per month, making the total amount paid £1134.72." |
|---|---|
| Bilal: | "That's about 13.47% above the amount borrowed; just a little over half the annual rate of 26.82%; I guess that makes sense because the debt has been decreasing each month till it's down to zero. But is there a way of calculating it accurately without using a spreadsheet and trial?" |

Teacher: "Yes, let's have a look at that. We'll start with a loan of £A and suppose the rate is $r$% per month. We'll call the monthly payment £P, which is what we want to find. So how much is still owing after one month?"

Alan: "The interest is $\frac{r}{100} \times A$, and the first payment is made, so the amount still owing is $A + \frac{rA}{100} - P$ pounds."

Bilal: "That's $A\left(1 + \frac{r}{100}\right) - P$ pounds."

Teacher: "That's right; and we'll call that $A_1$, the amount owing after one month, and also let $k$ stand for $1 + \frac{r}{100}$. Then we can say $A_1 = Ak - P$. Now what about $A_2$, the amount owing after two months?"

Bilal: "That would be $A_1k - P$, which is $(Ak - P)k - P = Ak^2 - Pk - P$."

Carol: "And then $A_3 = A_2k - P = Ak^3 - Pk^2 - Pk - P$."

Alan: "There's a pattern: it looks as if $A_4$ will be $Ak^4 - Pk^3 - Pk^2 - Pk - P$ and that $A_n$ is $Ak^n - Pk^{n-1} - Pk^{n-2} - \ldots - Pk - P$."

Teacher: "You're right; that's easy to see from the fact that you keep multiplying the latest amount by $k$ and then subtracting $P$. Also you can tidy up the result into $A_n = Ak^n - P\left(1 + k + k^2 + \ldots + k^{n-1}\right)$."

Bilal: "That makes it $Ak^n - P\frac{k^n - 1}{k - 1}$, from the work we did earlier."

Teacher: "Right. And can you now see how this can be used to find $P$? Let $n$ stand for the total number of months (which is 12 in our example.) Then what would $A_n$ have to be?"

Alan: "It has to be 0, so we have to solve $Ak^n - P\frac{k^n - 1}{k - 1} = 0$."

Carol: "That makes $P = \frac{Ak^n(k - 1)}{k^n - 1}$. And with $A = 1000, k = 1.02$ and $n = 12$ that makes 94.55959662, or £94.56 to the nearest penny; just what we found by trial!"

Teacher: "That's good! And since $k = 1 + \frac{r}{100}$, $k - 1 = \frac{r}{100}$ and so $P = \frac{Ark^n}{100(k^n - 1)} = \frac{Ar(k^n - 1 + 1)}{100(k^n - 1)}$ which makes $\frac{Ar}{100}\left(1 + \frac{1}{k^n - 1}\right)$. Can you see the point of writing it that way?"

Bilal: "The first bit $\frac{Ar}{100}$ is just the interest for the first month."

Alan: "That's what the borrower would pay every month if he was only paying interest on the loan and planning to repay the whole amount in one go at some later date."

Teacher: "Yes; some loans are arranged that way, with the borrower paying interest only, and separately saving up to repay the whole loan in the future. The second part in the bracket, $\dfrac{1}{k^n - 1}$, multiplied by $\dfrac{Ar}{10}$, gives the extra monthly amount that will enable the loan to be paid in $n$ months. Now what about a £100 000 mortgage (a loan to help buy a house) to be repaid in 20 years at an annual rate of 6%? What would be payable each month?"

Bilal: "Is the monthly rate just $6\% \div 12 = 0.5\%$?"

Alan: "No; if it was 0.5% per month we'd have to work out $1.005^{12} = 1.061677812$. That would make the annual rate 6.168% instead of 6%."

Carol: "So we have to work backwards; find the 12th root of 1.06; that's
$1.06^{\frac{1}{12}} = 1.004867551$, so the monthly rate is 0.4867551%."

Bilal: "So the multiplier $k$ is 1.004867551, and $n = 12 \times 20 = 240$, so the instalment works out at $£486.7551 \times (1 + 0.45307595) = £707.29$ per month."

Teacher: "Yes. That makes the total amount paid over 20 years to be £169 750; the interest comes to 69.75% of the loan, rather more than half of $20 \times 6\%$, which would be 120%."

# Binomial expansion and counting

| Teacher: | "What do you get when expanding $(a+b)(m+n)?$" |
| :--- | :--- |
| Carol: | "That's $am + an + bm + bn$." |
| Teacher: | "Right: now what about $(a+b)(m+n)(p+q)?$" |
| Bilal: | "You have to multiply the last answer by $p$ and also by $q$ and get $amp + amq + anp + anq + bmp + bmq + bnp + bnq$." |
| Alan: | "So you get all possible terms made by choosing one term from each bracket and multiplying the chosen terms together." |
| Teacher: | "That's right, and we'll be using that observation soon. Now what about $(a+b)^2$ and $(a+b)^3?$" |
| Bilal: | "They expand to $a^2 + 2ab + b^2$ and $a^3 + 3a^2b + 3ab^2 + b^3$." |
| Alan: | "And $(a+b)^4 = a^4 + 4a^3b + 6a^2b^2 + 4ab^3 + b^4$. Is there a pattern to help with higher and higher powers of $a + b$?" |
| Carol: | "The powers of $a$ and $b$ are quite predictable, starting with just $a$ to the highest power, than each time the power of $a$ reduces by 1 the power of $b$ increases by 1, till you have $b$ alone with the highest power. It's the coefficients that need working out each time." |
| Teacher: | "Well, let's look at those specifically; and to help us see the pattern we'll start with $(a+b)^0$." |
| Bilal: | "That's just 1 isn't it?" |
| Teacher: | "Yes it is, and of course $(a+b)^1$ is just $a + b$ which is the same as $1a + 1b$. So we get the table here, known as Pascal's triangle, after the famous mathematician, inventor and Christian philosopher Blaise Pascal, 1623–1662:" |

```
     1

     1    1

     1    2    1

     1    3    3    1

     1    4    6    4    1

     1    5   10   10    5    1
```

. . . and so on. If you look carefully you can see a way to continue it."

Alan: "Is the next line 1, 6, 15, 20, 15, 6, 1? I just added up neighbouring numbers in the line above."

Carol: "Yes, that's worked in the previous lines: 5 is 1 + 4, 10 is 4 + 6 and so on. But what's behind that?"

Teacher: "OK. When you expanded $(a+b)^4$ you got terms including $4a^3b$ and $6a^2b^2$. Now when you want to expand $(a+b)^5$ you will get a term with $a^3b^2$. How does that come?"

Bilal: "You have to multiply $4a^3b$ by $b$ and also $6a^2b^2$ by $a$, which makes $4a^3b^2 + 6a^3b^2$. That's how you get $10a^3b^2$ and the 10 is just 4 + 6."

Teacher: "That's right. If we now let $^nC_r$ stand for the coefficient of $a^{n-r}b^r$ in the expansion of $(a+b)^n$, then what Bilal has said means that $^5C_2 = {}^4C_1 + {}^4C_2$. More generally the term in $a^{n-r}b^r$ comes from multiplying $^{n-1}C_{r-1}\ a^{n-r}b^{r-1}$ by $b$ and also multiplying $^{n-1}C_r\ a^{n-r-1}b^r$ by $a$, from which we find that $^nC_r = {}^{n-1}C_{r-1} + {}^{n-1}C_r$. That makes it easy to continue the triangle to the next row and onwards, though it would still be challenging to find numbers, say, in row 100. Do you notice anything about the sum of the numbers in each row?"

Carol: "The sums are 1, then 2, then 4, then 8 and so on, doubling each time."

Alan: "So for row $n$ the sum is $2^n$, taking the top row as row 0. Why is that?"

Teacher: "Well, remember that we are looking at the coefficients of terms in the expansion of $(a+b)^n$. What if you let $a = b = 1$?"

Bilal: "Aha, then the expansion is just the sum of the coefficients, and of course $(1+1)^n = 2^n$."

Alan: "Is there a formula for calculating $^nC_r$ directly from $n$ and $r$ without using the previous row?"

| Teacher: | "There is, and we're going to be finding it; but we need to do some preliminary thinking. Let's start with a meal out: you have a choice of two starters, Risotto or Soup, and four main courses, Beef, Chicken, Duck or Eggs. How many different two course meals does that give? For instance RB would be Risotto then Beef." |
|---|---|
| Carol: | "You can have RB or RC or RD or RE and then SB, SC, SD or SE; that's 8 choices." |
| Bilal: | "It's the number of starter choices times the number of main course choices, because each of the two starters can be followed by any of four main courses." |
| Teacher: | "And what if there were three desserts: Lemon pie, Mousse or Nougat?" |
| Alan: | "Any of the eight choices so far can be followed by any of the three desserts, so that's $8 \times 3 = 24$ choices for a three course meal, from RBL up to SEN." |
| Carol: | "So if there are $x$ choices for starter, $y$ for main course and $z$ for dessert, that would make $xyz$ different three course meals, is that right?" |
| Teacher: | "Yes indeed; and this applies to any sequence of choices: if you know how many alternatives there are for each choice then you just multiply those together to get the total number of alternatives. For instance, suppose you are to write a six-digit number using each of the digits 1 to 6. How many different numbers can you write?" |
| Bilal: | "Any of the digits could be any of 1 to 6; so does that make $6^6$ choices? That's big!" |
| Alan: | "But that would include a number like 444 555 which only uses two digits." |
| Bilal: | "OK, so if I have six choices for the first digit, then just five for the second, then four for the third and so on." |
| Carol: | "That makes $6 \times 5 \times 4 \times 3 \times 2 \times 1$, that's 720." |
| Teacher: | "Good! And this sort of calculation comes up quite a lot, so we call it '6 factorial' written as 6! (Sometimes informally called '6 shriek'!)" |
| Alan: | "So $n! = n(n-1)(n-2)\ldots \times 2 \times 1$." |
| Teacher: | "Yes, and this gives the number of ways in which $n$ different items can be arranged in order, as we saw with the question about numbers made with 1 to 6: we just had to arrange those digits in order. We can also look at arranging things in order when they are not all different. How many different ways can you arrange the letters of the word ALLELE?" |
| Carol: | "With six different letters it would be the same as arranging the six digits, $6! = 720$. But it's a lot less than that because of the repeated letters." |

| Teacher: | "Let's write the word putting labels on the repeated letters: $AL_1L_2E_1L_3E_2$. Now suppose we were finding how many different ways the letters can be arranged, taking account of the different labels. That would be easy, because the labels make all the letters different so that the answer is again just 6!. But we could approach it a different way: We could start by making all the different 'words,' meaning arrangements there are of the unlabelled letters; let's say there are $w$ words." |
|---|---|
| Bilal: | "But we don't know what $w$ is, do we?" |
| Teacher: | "Not yet, but we will know it soon. Let's take any of these 'words,' say LALEELL. We now consider putting labels 1, 2, 3 on the L's and 1 and 2 on the E's. How many different ways can that be done?" |
| Alan: | "We have three choices for which L will get label 1, then two choices for label 2 and one for label 3; that makes 3! ways to label the Ls." |
| Bilal: | "And 2! ways to label the E's; so altogether 3! × 2! ways to do the labelling." |
| Teacher: | "Right; so each of the $w$ unlabelled words can be labelled in 3! × 2! ways. So then what's the total number of ways of arranging the labelled letters?" |
| Alan: | "It's $w \times 3! \times 2!$, but we know it's also 6!, so that must mean that $w = \dfrac{6!}{3! \times 2!}$." |
| Carol: | "That's $\dfrac{720}{6 \times 2} = 60$ 'words' you can make from ALLELE." |
| Teacher: | "Yes. Can you see how many 'words' you could make using $p$ As and $q$ Bs?" |
| Bilal: | "If they are labelled there are $(p+q)!$ ways to arrange them; and each unlabelled 'word' can be labelled in $p! \times q!$ ways, so the number of words must be $\dfrac{(p+q)!}{p!q!}$." |
| Teacher: | "Good. That brings us back to where we started with expanding brackets. You remember that you get all possible terms made by choosing one term from each bracket and multiplying them together: for instance what was $(a+b)(m+n)(p+q)$?" |
| Carol: | "That was $amp + amq + anp + anq + bmp + bmq + bnp + bnq$." |
| Teacher: | "Right; so what would $(a+b)(a+b)(a+b)$ make when expanded in that way?" |
| Bilal: | "That would be $aaa + aab + aba + abb + baa + bab + bba + bbb$." |
| Alan: | "Aha, it's all about how many words you can make with given numbers of $a$s and $b$s. With two $a$s and one $b$ you get $aab$, $aba$ and $baa$, which adds up to $3a^2b$, and that 3 is also $\dfrac{3!}{2! \times 1!}$, using the general method you showed us. So does that mean that when you expand $(a+b)^n$, the coefficient of $a^p b^q$ will be $\dfrac{(p+q)!}{p!q!}$?" |

| | |
|---|---|
| Teacher: | "Yes it does; only remember that $p + q = n$, so we generally think of the coefficient of $a^{n-r}b^r$, which we called $^nC_r$." |
| Bilal: | "So $^nC_r = \dfrac{n!}{r!(n-r)!}$, does it?" |
| Teacher: | "It does, and now we can have a look at what that gives for specific values of $r$. If we start at $r = 0$ we are looking at the coefficient of $a^n$, which of course is 1. Our formula gives $\dfrac{n!}{0!n!}$." |
| Carol: | "So 0! Has to be 1, does it? Why is that?" |
| Teacher: | "Well, how do you go from 3! To 2! ?" |
| Carol: | "Divide by 3. And from 2! To 1! divide by 2; Oh, so from 1! divide by 1; that's how you get 1 for 0!" |
| Qasim: | "What about $(-1)!$ then? Do you divide 1 by 0?" |
| Alan: | "You can't do that; there's no number that multiplied by 0 makes 1." |
| Teacher: | "That's right, so $(-1)!$ is not defined. Or, if you like you can say it's infinity, since $\dfrac{1}{x}$ tends to infinity, that means it grows beyond all limits, when $x$ tends to 0. Infinity or $\infty$ is not a number, it's an extra symbol; but if you try for instance to find the coefficient of $b^5$ in the expansion of $(a+b)^4$ what would you get?" |
| Alan: | "You shouldn't be doing that! There's no term in $b^5$ when you expand $(a+b)^4$." |
| Teacher: | "Quite right; but if you try the formula you get $\dfrac{4!}{5!(-1)!}$." |
| Alan: | "Oh, so that fraction has infinity in the denominator, so would it give 0?" |
| Teacher: | "Yes. But if you do things right you shouldn't be having to work with factorial of $-1$, or of any negative number. Now let's look at $^nC_1$." |
| Carol: | "That's $\dfrac{n!}{1!(n-1)!}$. Does that just come down to $n$?" |
| Teacher: | "Yes it does, and if you think of all the 'words' you can make using $n-1$ $a$ s and 1 $b$, you can see that the $b$ can either be the first letter, or the second, or the third, . . . or the $n$th, giving just $n$ possibilities. What about $^nC_2$?" |
| Qasim: | "That's $\dfrac{n!}{2!(n-2)!}$, cancels down to $\dfrac{n(n-1)}{2!}$." |
| Alan: | "So $^nC_3$ becomes $\dfrac{n(n-1)(n-2)}{3!}$ and so on; what about $^nC_r$? Would that be $\dfrac{n(n-1)(n-2)\ldots(n-[r-1])}{r!}$ ?" |
| Carol: | "That would simplify to $\dfrac{n(n-1)(n-2)\ldots(n-r+1)}{r!}$, wouldn't it?" |
| Teacher: | "That's right. Now we're going to look at another use of $^nC_r$. Suppose you are in charge of a cricket squad of 15, and you need to choose 11 of these to be" |

the team for the next match and arrange them in batting order. The number of ways to do this is called $^{15}P_{11}$, the P standing for permutations, since we're choosing and arranging players in order. How do we find this?"

Alan: "You have 15 choices for who's to bat first, then 14 for who bats second, and so on, down to 5 for who bats last, so that's $15 \times 14 \times 13 \times 12 \times \ldots 5$. It's like 15! But missing out on the numbers 4 down to 1."

Qasim: "So that makes it the same as $\frac{15!}{4!}$, doesn't it?"

Teacher: "That's right. But there is another way to tackle the same problem: you could start by choosing who will be in the team, regardless of order, and then arrange the 11 chosen players in batting order."

Carol: "We don't know yet how many ways there are to choose 11 players from 15."

Teacher: "That's right, so I'm going to call that C for now."

Carol: "Then there are 11! ways to arrange them in order, so that makes $^{15}P_{11} = C \times 11!$."

Alan: "In that case C must be $^{15}P_{11} \div 11!$ which is $\frac{15!}{11! \times 4!}$; hey, that's $^{15}C_{11}$ isn't it?"

Teacher: "Yes it is; and you can redo the whole argument to show that the number of ways to choose and arrange $r$ items from a set of $n$ is $\frac{n!}{(n-r)!}$ and that the number of ways to choose $r$ items from a set of $n$ is $\frac{n!}{r!(n-r)!}$ which is called $^nC_r$, the number of combinations of $r$ items from a set of $n$ different items. From this you can see another reason why $^nC_r = {}^{n-1}C_{r-1} + {}^{n-1}C_r$: suppose the cricket squad includes a talented player who is not so good at working with others on the team – let's call him Rob. How many teams of $r$ from $n$ can you make that include Rob?"

Qasim: "If you choose Rob you still have to choose $r-1$ from the other $n-1$, so that's $^{n-1}C_{r-1}$ ways."

Carol: "And if you don't choose Rob you have to choose $r$ from $n-1$ players, making it $^{n-1}C_r$ ways; so that's how $^nC_r = {}^{n-1}C_{r-1} + {}^{n-1}C_r$ is it?"

Teacher: "Yes, and you can also prove it from the formula using factorials. Try that, and also see if you can show that the sum of row $n$ in Pascal's triangle is $2^n$ by thinking about how many subsets a set of $n$ items has altogether, of any size, from the empty set up to the whole set. For a bigger challenge, investigate the following: if the numbers from 1 to $n$ start off in the correct order 1, 2, 3, ...$n$ and are then randomly rearranged, what is the probability that none of the numbers is in its original place? Start with just one number, then 2 and so on; but don't be worried if you find it difficult!"

# How to make your own logarithms

Alan: "Sir, do we still need logarithms? My dad says he used them for doing heavy arithmetic, but now we've got calculators to do that?"

Teacher: "Yes; we don't need logarithms for all the things we used to need them for. But consider this question: A population grows at 8% per year. How long does it take to (a) double, (b) increase tenfold?"

Carol: "That means it multiplies by 1.08 very year, so after $x$ years it has multiplied by $1.08^x$, so we have to solve $1.08^x = 2$ and $1.08^x = 10$."

Bilal: "Do we know a way to solve those?"

Teacher: "Not yet; you are trying to get the inverse of the function $1.08^x$; so far there is no inverse for this function, and we'll have to use trial or a graph to solve the equations. Using a spreadsheet it is easy to construct a table of powers of 1.08, as follows:"

| Powers of 1.08 | | | | | |
|---|---|---|---|---|---|
| $n$ | $1.08\text{^}n$ | $n$ | $1.08\text{^}n$ | $n$ | $1.08\text{^}n$ |
| 1 | 1.0800 | 11 | 2.3316 | 21 | 5.0338 |
| 2 | 1.1664 | 12 | 2.5182 | 22 | 5.4365 |
| 3 | 1.2597 | 13 | 2.7196 | 23 | 5.8715 |
| 4 | 1.3605 | 14 | 2.9372 | 24 | 6.3412 |
| 5 | 1.4693 | 15 | 3.1722 | 25 | 6.8485 |
| 6 | 1.5869 | 16 | 3.4259 | 26 | 7.3964 |
| 7 | 1.7138 | 17 | 3.7000 | 27 | 7.9881 |
| 8 | 1.8509 | 18 | 3.9960 | 28 | 8.6271 |
| 9 | 1.9990 | 19 | 4.3157 | 29 | 9.3173 |
| 10 | 2.1589 | 20 | 4.6610 | 30 | 10.0627 |

Alan:    "That shows $1.08^9$ is close to 2, while $1.08^{30}$ is a little over 10, so the population takes about nine years to double and about 30 years to increase tenfold."

Teacher:    "Right. Now how long does it take a culture of bacteria to double, given that it increases by a factor of ten in one week?"

Carol:    "It multiplies by $10^x$ in $x$ weeks, so we have to solve $10^x = 2$."

Alan:    "From the table we got $2 \approx 1.08^9 \approx (10^{1/30})^9 = 10^{\frac{1}{30} \times 9} = 10^{0.3}$, so that the doubling time is about 0.3 weeks, just over two days."

Teacher:    "Yes. Another way to see this is to observe that $2^{10} = 1024 \approx 10^3$ so that $2 \approx (10^3)^{1/10} = 10^{0.3}$. But that is still only approximate. We would really like to be able to invert the function $10^x$, and no elementary inverse exists. This gap is filled by introducing the logarithm function: the logarithm of $N$ to base $b$, $\log_b N$ is defined as *the power to which $b$ must be raised to make $N$*. This definition is worth memorising, and can be expressed symbolically by the fact that if $\log_b N = L$ then $N = b^L$; thus the logarithm to base $b$ is the inverse of the function $b^x$. Can you tell me the logarithm of 2 to base 10?"

Bilal:    "It must be about 0.3, since $10^{0.3} \approx 2$. But how do we get it more accurately?"

Alan:    "My calculator makes it 0.301029996. But my dad used logs long before there were any electronic calculators. They had a book of four figure tables that included logarithms."

Teacher:    "Yes. Logarithm tables began to be published soon after 1600, as an aid to doing multiplication, division, powers and roots, based on the principle that, if $M = b^x$ and $N = b^y$ then $MN = b^{x+y}$, $M \div N = b^{x-y}$ and $M^n = b^{nx}$ while $\sqrt[n]{M} = M^{1/n} = b^{x/n}$. Here $x$ and $y$ are of course the logs of $M$ and $N$ to base $b$, and adding or subtracting them is much less work than multiplying or dividing the original numbers."

Carol:    "So how did they make those tables when they didn't have calculators or computers?"

Teacher:    "The basic principle was to start with a number close to 1 and work out powers of this number by multiplication, all done by hand of course. Joost Bürgi, a Swiss astronomer and mathematician, used the multiplier 1.0001. Can you work out its powers up to the fourth? Round them to 9DP."

Bilal:    "I get 1.000 200 010, 1.000 300 030 and 1.000 400 060."

Teacher:    "That's right. Now imagine going on and on till you reach 10. At the 23 027th power we get 9.999 997 797, and the 23 028th power of 1.0001 is at last 10.000 997 797, just over 10."

Carol:    "Wow! That takes some work doing 23 000 multiplications by hand! We could never do that."

Alan: "Though each one is fairly easy to do, as it's just multiplying again by 1.0001. But it must be tricky to make sure you never go wrong, because one mistake would affect all the later powers as well."

Teacher: "Yes indeed; it took a lot of dedication, patience and hard work. We are going to do something like what Bürgi did[1] without all the hard labour by using a spreadsheet; that's how I found the powers mentioned above. We begin with 1.0001 stored in the cell A3, then column B headed $n$ and column C headed $1.0001^n = x$, as shown. The numbers 1, 2, 3 ... are made by repeatedly adding 1, and the values of $x$ by repeatedly multiplying by A\$3, i.e. by 1.0001.

These have to be replicated in the usual way, but down a long way! Eventually the power of 1.0001 reaches 10, as shown in the next extract, from which we see that 10 is between $1.0001^{23027}$ and $1.0001^{23028}$.

| $n$ | $1.0001^n = x$ |
|---|---|
| 1 | 1.000100000 |
| 2 | 1.000200010 |
| 3 | 1.000300030 |
| 4 | 1.000400060 |
| 5 | 1.000500100 |
| 6 | 1.000600150 |
| 7 | 1.000700210 |
| 8 | 1.000800280 |
| 9 | 1.000900360 |
| 10 | 1.001000450 |

| $n$ | $1.0001^n = x$ |
|---|---|
| 23019 | 9.992001397 |
| 23020 | 9.993000598 |
| 23021 | 9.993999898 |
| 23022 | 9.994999298 |
| 23023 | 9.995998797 |
| 23024 | 9.996998397 |
| 23025 | 9.997998097 |
| 23026 | 9.998997897 |
| 23027 | 9.999997797 |
| 23028 | 10.000997797 |

Thus thousands of numbers between 1 and 10 have been expressed as powers of 1.0001."

Carol: "To begin with the numbers are very close, changing only in the fourth place of decimals."

Bilal: "Yes, but the spacing between neighbouring values increases, so that as 10 is approached the third decimal place changes from each power to the next."

Teacher: "Yes. If we round all the powers to three places, i.e. four significant figures, we then get all values from 1.000 to 9.999 expressed as powers of 1.0001. This rounding is achieved in column D, headed 'x to 3DP' with the instruction = INT(C2*1000 + 0.5)/1000 put into D2 and then replicated down.

The beginning and end now look like this:"

| $n$ | $1.0001^n = x$ | x to 3DP | $n$ | $1.0001^n = x$ | x to 3DP |
|---|---|---|---|---|---|
| 1 | 1.000100000 | 1.000 | 23009 | 9.982014889 | 9.982 |
| 2 | 1.000200010 | 1.000 | 23010 | 9.983013091 | 9.983 |
| 3 | 1.000300030 | 1.000 | 23011 | 9.984011392 | 9.984 |
| 4 | 1.000400060 | 1.000 | 23012 | 9.985009793 | 9.985 |
| 5 | 1.000500100 | 1.001 | 23013 | 9.986008294 | 9.986 |
| 6 | 1.000600150 | 1.001 | 23014 | 9.987006895 | 9.987 |
| 7 | 1.000700210 | 1.001 | 23015 | 9.988005596 | 9.988 |
| 8 | 1.000800280 | 1.001 | 23016 | 9.989004396 | 9.989 |
| 9 | 1.000900360 | 1.001 | 23017 | 9.990003297 | 9.990 |
| 10 | 1.001000450 | 1.001 | 23018 | 9.991002297 | 9.991 |
| 11 | 1.001100550 | 1.001 | 23019 | 9.992001397 | 9.992 |
| 12 | 1.001200660 | 1.001 | 23020 | 9.993000598 | 9.993 |
| 13 | 1.001300780 | 1.001 | 23021 | 9.993999898 | 9.994 |
| 14 | 1.001400910 | 1.001 | 23022 | 9.994999298 | 9.995 |
| 15 | 1.001501050 | 1.002 | 23023 | 9.995998797 | 9.996 |
| 16 | 1.001601201 | 1.002 | 23024 | 9.996998397 | 9.997 |
| 17 | 1.001701361 | 1.002 | 23025 | 9.997998097 | 9.998 |
| 18 | 1.001801531 | 1.002 | 23026 | 9.998997897 | 9.999 |
| 19 | 1.001901711 | 1.002 | 23027 | 9.999997797 | 10.000 |
| 20 | 1.002001901 | 1.002 | 23028 | 10.000997797 | 10.001 |

Alan: "In the early stages there's a lot of repetition in the third column: I suppose the changes from each row to the next are so small that they disappear in the rounding."

Bilal: "Yes, but near the end it's different: each number occurs just once in the third column."

Carol: "How does this give us logs to base 10?"

Teacher: "Well, we can see that it is the 23027th power of 1.0001 that is closest to 10. Thus 1.0001 is very close to $10^{1/23027}$, and we can use this to express numbers from 1 to 10 as powers of 10, i.e. to find their logarithms to base 10.

For example, to get log2 we scroll down and find that the powers $1.0001^{6930}$ up to $1.0001^{6934}$ are all given as 2.000 when rounded to 4SF."

| | | |
|---|---|---|
| 6928 | 1.999236509 | 1.999 |
| 6929 | 1.999436433 | 1.999 |
| 6930 | 1.999636377 | 2.000 |
| 6931 | 1.999836340 | 2.000 |
| 6932 | 2.000036324 | 2.000 |
| 6933 | 2.000236327 | 2.000 |
| 6934 | 2.000436351 | 2.000 |
| 6935 | 2.000636395 | 2.001 |
| 6936 | 2.000836458 | 2.001 |

Alan: "It is $1.0001^{6932} = 2.000\ 036\ 324$ which is nearest[2] to 2, isn't it?"

Teacher: "Yes. We can now say that 2 is close to $(10^{1/23027})^{6932} = 10^{0.301\ 037\ 912}$, giving 0.301 037 912 for log2. This differs from the correct value 0.301 029 996 (given by the LOG function in the spreadsheet) by about $7.9 \times 10^{-6}$; in this example the result is correct to 4SF and nearly correct in the 5th figure."

Alan: "So to make a table of logs to base 10 of all numbers from 1 to 10 in steps of 0.001 we need to repeat the procedure above, namely identifying, for each four-digit input number, which of the 10 digit numbers it has been rounded from is closest to it, then dividing the relevant index (power to which 1.0001 was raised) by 23027? But how do you find automatically which is the closest 10 digit number?"

Teacher: "We do that by the instruction, placed in E6 to the right of D6 where the value of $1.0001^5$ is given in rounded form as 1.001, =IF(ABS($C6-$D6)<=MIN(ABS($C5-$D6),ABS($C7-$D6)),B6/23027,"")."

The first part of this is a test to see whether the unrounded value in C6 is nearer to the rounded value in D6 than are the two neighbouring unrounded values in C5 and C7. (The $ signs are inserted because this test is needed again in later columns, and can thus be copied over without the C and D changing e.g. to E and F.) If so, the index in B6 is divided by 23027 to give the base 10 logarithm of the rounded number in C6. Otherwise the "" puts an empty string in the cell, leaving it blank. In the slot E6 (where $n = 5$, the first slot in which the rounded $x$ is 1.001) the condition is not fulfilled. As we replicate down it is not till we get to the 10th power of 1.0001, in B11, that we have the number nearest to 1.001 and are given its log, 0.000434273."

| n | 1.0001^n = x | x to 3DP | logx to base 10 |
|---|---|---|---|
| 1 | 1.000100000 | 1 | |
| 2 | 1.000200010 | 1 | |
| 3 | 1.000300030 | 1 | |
| 4 | 1.000400060 | 1 | |
| 5 | 1.000500100 | 1.001 | |
| 6 | 1.000600150 | 1.001 | |
| 7 | 1.000700210 | 1.001 | |
| 8 | 1.000800280 | 1.001 | |

| n | 1.0001^n = x | x to 3DP | logx to base 10 |
|---|---|---|---|
| 9 | 1.000900360 | 1.001 | |
| 10 | 1.001000450 | 1.001 | 0.000434273 |
| 11 | 1.001100550 | 1.001 | |
| 12 | 1.001200660 | 1.001 | |
| 13 | 1.001300780 | 1.001 | |
| 14 | 1.001400910 | 1.001 | |
| 15 | 1.001501050 | 1.002 | |
| 16 | 1.001601201 | 1.002 | |

Bilal: "So how accurate are the results?"

Teacher: "To get an idea of that we can use the next column to calculate the difference between our home-made logarithms and those given by the spreadsheet's own LOG function. At the bottom of the column I had the maximum and minimum of these differences worked out, which came to about $2.18 \times 10^{-5}$ and $-2.16 \times 10^{-5}$ respectively. Thus the home-made logs will generally be accurate to 4DP but may be wrong by 1 unit in the 4th place."

Carol: "That's pretty good; but can we do better still?"

Teacher: "Yes, we can improve the values using linear interpolation. For example, the sheet shows that $1.0001^{6932} = 2.000036324$, close to 2 but slightly above 2.

| 6930 | 1.999636377 | 2.000 | |
|---|---|---|---|
| 6931 | 1.999836340 | 2.000 | |
| 6932 | 2.000036324 | 2.000 | 0.301037912 |
| 6933 | 2.000236327 | 2.000 | |

To get nearer to 2 we need a slightly lower power of 1.0001. When the index $n$ is increased by 1, the power $x = 1.0001^n$ increases by 0.0001 of its current value. Thus the gradient $\delta x/\delta n$ is $0.0001x$, making $\delta n/\delta x$ the reciprocal of this, namely $10\,000/x$. The desired change in $x$, here $2 - 2.000\,036324$, is thus multiplied by $10\,000/2.000\,036324$ to give the change in the index $n$, namely $-0.181\,616$, so we add this to 6932 and estimate that $1.0001^{6931.818384}$ will be considerably closer to 2 than $1.0001^{6932}$.

A similar calculation makes us change the power of 1.0001 that gives 10 from 23 027 to 23 027.002 203, so that the revised estimate for log2 to base 10 is 6931.818 384/23027.002203 = 0.301 029 996."

Carol:       "That is better! It agrees with the spreadsheet's own LOG function to 9 DP."

Teacher:     "Yes; when you ask for the difference between the two this is given as $4.67 \times 10^{-10}$, quite an improvement."

Bilal:       "Is there a way to do that to the other values?"

Teacher:     "Yes, by replicating a suitable instruction. We put the following into column I and row 11 where 1.0001 is raised to power 10, giving the power closest to 1.001: = IF(ABS($C11–$D11)<= MIN(ABS($C10–$D11), ABS($C12–$D11)), B11+(D11–C11)*10000/C11,'''). That gives the adjusted log to base 1.0001. Again it starts with a test to make sure that we only use the power of 1.0001 that is closest to 1.001. We replicate that all the way down and then in column J and row 11 we do = IF(ABS($C11–$D11)<= MIN(ABS($C10–$D11),ABS($C12–$D11)),I11/I$23028,''') which divides the adjusted log to base 1.0001 by the adjusted log of 10 to base 1.0001."

Carol:       "So how much better is that than before?"

Teacher:     "We can make the sheet calculate the difference between the adjusted value of the log and the value given by the LOG function; the errors thus found vary between $-5.4 \times 10^{-10}$ and $+1.63 \times 10^{-9}$. So our home-made logarithms are now liable to be wrong in the 9th or 10th decimal place, but mostly correct to 8DP."

## Notes

1  Bürgi in fact multiplied the powers $x$ that he calculated by $10^8$, rounded the results to make integers (which he called "black numbers"), and also multiplied the values of $n$ by 10 (to give "red numbers.") The idea of a logarithm as a power to which 10 is raised was introduced by Henry Briggs.
2  The reader may notice that 6932 is about $10\,000 \times \ln 2$, as $\ln 2 = 0.6931$ to 4DP. This closeness to $10^4$ times a log to base e applies to all the base 1.0001 logarithms, because $\log_{1.0001} x = \ln x / \ln 1.0001$, and from the series for $\ln(1 + x) = x - x^2/2 + x^3/3 \ldots$ we have $\ln 1.0001 \approx 0.0001$. However, the class may not yet be in a position to find this connection meaningful.

# The mysterious integral of $\dfrac{1}{x}$

Teacher: "Do you remember how to integrate $x^n$?"

Alan: "It makes $\dfrac{x^{n+1}}{n+1}$."

Teacher: "Is that the complete answer? And does it work for all $n$?"

Bilal: "It should have $+ c$, and it works for all $n$ except $n = -1$."

Carol: "So you can integrate $x^{-1.00136}$ but not $x^{-1}$ which is just $\dfrac{1}{x}$, a much simpler function? That seems weird!"

Teacher: "Well, try replacing $n$ by $-1$ in $\dfrac{x^{n+1}}{n+1}$. What do you get?"

Carol: "It makes $\dfrac{1}{0}$; I can see that's a problem; $0 \times$ anything is always 0, never 1. But if we can use the formula for every other value of $n$, is there a way of dealing with $-1$ by using numbers very close to $-1$?"

Teacher: "OK; let's try integrating $x^{-1+\varepsilon}$. What happens to that when $\varepsilon$ gets small?"

Bilal: "The integral is $\dfrac{x^{\varepsilon}}{\varepsilon}+c$. That just approaches $\dfrac{1}{0} + c$, so it's tending to infinity is it? And what about the $c$? Does that change?"

Teacher: "You're highlighting the problem with an indefinite integral; there's the undetermined constant $c$ which can take any value. Let's avoid that by making the integral definite, but with $x$ as upper limit. That means that, if the indefinite integral is $F(x)+c$, we have instead the definite integral $F(x)-F(a)$, where $a$ stands for the lower limit, whatever we make that to be."

Alan: "What, like $\displaystyle\int_{0}^{x} x^{-1+\varepsilon}dx$? That's $\dfrac{x^{\varepsilon}}{\varepsilon} - \dfrac{0^{\varepsilon}}{\varepsilon}$ which still goes wild when $\varepsilon$ is small."

Teacher: "Yes, and in fact $0^{\varepsilon}$ itself is undefined/infinite when $\varepsilon$ is negative. The problem arises from using 0 as the lower limit, since $\dfrac{1}{x}$ itself tends to infinity as $x$ tends to 0. Let's try using 1 as lower limit. We'll look at $\displaystyle\int_{1}^{x} t^{-1+\varepsilon}dt$."

Alan: "What's the $t$ doing there? Isn't it a function of $x$ that we're integrating?"

Teacher: "Yes, but $x$ is the upper limit, while $t$ is the variable of integration, going from 1 to $x$. It's not a good idea to use the same letter for different variables in the same expression."

Alan: "Does it really matter?"

Teacher: "Not seriously in what we're doing. But it can cause real problems in other cases. Think of $\int_0^x (t+x)\,dt$. What does that work out to?"

Bilal: "It's $\left[\dfrac{t^2}{2}+xt\right]_0^x$ which makes $\dfrac{3x^2}{2}$."

Teacher: "That's right; and you'd get the same if you started with $\int_0^x (u+x)\,du$; the change from $t$ to $u$ as a variable of integration makes no difference. But what does $\int_0^x (x+x)\,dx$ equal?"

Carol: "That's just $x^2$, not the same as the other integral."

Alan: "OK, I can see that using the same letter for different variables can mess things up."

Teacher: "Good. So let's get back to our integral, $\int_1^x t^{-1+\varepsilon}\,dt$."

Carol: "That makes $\dfrac{x^\varepsilon}{\varepsilon}-\dfrac{1^\varepsilon}{\varepsilon}=\dfrac{x^\varepsilon-1}{\varepsilon}$."

Teacher: "Right; so what happens when $\varepsilon$ tends to 0?"

Bilal: "Top and bottom both tend to 0. What can you do with $\dfrac{0}{0}$? $0\times$ anything is 0."

Teacher: "That's right; whereas $\dfrac{1}{0}$ is impossible, $\dfrac{0}{0}$ is indeterminate. So we can't get anywhere by making $\varepsilon=0$. Instead, let's take some small values for $\varepsilon$ and see what we get."

The class does some calculation using a spreadsheet or scientific calculators and produces the following table of values of $\dfrac{x^\varepsilon-1}{\varepsilon}$ to 6DP, with $x$ from 2 to 6 and $\varepsilon$ starting at 0.01 and being divided several times over by 100.

| | $\varepsilon$ | 0.01 | 0.0001 | 0.000001 | 1E–08 | 1E–10 |
|---|---|---|---|---|---|---|
| $x$ | | | | | | |
| 2 | | 0.695555 | 0.693171 | 0.693147 | 0.693147 | 0.693148 |
| 3 | | 1.104669 | 1.098673 | 1.098613 | 1.098612 | 1.098612 |
| 4 | | 1.395948 | 1.386390 | 1.386295 | 1.386294 | 1.386293 |
| 5 | | 1.622459 | 1.609567 | 1.609439 | 1.609438 | 1.609437 |
| 6 | | 1.807908 | 1.791920 | 1.791761 | 1.791759 | 1.791760 |

Teacher:    "So what does this tell us?"

Alan:    "The results seem to settle down by the time you get to $\varepsilon = 10^{-10}$. At least the first five figures after the decimal point have stabilised."

Teacher:    "Right; so let's take the last column as giving us good approximations to the limit we are trying to find, the limit of $\frac{x^{\varepsilon}-1}{\varepsilon}$ as $\varepsilon \to 0$. It depends on x, so let's call it $L(x)$. What do you notice about $L(2) + L(3)$?"

Bilal:    "That's 0.69315 + 1.09861 = 1.79176. Oh, that looks like $L(6)$."

Carol:    "And $L(4)$ looks as if it's just double $L(2)$."

Teacher:    "Yes; so what does that suggest may be happening?"

Alan:    "Perhaps that $L(a) + L(b) = L(ab)$?"

A bit more calculation seemed to confirm this result.

Bilal:    "How can we be sure though that it's always true? No amount of numerical experimenting will guarantee that, will it?"

Teacher:    "That's right. We need an approach that doesn't depend on trying things out with particular numbers. Now, what were we originally trying to find that led us to $L(x)$?"

Carol:    "The integral of $\frac{1}{x}$, but made into a definite integral between 1 and x."

Teacher:    "Right; so let's look at $L(ab) = \int_{1}^{ab} \frac{1}{x} dx$; we can write this as $\int_{1}^{a} \frac{1}{x} dx + \int_{a}^{ab} \frac{1}{x} dx$. What's the point of doing that?"

Alan:    "The first part on the right hand side is $L(a)$. Could the second term be equal to $L(b)$?"

Teacher:    "Good. Can anyone see how?"

Bilal:    "What if we did a substitution $x = au$ in the second integral? Then $dx = adu$ and we get $\int_{a}^{ab} \frac{1}{x} dx = \int_{1}^{b} \frac{1}{au} adu$. Ah, the $a$'s cancel and then the integral is just of $\frac{1}{u}$ from 1 to b, which is $L(b)$!"

Teacher:    "Well done! So now we have established that $L(a) + L(b) = L(ab)$ is true generally. Does that remind you of any function you've met so far?"

Carol:    "A logarithm function?"

Teacher:    "Good; the logarithm function has that property, which motivated its introduction by the pioneers who first made log tables to ease the enormous work of multiplying and dividing long numbers."

Alan: "But if it's a log, what's the base? It's not likely to be 10, is it?"

Teacher: "If the base is 10, then what should $L(10)$ be? And what is it actually?"

Carol: "It should be 1, but it seems [after some calculation] to be 2.30259; so the base is not 10."

Teacher: "OK, so if the base is $b$, what can you say about $L(b)$? And how will that help?"

Bilal: "$L(b)$ has to be 1, that means that the limit of $\dfrac{b^\varepsilon - 1}{\varepsilon}$ as $\varepsilon$ tends to 0 is 1."

Teacher: "Right. That means that, when $\varepsilon$ is very small, $\dfrac{b^\varepsilon - 1}{\varepsilon}$ is close to 1; so then $b^\varepsilon - 1 \approx \varepsilon$, so $b^\varepsilon \approx 1 + \varepsilon$. How do we get $b$ from that?"

Alan: "You have to undo raising to power $\varepsilon$ by taking the $\varepsilon$th root; that's the same as raising to power $\dfrac{1}{\varepsilon}$ isn't it?"

Bilal: "Right, so we get $b \approx (1 + \varepsilon)^{\frac{1}{\varepsilon}}$. Now what?"

Teacher: "Now we need some numerical work. Find $(1 + \varepsilon)^{\frac{1}{\varepsilon}}$ starting with $\varepsilon = 0.01$, then 0.0001 and so on."

The calculations give the following results:

| $\varepsilon$ | 0.01 | 0.0001 | 0.000001 | 1E–08 | 1E–10 |
|---|---|---|---|---|---|
| (1+ε)^(1/ε) | 2.704814 | 2.718146 | 2.718280 | 2.718282 | 2.718282 |

Carol: "So the base is about 2.718282?"

Teacher: "Yes, it's the number called $\varepsilon$. If we replace e by $\dfrac{1}{n}$ then $\varepsilon \to 0$ as $n \to \infty$ and e can be defined as $\lim\limits_{n\to\infty}\left(1 + \dfrac{1}{n}\right)^n$."

This next bit can be omitted unless the class actually reacts like Bilal, which will not be often!

Bilal: "But does this mean that $L(x)$ really has to be the log of $x$ to base e?"

Teacher: "Let's see how we can check that. Using the identity
$L(a) + L(b) = L(ab)$ we find that, since $L(e) = 1$,
$L(e^2) = 1 + 1 = 2, L(e^3) = L(e^2 \times e) = 2 + 1 = 3, L(e^4) = 3 + 1 = 4$. What about $L(e^5)$ and onwards?"

Bilal: "$L(e^5)$ will be $4 + 1 = 5$, $L(e^6)$ is 6 and so on; $L(e^n) = n$ for all positive integers $n$."

Alan:     "What about $L\left(e^x\right)$ if $x$ is not an integer, or if $x$ is negative?"

Teacher:  "If $x = \frac{p}{q}$ where $p$ and $q$ are positive integers then $L\left(e^x\right)$ can be found

from the facts that $L\left(\left(e^{\frac{p}{q}}\right)^q\right)$ on the one hand equals $L\left(e^p\right) = p$ and on the

other hand equals $L\left(e^{\frac{p}{q}}\right) \times q$, so that $L\left(e^{\frac{p}{q}}\right) = \frac{p}{q}$. Thus $L\left(e^x\right) = x$ is true for

positive rational $x$. Finally $L\left(e^{-x}\right) + L\left(e^x\right) = L\left(e^{-x} \times e^x\right) = L\left(1\right) = 0$, so that

$L\left(e^{-x}\right) = -L\left(e^x\right) = -x$. That deals with $L\left(e^x\right)$ for all rational $x$."

Carol:    "What if $x$ is irrational?"

Teacher:  "That's getting a bit advanced! You'd have to form a sequence of rational
numbers $r_n$ that tend to $x$, then use the fact that both $L(x)$ and $e^x$ are
continuous functions to deduce that the limit as $n \to \infty$ of $L\left(e^{r_n}\right) = r_n$ is $L\left(e^x\right)$
as well as being $x$. Are you satisfied now that $L$ is the inverse function to $e^x$ and
is therefore the log of $x$ to base $e$?"

Carol:    "Yes, that figures."

End of section to be omitted with most classes.

Teacher:  "The log to base $e$ is also called natural logarithm, ln for short. Do we now have

a way to integrate $\frac{1}{x}$ for positive $x$?"

Alan:     "Doesn't it make $\ln x + c$?"

Teacher:  "Yes, and that is quite surprising seeing that integrating any other power of $x$
just produces a multiple of the next power up."

Bilal:    "So does that mean we can differentiate $\ln x$ and get $\frac{1}{x}$?"

Teacher:  "Yes; we should be seeing that again shortly."

# Differentiating exponential functions

Teacher: "If a population size is $A$ at a certain time, and then grows by 3% each year, how big is it after one year?"

Alan: "It's $A + 0.03 \times A$; that's $1.03A$, isn't it?"

Teacher: "That's right. So how can we increase a number by 3% with a single operation?"

Carol: "Multiply it by 1.03."

Teacher: "Good; so what is the population size after 2 years? Or 3?"

Carol: "$A \times 1.03^2$ after 2 years and $A \times 1.03^3$ after 3 years."

Teacher: "Right; so what about after $x$ years?"

Bilal: "It would be $A \times 1.03^x$, wouldn't it?"

Teacher: "Yes; and that is an example of an *exponential function*, because the variable $x$ is in the exponent or index; this is quite different from the polynomial functions you first worked with, where $x$ is the base of each power and the powers are fixed numbers: 1, 2, 3 and so on. Can you think of another situation where a quantity increases by 3% every year?"

Alan: "A savings account offering 3% interest?"

Teacher: "Yes, provided the interest earned each year is added to the investment so that it can earn interest in following years. That's called *compound* interest, and means that the amount saved is multiplied by 1.03 each year, leading to the same formula we've just had for the amount after $x$ years. If interest is *not* added to the investment then we have *simple* interest, and the total amount just increases by 3% of the original investment each year, giving a linear growth with constant rate of growth. What we are looking at is exponential growth. If we plotted the graph of $y = 1.03^x$ what would the gradient function be?"

Bilal: "The growth each year is 3% of the amount at the start, so is the gradient $0.03 \times 1.03^x$?"

Teacher: "That's close, but it's not quite what we're after. If you plotted $y = 1.03^x$ for integer values of $x$ only, and then joined the points by straight lines, you'd get a sort of polygon, and the line joining $(x, 1.03^x)$ to $(x+1, 1.03^{x+1})$ would have gradient $0.03 \times 1.03^x$ as you said; that's an average gradient for the interval from $x$ to $x + 1$. However, we want to envisage $y = 1.03^x$ plotted for non-integer values as well, making a smooth curve, and we want the gradient of this curve *at the point* $(x, 1.03^x)$ So, instead of joining this to $(x+1, 1.03^{x+1})$ we join it to $(x+\delta x, 1.03^{x+\delta x})$ and find the gradient of that line."

Alan: "That would be $\frac{1.03^{x+\delta x} - 1.03^x}{\delta x}$, but then what?"

Carol: "You can rewrite $1.03^{x+\delta x}$ as $1.03^x \times 1.03^{\delta x}$ and then take out $1.03^x$ as a common factor."

Teacher: "Good, that makes $1.03^x \times \frac{1.03^{\delta x} - 1}{\delta x}$. What happens next?"

Bilal: "You have to find the limit of $\frac{1.03^{\delta x} - 1}{\delta x}$ as $\delta x$ tends to 0. But you can't divide top and bottom by $\delta x$, and they both tend to 0. What can you do with $\frac{0}{0}$?"

Teacher: "Yes, that doesn't tell you much. You're asking 'What times 0 makes 0?' or 'How many 0's make 0?' The answer of course is, Any number; so $\frac{0}{0}$ is completely uninformative. (By contrast, something like $\frac{5}{0}$ is impossible, because no number of 0's can ever make 5.) What we can do, however, given modern calculators, is to work out $\frac{1.03^{\delta x} - 1}{\delta x}$ for some small but non-zero values of $\delta x$ and see what happens. Try it with $\delta x = 0.001$, 0.000 01 and 0.000 000 1."

The class got 0.029559, 0.0295588 and 0.02956 respectively.

Teacher: "Well, those agree to 4 SF, so we can be confident that the gradient of $1.03^x$ is close to $0.02956 \times 1.03^x$, which incidentally is not far from Bilal's original answer of $0.03 \times 1.03^x$."

Carol: "What about the more general case with $y = a^x$?"

Teacher: "Yes, that's the next question. A similar process to the above leads us to a gradient function $\frac{dy}{dx} = a^x \times \lim_{\delta x \to 0} \frac{a^{\delta x} - 1}{\delta x}$."

Bilal: "So we're still faced with that tricky limit that we can only approximate numerically?"

Alan: "Hang on, haven't we met that limit before, when we were dealing with the integral of $\frac{1}{x}$ via the limit of $\int_1^x t^{-1+\varepsilon} dt$, which became the limit of $\frac{x^\varepsilon - 1}{\varepsilon}$ as $\varepsilon \to 0$?"

Carol: "Yes, we called it $L(x)$ and found that this behaves like a logarithm. Only this time we have $a$ instead of $x$ and $\varepsilon$ instead of $\delta x$."

Bilal: "Yes, and we got the base $b$ of the logarithm by requiring that the limit as $\varepsilon \to 0$ of $\dfrac{b^{\varepsilon} - 1}{\varepsilon}$ should be 1, which led to $b \approx (1 + \varepsilon)^{\frac{1}{\varepsilon}}$ and we found $b$ is about 2.71828,"

Alan: "Which is called e."

Teacher: "Yes, that's good. Now we can use the same approach here. The gradient of $a^x$ turns out to be proportional to $a^x$ itself, with the proportionality constant $\lim\limits_{\delta x \to 0} \dfrac{a^{\delta x} - 1}{\delta x}$ depends on $a$, and we can choose $a$ to make this constant equal 1 by requiring that $a \approx (1 + \delta x)^{\frac{1}{\delta x}}$ when $\delta x$ is small, which leads again to the number e. We find that $y = e^x$ leads to $\dfrac{dy}{dx} = e^x$ ; this special exponential function has its gradient equal to itself."

Carol: "What about when $a$ is not e? Do we still need that limit of $\dfrac{a^{\delta x} - 1}{\delta x}$ ?"

Teacher: "Yes, in a way we do. But here's another approach: express $y = a^x$ as a power of e. What is $a$ itself as a power of e?"

Carol: "I guess it must be $e^{\ln a}$, because that's what a logarithm is about: the power to which the base is raised to give the number."

Teacher: "Good. Now what about $a^x$ as a power of e?"

Alan: "That would be $(e^{\ln a})^x$ which makes $e^{x \ln a}$."

Bilal: "So you can differentiate that using the chain rule: let $u = x \ln a$ and $y = e^u$ , then $\dfrac{dy}{dx} = \dfrac{dy}{du} \times \dfrac{du}{dx} = e^u \times \ln a = e^{x \ln a} \times \ln a$ ."

Carol: "And that's the same as $a^x \times \ln a$, so that limit reduces to the natural log of $a$ again."

Teacher: "Right. Another thing, we can now confirm the result about the integral of $\dfrac{1}{x}$ . Suppose we have $y = \ln x$. Then what is $x$ in terms of $y$?"

Alan: "$x$ would be $e^y$, because $y$ is the power to which e is raised to give $x$."

Bilal: "So then $\dfrac{dx}{dy} = e^y$ . That means $\dfrac{dy}{dx} = \dfrac{1}{e^y}$ ."

Carol: "But that's the same as $\dfrac{1}{x}$ ; So the gradient function for $\ln x$ is $\dfrac{1}{x}$ ."

Teacher: "Yes, and thus we see again that ln $x$ is the result of integrating $\frac{1}{x}$, at least provided $x$ is positive."

Alan: "Why does $x$ have to be positive? What if it's negative?"

Bilal: "Can a negative number have a log to base e? If the log is $L$, then $x = e^L$; but $e^L$ is never negative, is it?"

Teacher: "That's right; in fact it's never even 0, though $e^L$ tends to 0 when $L$ tends to $-\infty$. So only positive numbers have logs. However, that doesn't stop us from integrating $\frac{1}{x}$ for negative $x$."

Carol: "It can't be difficult, because the graph of $\frac{1}{x}$ for negative $x$ is like the one for positive $x$ only with negative instead of positive values."

Teacher: "That's right; and if $x$ is negative, let $y = \ln(-x)$. Call this ln $u$ with $u = -x$ and you get $\frac{dy}{dx} = \frac{1}{u} \times (-1) = \frac{1}{x}$. Thus, for negative $x$, $\int \frac{1}{x} dx = \ln(-x) + c$. Combining this with the case when $x$ is positive we can say $\int \frac{1}{x} dx = \ln|x| + c$, where $|x|$ is the modulus or numerical size of $x$, so equals $x$ when $x$ is positive and equals $-x$ when $x$ is negative."

Alan: "Isn't there a series that can be used to calculate $e$ and $e^x$ ?"

Teacher: "Yes. If you consider the limit as $n \to \infty$ of $\left(1 + \frac{x}{n}\right)^n$, this can be written as the limit as $\varepsilon \to 0$ of $(1 + \varepsilon)^{\frac{x}{\varepsilon}} = \left((1 + \varepsilon)^{\frac{1}{\varepsilon}}\right)^x$, where $\varepsilon = \frac{x}{n}$. What happens in the limit?

Bilal: "The $(1 + \varepsilon)^{\frac{1}{\varepsilon}}$ part tends to $e$, doesn't it?"

Carol: "So the whole thing tends to $e^x$ as $\varepsilon \to 0$. But how does that give a series?"

Teacher: "We can expand $\left(1 + \frac{x}{n}\right)^n$ using the binomial theorem."

Carol: "That gives $1 + n\left(\frac{x}{n}\right) + \frac{n(n-1)}{2!}\left(\frac{x}{n}\right)^2 + \frac{n(n-1)(n-2)}{3!}\left(\frac{x}{n}\right)^3 + \ldots$ "

Teacher: "Good, and you can rewrite that as $1 + x + \frac{x^2}{2!}\left(1 - \frac{1}{n}\right) + \frac{x^3}{3!}\left(1 - \frac{1}{n}\right)\left(1 - \frac{2}{n}\right) + \ldots$ "

Alan: "So then you have to let $n$ tend to infinity?"

Teacher: "Yes; can you see what happens to the factors $\left(1 - \frac{1}{n}\right)$, $\left(1 - \frac{2}{n}\right)$, $\left(1 - \frac{3}{n}\right)$ and so on?"

Alan: "They would all tend to 1 as $n$ gets bigger and bigger."

Bilal:    "So that gives $e^x = 1 + x + \dfrac{x^2}{2!} + \dfrac{x^3}{3!} + \dfrac{x^4}{4!} \ldots$ and so on."

Teacher:    "Good. You can see this is like a polynomial, but one that goes on for ever. However, the ratio of the $(n + 1)$th term to the $n$th is $\dfrac{x}{n}$, which for any value of $x$ will tend to 0 as $n \to \infty$. When you compare this with a geometric series like $1 + x + x^2 + x^3 + \ldots$ which converges so long as $-1 < x < 1$, you can see that the series for $e^x$ converges for every value of $x$."

Carol:    "Then e must be $1 + 1 + \dfrac{1}{2!} + \dfrac{1}{3!} + \dfrac{1}{4!} + \ldots$"

Alan:    "Yes, the first six terms make 2.716667, and from about 10 terms on it's 2.718282."

Bilal:    "Is there an easier way to get the series without needing all that binomial stuff?"

Teacher:    "Yes; let's assume there is a series $a_0 + a_1 x + a_2 x^2 + a_3 x^3 + \ldots$ for $e^x$. What can we deduce from the fact that when $x = 0$ the series must give 1?"

Carol:    "That must make $a_0 = 1$, mustn't it?"

Teacher:    "And now what about the fact that $\dfrac{d\left(e^x\right)}{dx} = e^x$?"

Bilal:    "Differentiating the series gives $a_1 + 2a_2 x + 3a_3 x^2 + \ldots$"

Alan:    "So if that's to equal the original series, then we must have $a_1 = a_0, 2a_2 = a_1, 3a_3 = a_2$ and so on."

Carol:    "So $a_0 = a_1 = 1, a_2 = \dfrac{1}{2}, a_3 = \dfrac{1}{3 \times 2}, a_4 = \dfrac{1}{4 \times 3 \times 2}, \ldots$"

Bilal:    "So $a_n = \dfrac{1}{n!}$"

Teacher:    "Yes, we get the same series again, and whereas a polynomial when differentiated gives a lower order polynomial, this infinite series differentiates to give itself."

# Why do the trig ratios have those names?

Teacher: "We're looking at trigonometry, which of course you have studied before. Do you remember what these letters stand for?"

O    A    O

S   H C   H T   A

Alan: "Sine = Opposite over Hypotenuse, Cosine = Adjacent over Hypotenuse . . ."

Bilal: "And Tangent = Opposite over Adjacent. But why do sine, cosine and tangent have those names?"

Teacher: "Good question! The name 'sine' has a rather complicated history; the Indian mathematician Aryabhata (around AD 500) used the term *jya* which means a chord of a circle (since it's via sine of an angle at the centre of the circle that a chord is related to the radius.) Arabs translated this to *jiba* and wrote that as *jb*. Europeans misread that as *jaib*, meaning bulge or bay, and it got translated into Latin as *sinus* and then turned into English sine."

Carol: "Is sinus related to the sinuses in anatomy?"

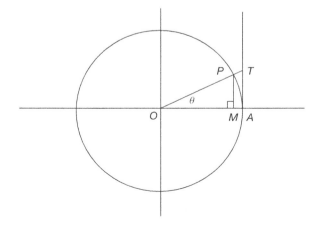

Teacher: "Yes, they are curved cavities behind the face, hence that name."

Alan: "Do we have to know all this about sine?"

Teacher: "No, it's not something you'll be asked about. And you won't be asked about the reasons for the names of other trig ratios; but the reasons behind those will help you understand and remember the things you do need to know; so now we'll look at tangent and secant. How long is *AT* in the diagram, in which the circle has radius 1?"

Bilal: "*AT* is the opposite in the triangle *OAT* in which the adjacent *OA* = 1, so *AT* = tan$\theta$."

Carol: "How do you know that the triangle is right-angled at *A*?"

Alan: "Because *OA* is a radius and *AT* is a tangent; Oh, so *that's* why that ratio is called tangent, is it?"

Teacher: "Yes, that's how it gets that name. It comes from the Latin word *tangere*, to touch, with past participle *tactum*, from which we get words like 'contact.' A tangent touches a circle at one point instead of cutting it in two points, and the trig ratio called tangent is what gives us the length of the tangent cut off by the radius *OP* when extended. Now what about the length of *OT*, the line that cuts off the tangent?"

Bilal: "That's the hypotenuse, with the adjacent being 1, so it's sec $\theta$. And sec is short for secant; does that relate to the fact that it cuts off the tangent?"

Teacher: "Yes indeed, from the Latin *seco*, I cut, from which we get 'section,' 'secateurs' and many other words. The Latin forms *tangens, secans* of the names were given by the Danish astronomer and mathematician Thomas Fincke in 1583. Looking at triangle *OAT*, what does Pythagoras' theorem tell you?"

Alan: "The hypotenuse is sec $\theta$ and the other sides are 1 and tan $\theta$, so $1 + tan^2\theta = sec^2\theta$."

Teacher: "Good; that's an important identity you need to remember and be ready to use at times. And what about triangle *OPM*?"

Carol: "That gives us $cos^2\theta + sin^2\theta = 1$. But why the name cosine?"

Teacher: "Good, I was coming to that. When you label the sides Hyp, Opp and Adj, Hyp is always the longest side, opposite the right angle; but how do you decide which is Opp and which is Adj?"

Bilal: "Opp is opposite the marked angle and Adj is adjacent to it."

Teacher: "Yes; now suppose your marked angle is 40°; then what is the third angle? It's 90° − 40° = 50° of course. Now suppose the 50° angle was your marked angle; how would that affect Opp and Adj?"

Carol: "They would change places: Opp would now be opposite the 50° angle, where Adj was previously. Oh, so that means that sin50° is the same as cosine40°."

Teacher: "Yes, and in general cos $\theta$ is the same as sin(90° − $\theta$), the sine of the complement of $\theta$, hence the name co-sine, introduced by Edmund Gunter in 1620 as *cosinus* to replace *sinus complementi*, while *tangens complementi* was shortened to *cotangens*, now cotangent."

Alan: "And cosecant is secant of the complement?"

Teacher: "That's right. Looking at the diagram, with a circle of radius 1, the angle BOP is 90° − $\theta$. Can you see which length equals cos $\theta$?"

Alan: "It's OM which is the adjacent to $\theta$ in triangle OPM, while the hypotenuse OP = 1."

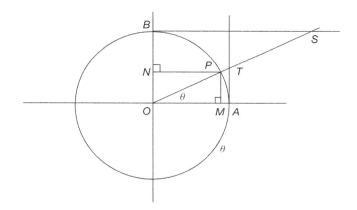

Carol: "That's the same as NP, which is the opposite to 90 − $\theta$."

Teacher: "Good, showing again that cos $\theta$ is sin(90° − $\theta$); and what about cotan and cosec of $\theta$?"

Bilal: "Cot $\theta$ must be the cotangent BS, as that's the opposite to 90 − $\theta$ in triangle OBS and the adjacent OB is 1."

Carol: "And OS must be the cosec; it's the line cutting off the cotangent."

Teacher: "That's right. Now, looking at the figure, what happens to sine, tan and sec of $\theta$ when $\theta$ increases from 0 towards 90°?"

Alan: "They all increase; sine and tan start at 0, sec starts at 1, and they get bigger."

Bilal: "So what about cosine, cotan and cosec? Does that mean they get smaller?"

Teacher: "Yes. You can see that either from the diagram or just from the fact that when $\theta$ increases, 90 − $\theta$ must decrease. This will help you to remember for instance that cosec $\theta$ is $\frac{1}{\sin\theta}$, not $\frac{1}{\cos\theta}$."

Carol:     "Why is that?"

Bilal:     "Is it because sine increases, so 1/sine must decrease, hence must be a co-ratio?"

Teacher:   "Yes, and cosine decreases, so 1/cosine is increasing, so you know that's sec. Another useful result: every trig identity is still true when ratios are replaced by co-ratios. For instance, what identity do you know that involves $sec^2\theta$?"

Alan:      "We had that today: $sec^2\theta = 1 + tan^2\theta$. So you just replace $\theta$ by $90° - \theta$ and that gives . . ."

Bilal:     "$cosec^2\theta = 1 + cot^2\theta$."

Teacher:   "That's right; it's not an identity you need as often as the sec one; but it's there and you don't need to make it an extra burden on your memory. Can you think of another?"

Carol:     "What about $tan\theta = \dfrac{sin\theta}{cos\theta}$? But what would be the co-ratio for cos?"

Alan:      "That's sine, because $90 - (90 - \theta) = \theta$."

Carol:     "So then you get $cot\theta = \dfrac{cos\theta}{sin\theta}$."

Teacher:   "Good. There's also $cos^2\theta + sin^2\theta = 1$, but that doesn't produce anything new when you replace ratios by co-ratios. We'll see another sign that all the co-ratios are decreasing when we look at differentiating the trig ratios: all the co-ratios have derivatives with a minus sign in front. But that's for another time."

# Compound angle formulae

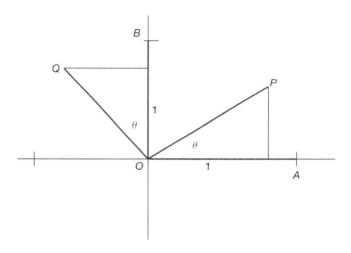

Teacher: "In the diagram **OA** and **OB** are vectors of length 1 in the $x$ and $y$ directions…"

Bilal: "Are they **i** and **j** then?"

Teacher: "That's right. **OP** and **OQ** are the results of rotating **i** and **j** through angle $\theta$ about the origin $O$. We'll express that by saying **OP** $= R_\theta\mathbf{i}$ and **OQ** $= R_\theta\mathbf{j}$", but can we express them also in terms of **i, j** and $\theta$?"

Carol: "That's just basic trig isn't it? If $P$ has coordinates $(x, y)$ then since $OP = 1$, same as $OA$, $x = \cos\theta$ and $y = \sin\theta$, so **OP** $= \cos\theta\,\mathbf{i} + \sin\theta\,\mathbf{j}$."

Alan: "I can see that in the diagram, with $\theta$ being a positive acute angle, but is it true for other values of $\theta$?"

Teacher: "Good question, Alan. The answer is Yes, because we *define* sine and cosine for general $\theta$ by saying that $P$ has coordinates $x = \cos\theta$, $y = \sin\theta$, when $OP$ has length 1 and makes angle $\theta$ with $OA$."

Bilal: "And at $Q$, $x = -\sin\theta$ and $y = \cos\theta$, so $OQ = -\sin\theta\,\mathbf{i} + \cos\theta\,\mathbf{j}$."

Teacher: "That's right. We can also express those by saying that $R_\theta\mathbf{i} = \cos\theta\,\mathbf{i} + \sin\theta\,\mathbf{j}$ while $R_\theta\mathbf{j} = -\sin\theta\,\mathbf{i} + \cos\theta\,\mathbf{j}$. Now suppose we rotate $OP$ further through an angle $\varphi$ to make $R_\varphi OP = R_\varphi R_\theta\mathbf{i}$ Can we work out what that will be?"

Bilal: "It's $R_\varphi(\cos\mathbf{i} + \sin\mathbf{j})$, so that should be $\cos\theta\,R_\varphi\mathbf{i} + \sin\theta\,R_\varphi\mathbf{j}$, is that right?"

Teacher: "Yes, because when you rotate two vectors and their sum, the rotated version of the sum is the sum of the rotated versions of the two vectors; if you think of the triangle law for adding vectors, the triangle can be rotated as a whole."

Carol: "Then that's $\cos\theta(\cos\varphi\mathbf{i} + \sin\varphi\mathbf{j}) + \sin\theta(-\sin\varphi\mathbf{i} + \cos\varphi\mathbf{j})$, which makes $(\cos\theta\cos\varphi - \sin\theta\sin\varphi)\mathbf{i} + (\cos\theta\sin\varphi + \sin\theta\cos\varphi)\mathbf{j}$."

Teacher: "Good. So that's what you get when you rotate the vector $\mathbf{i}$ through angle $\theta$ and then through angle $\varphi$. Can you see another way to express this result?"

Alan: "Hang on, doesn't that simply mean that $\mathbf{i}$ has been rotated through $\theta + \varphi$? In that case we should be able to use the original formula for $R_\theta\mathbf{i}$ but with $\theta$ replaced by $\theta + \varphi$, which makes $\cos(\theta + \varphi)\mathbf{i} + \sin(\theta + \varphi)\mathbf{j}$."

Teacher: "That's right; so now we have two different expressions for exactly the same vector. What can we conclude?"

Bilal: "Well, if they're both right they must actually be equal even if they look different."

Carol: "Then $\cos\theta\cos\varphi - \sin\theta\sin\varphi$ must be the same as $\cos(\theta + \varphi)$."

Alan: "And $\cos\theta\sin\varphi + \sin\theta\cos\varphi$ is the same as $\sin(\theta + \varphi)$, is that right?"

Teacher: "Yes, you have discovered the compound angle formulae, usually written in the form $\sin(\theta + \varphi) = \sin\theta\cos\varphi + \cos\theta\sin\varphi$ and $\cos(\theta + \varphi) = \cos\theta\cos\varphi - \sin\theta\sin\varphi$."

Carol: "Do we have to remember those?"

Teacher: "Yes; and here's a way to do that. First, the plus sign in $\sin\theta\cos\varphi + \cos\theta\sin\varphi$ is because sine is an increasing function, while the minus in $\cos\theta\cos\varphi - \sin\theta\sin\varphi$ comes from cosine being a decreasing function, in the first quadrant. Next, think of $\varphi$ as being a small angle. What can you then say about $\cos\varphi$ and $\sin\varphi$?"

Bilal: "$\cos\varphi$ will be close to 1 and $\sin\varphi$ close to 0."

Teacher: "That's right. So, in $\sin\theta\cos\varphi + \cos\theta\sin\varphi$, the first term will be close to $\sin\theta \times 1$ or $\sin\theta$, while the second term will be small; so the whole thing is close to $\sin\theta$ as it should be when $\varphi$ is small."

Carol: "And the same works with $\cos\theta\cos\varphi - \sin\theta\sin\varphi$ ; it's close to $\cos\varphi$ when $\varphi$ is small."

Teacher: "That's right. Bearing those in mind should help you not to get muddled about those formulae. Now what about $\tan(\theta + \varphi)$?"

Alan: "That would be $\dfrac{\sin(\theta + \varphi)}{\cos(\theta + \varphi)} = \dfrac{\sin\theta\cos\varphi + \cos\theta\sin\varphi}{\cos\theta\cos\varphi - \sin\theta\sin\varphi}$ , but how to get that in terms of tan of $\theta$ and $\varphi$?"

Teacher: "Divide top and bottom by $\cos\theta\cos\varphi$."

Alan: "Oh, that makes $\dfrac{\tan\theta + \tan\varphi}{1 - \tan\theta\tan\varphi}$."

Teacher: "Yes; and to help remember that, look at this figure, which shows some trig ratios for a small angle $\theta$. The arc is of a circle of radius 1. Can you say which lengths are $\sin\theta$, $\tan\theta$ and $\theta$ itself?"

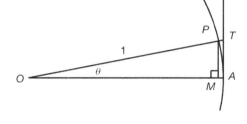

Bilal: "$\sin\theta$ is $PM$ and $\tan\theta$ is $AT$."

Carol: "And $\theta$ is the length of the arc $PA$, if we're using radians; is that right?"

Teacher: "Yes, that's why radians are so useful in this context. Now what can you say about the relative size of $\sin\theta$, $\tan\theta$ and $\theta$?"

Alan: "They seem much the same, though $\sin\theta$ looks a bit less than $\theta$ which seems a bit less than $\tan\theta$."

Teacher: "That's right. In fact you can prove those comparisons by considering the areas of triangle $OAP$, the sector $OAP$ and triangle $OAT$; I'll leave that for you as an exercise. But the point at the moment is that $\sin\theta$ and $\tan\theta$ are both very close to $\theta$ when $\theta$ is very small."

Alan: "So that makes $\tan(\theta + \varphi)$ very close to $\theta + \varphi$ when both angles are small, and $\tan\theta + \tan\varphi$ is also close to $\theta + \varphi$."

Bilal: "And the denominator $1 - \tan\theta\tan\varphi$ is then close to 1, which checks that the formula seems to be right. But what if $1 - \tan\theta\tan\varphi$ gets close to or equal to 0?"

Carol: "That's when $\tan\theta$ is close to $\dfrac{1}{\tan\varphi}$, which is $\cot\varphi$."

Alan: "That's also $\tan\left(\dfrac{\pi}{2} - \varphi\right)$, so that would happen when $\theta + \varphi$ is close to a right angle; aha, that's when tan gets unbounded because the adjacent approaches 0. So that's what the formula should be doing when the two angles add up to a right angle."

Teacher: "Good! Between us we've seen ways to make the formula more memorable. Now let's look at the double angle formulae that we get by taking $\varphi$ to equal $\theta$."

Carol: "So $\sin 2\theta = 2\sin \theta \cos \theta$, is that right?"

Teacher: "Yes; and can you incidentally see an easy way to prove that directly? It involves finding the area of an isosceles triangle, with equal sides of length 1 having an angle $2\theta$ between them."

Alan: "That's $\frac{1}{2} \times 1 \times 1 \times \sin 2\theta$."

Bilal: "But if you take the third side as base, its length is $2 \times 1 \times \sin\theta$ and the height is then $1 \times \cos\theta$ which makes the area $\sin \theta \cos \theta$."

Carol: "So $\frac{1}{2}\sin 2\theta = \sin\theta \cos\theta$; aha! That proves $\sin 2\theta = 2\sin\theta \cos\theta$."

Alan: "Also $\cos 2\theta = \cos^2\theta - \sin^2\theta$ ; is that right?"

Teacher: "Yes, but there are two other forms for that, because $\cos^2\theta + \sin^2\theta$ is always 1."

Bilal: "So we can make $\cos 2\theta = 1 - 2\sin^2\theta$ or $2\cos^2\theta - 1$."

Teacher: "That's right; and one of those forms can be proved directly by using the cosine formula in the same triangle we just used for $\sin 2\theta$; I'll leave that for you as an exercise. Those two forms can be rewritten to express $\sin^2\theta$ and $\cos^2\theta$ in terms of $\cos 2\theta$."

Carol: "So $\sin^2\theta = \frac{1}{2}(1 - \cos 2\theta)$ and $\cos^2\theta = \frac{1}{2}(1 + \cos 2\theta)$. "

Teacher: "Good. You will need those when you want to integrate $\sin^2\theta$ and $\cos^2\theta$. To remember them, think of the sum of $\sin^2\theta$ and $\cos^2\theta$ being 1, so that on average they are $\frac{1}{2}$ each. For the − and + signs use the fact that cosine is a decreasing function, so the $-\cos 2\theta$ makes an increasing function, which $\sin^2$ is, while the $+\cos 2\theta$ makes it decreasing, as it should be."

*Addendum from a later lesson, when the factor formulae have been derived.*

Carol: "Sir, how are we going to remember these?"

Teacher: "OK; let's start with $\sin P + \sin Q = 2\sin \frac{1}{2}(P+Q) \cos\frac{1}{2}(P-Q)$. Think of $P$ and $Q$ being nearly equal to each other; then the left side should be nearly $2\sin P$, and on the right side $2\sin\frac{1}{2}(P+Q)$ is nearly $2\sin P$, while $\frac{1}{2}(P-Q)$ is small, so its cosine is close to 1; that makes the two sides match each other."

Alan: "So with $\sin P - \sin Q = 2\sin\frac{1}{2}(P-Q)\cos\frac{1}{2}(P+Q)$ do we use the same approach?"

Teacher: "Yes, let $P$ be slightly greater than $Q$; that makes $P - Q$ a very small angle, so $2\sin\frac{1}{2}(P-Q)$ is close to $2 \times \frac{1}{2}(P-Q) = P - Q$, while $\cos\frac{1}{2}(P+Q)$ is close to $\cos Q$; so $\sin P - \sin Q$ is nearly the same as $(P - Q)\cos Q$."

Carol: "But how does that help?"

Bilal: "Isn't this to do with differentiating sine and getting cosine? You increase the angle from $Q$ by a small amount to $P$ and the change in the sine is $\cos Q$ times the change in the angle."

Teacher: "Well done, that's exactly it; in fact this approach can be used to establish that the gradient of sine is cosine, starting with the factorisation of $\sin(\theta + \delta\theta) - \sin\theta$ as $2\sin\frac{1}{2}\delta\theta\cos\left(\theta+\frac{1}{2}\delta\theta\right)$."

Alan: "Does that work with cosine as well? $\cos P - \cos Q = -2\sin\frac{1}{2}(P+Q)\sin\frac{1}{2}(P-Q)$, so that's nearly the same as $-2\sin Q\frac{1}{2}(P-Q) = -\sin Q(P-Q)$, the change in the angle times the derivative $-\sin Q$ of $\cos Q$?"

Teacher: "Yes, that's it, and the minus sign reminds you that cosine decreases in the first quadrant. As for $\cos P + \cos Q$, you can do the check for yourselves. And for another exercise, see if you can work on $\tan(\theta+\delta\theta) - \tan\theta$ to get the derivative of $\tan\theta$."

# Differentiating the trigonometric ratios

Teacher: "We're going to be differentiating the trig ratios sinθ etc. with respect to θ. First we need to think about how we measure the angle θ."

Alan: "Why does that matter?"

Teacher: "Because we'll be dividing the change in sinθ by the change in θ; and you need a numerical measure for the change in the angle. If you look at the diagram, we have a circle of radius 1, and we are going to use the length of the arc PP' as our measure for the angle δθ."

Carol: "Is that to do with radians?"

Teacher: "Yes indeed: the radian measure of the angle is the arc length divided by the radius, and here the radius is 1 so that just becomes the arc length itself. In the diagram what is the length of P'Q?"

Bilal: "It's the difference between P'M and PM, so that's sin(θ + δθ) − sinθ."

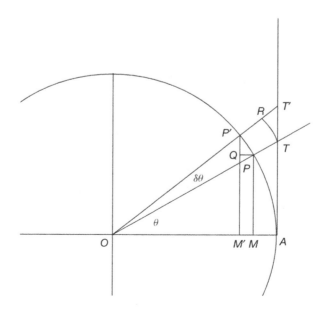

208

Teacher:  "Right. Now look at the next diagram, which shows the 'triangle' *P'QP* enlarged. You can see it is not really a triangle, because *P'P* is an arc, not a straight line."

Alan:  "And shouldn't the angle at *P'* be $\theta + \delta\theta$? Because *OP'M* = 90° − ($\theta + \delta\theta$) and *P'P* is sort of perpendicular to *OP'*. Well, at least the tangent at *P'* is at right angles to the radius *OP'''*

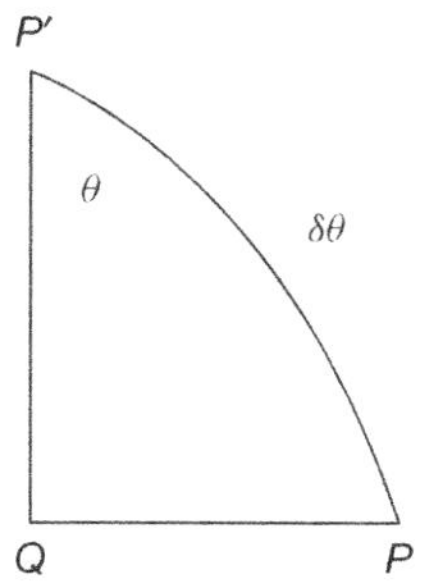

Carol:  "Yes, but by similar reasoning the angle *QPP'* should equal 90° − $\theta$, at least that's the angle between *OP* and the tangent at *P*."

Bilal:  "That means the angles don't add up to 180°!"

Teacher:  "Of course they don't, because *PP'* is not a straight line! Also we should really be talking about $\pi$ radians rather than 180°; though it's clear what you mean, and it's when we want to divide by $\delta\theta$ that the use of radians really matters. But now imagine that $\delta\theta$ is seriously small, say about $10^{-16}$, so that no calculator could distinguish between $\theta$ and $\delta\theta$."

Carol:  "What does that mean?"

Teacher:  "Well, try adding $10^{-16}$ onto 1.5 in your calculator, then subtract 1.5. What do you get?"

Carol:  "It makes 0!"

Alan:  "That's because the true answer when you add them is 1.500 000 000 000 000 1 and the calculator can't display or even store that many digits, so it makes it the same as 1.5."

Teacher:  "Exactly. Now imagine the enlarged diagram drawn with this value of $\delta\theta$ and then magnified about $10^{16}$ times to make it visible. Suppose that also the tangents at *P* and at *P'* were included in the enlarged diagram. Would you be able to tell which line is the tangent at *P*, which is the tangent at *P'* and which is the arc *PP'*?"

Bilal:  "No way; they would all look like a straight line from *P* to *P'*."

Teacher:  "That's right; and the length of that line is still the tiny $\delta\theta$, and it makes with *P'Q* an angle that can hardly be distinguished from $\theta$. So now what is the length of *P'Q*, using simple trigonometry?"

Carol:  "It's *P'P* × cos $\theta$, that's $\delta\theta$ cos $\theta$."

Teacher:  "Right; and remember that *PQ'* = sin ($\theta + \delta\theta$) − sin$\theta$. so what can you deduce about $\frac{\sin(\theta+\delta\theta) - \sin\theta}{\delta\theta}$ ?"

Alan:  "It's cos$\theta$, or at least practically indistinguishable from cos$\theta$."

Teacher:   "Good. So that's how you can see that the derivative of $\sin\theta$ is $\cos\theta$. Now can we similarly differentiate $\cos\theta$?"

Bilal:   "In the first diagram $\cos\theta = OM$ and $\cos(\theta+\delta\theta) = OM'$, so $\cos(\theta+\delta\theta) - \cos\theta = OM' - OM$…"

Alan:   "And that equals $-QP$ which equals $-PP' \times \sin\theta = -\delta\theta\,\sin\theta$."

Carol:   "So the derivative of $\cos\theta$ is $-\sin\theta$, is it?"

Teacher:   "That's right. Well done all of you. Remember that cosine is a decreasing function, hence the minus sign in the derivative. The fact that it *is* cosine gives another way of finding the derivative, which we'll see a bit later on. But now look at this third diagram, which enlarges another part of the first. What can you say about $TT'$?"

Alan:   "It's the difference between $AT'$ and $AT$, so that's $\tan(\theta+\delta\theta) - \tan\theta$."

Carol:   "Why does $RT = \sec\theta\,\delta\theta$ ?"

Bilal:   "Because it's an arc of a circle with radius $OT = \sec\theta$, and $\delta\theta$ is the angle at the centre."

Carol:   "OK, then it looks as if $TT' = RT\sec\theta = \sec^2\theta\,\delta\theta$."

Teacher:   "Yes; again that's not absolutely exact, because $RT$ is not really a straight line at right-angles to $RT'$, but when $\delta\theta$ gets really small the inaccuracy can be ignored."

Alan:   "So then $\dfrac{\tan(\theta+\delta\theta) - \tan\theta}{\delta\theta}$ almost equals $\sec^2\theta$, is that right?"

Teacher:   "Yes, and that gives the answer when $\tan\theta$ is differentiated. Can you also see how to differentiate $\sec\theta$ from the same figure?"

Bilal:   "That must be using $RT'$ That's $\sec(\theta+\delta\theta) - \sec\theta$."

Carol:   "And $RT' = RT\tan\theta = \sec\theta\,\delta\theta \times \tan\theta$."

Alan:   "So $\dfrac{\sec(\theta+\delta\theta) - \sec\theta)}{\delta\theta}$ is nearly $\sec\theta\,\tan\theta$, which must be the derivative of $\sec\theta$."

Teacher:   "Well done; that's right. Now what about $\operatorname{cosec}\theta$ and cotan?"

Carol:   "Do we need a new figure, or can we use $\operatorname{cosec}\theta = \sec(90° - \theta)$?"

Teacher:   "Yes, we'll use that way to define cosec; but to be consistent we'll express 90° in radians. So let $y = \operatorname{cosec}\theta = \sec\left(\dfrac{\pi}{2} - \theta\right)$; we'll call that sec$u$."

Bilal:   "So are we going to use the chain rule, $\dfrac{dy}{d\theta} = \dfrac{dy}{du} \times \dfrac{du}{d\theta}$ ?"

Teacher:   "Yes indeed."

Bilal:   "So that makes $\dfrac{dy}{d\theta} = \sec u \tan u \times (-1)$."

Alan:   "That's $-\sec\left(\dfrac{\pi}{2} - \theta\right)\tan\left(\dfrac{\pi}{2} - \theta\right)$. Oh, of course that's $-\csc\theta \cot\theta$."

Teacher:   "Good. The minus sign reminds us that cosec is decreasing in the first quadrant, and apart from that the sec and tan become cosec and cot."

Carol:   "So is the derivative of $\cot\theta$ just $-\csc\theta^2\theta$?"

Teacher:   "Exactly! The $\sec^2$ becomes $\csc^2$ and the minus sign is there because you're dealing with a co-ratio."

# Fermat centre of a triangle

Teacher: "A company has offices in three different locations *A*, *B* and *C*, and wants to link them with fibre optic cables to a centre point *P*. Where should *P* be located to minimise the total amount of cable? Let's start by assuming the triangle *ABC* is isosceles with *AB = AC*. Look at the diagram. I'm assuming that the centre point will be on the line of symmetry." [Note: this can be proved if necessary using the methods of Chapter 28 on Minimising via Reflection.]

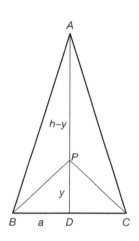

Bilal: "So *BC* = 2*a* and the height is *h*, and we want to minimse *AP* + *BP* + *CP*. That's the same as $h - y + 2\sqrt{a^2 + y^2}$ ."

Teacher: "Good. Let's call that *L* for total length of cable."

Alan: "Then $\dfrac{dL}{dy} = -1 + 2 \times 2y \times \dfrac{1}{2}\left(a^2 + y^2\right)^{-\frac{1}{2}} = \dfrac{2y}{\sqrt{a^2 + y^2}} - 1.$"

Carol: "So for a minimum that has to be 0, then $2y = \sqrt{a^2 + y^2}$ ; that means $4y^2 = a^2 + y^2$. That makes $y = \dfrac{a}{\sqrt{3}}$, does it?"

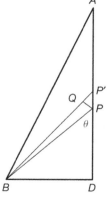

Teacher: "That's right. Now can you work out the angle *BPD*?"

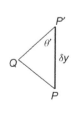

Bilal: "That's $\tan^{-1}\dfrac{a}{a/\sqrt{3}} = \tan^{-1}\sqrt{3}$; it's 60°."

Alan: "So then the three cables are at 120° with each other. Is that right?"

Teacher: "Yes they are; now look at the next diagram, in which we have half of triangle $ABC$, and we consider $P$ moving a small amount $\delta y$ up to $P'$. This obviously reduces the distance from $A$ by $\delta y$, but increases the distance from $B$ by the length $QP'$ which is the difference between $BP$ and $BP'$. Think of $PQ$ as a tiny arc with centre $B$. When $\delta y$ is seriously small we can treat $PP'Q$ as a triangle right-angled at $Q$, and we can also ignore the difference between $\theta$ and $\theta'$, so we have $QP' \approx \delta y \cos\theta$."

Alan: "So does that make the overall change in cable length $\delta L \approx (2\cos\theta - 1)\delta y$ ?"

Teacher: "Yes it does, and the approximation gets better and better as you let $\delta y$ tend to 0."

Carol: "So that $\dfrac{dL}{dy} = 2\cos\theta - 1$, which is 0 when $\cos\theta = \dfrac{1}{2}$, again making $\theta = 60°$."

Alan: "Just looking back at $\dfrac{dL}{dy} = \dfrac{2y}{\sqrt{a^2 + y^2}} - 1$ which we got before, you can see that $\dfrac{y}{\sqrt{a^2 + y^2}} = \dfrac{DP}{BP} = \cos\theta$ which makes $\dfrac{dL}{dy} = 2\cos\theta - 1$."

Bilal: "Hang on; couldn't we have expressed $L$ in terms of $\theta$ to start with? $AP = h - a\cot\theta$ and $BP = a\csc\theta$, so $L = h - a\cot\theta + 2a\csc\theta$."

Carol: "So then $\dfrac{dL}{d\theta} = a\csc^2\theta - 2a\csc\theta \cot\theta$."

Bilal: "That seems a lot more complicated than $2\cos\theta - 1$."

Teacher: "Yes, but remember we are now doing $\dfrac{dL}{d\theta}$, instead of $\dfrac{dL}{dy}$, and $y = a\cot\theta$ makes $dy = -a\csc^2\theta\, d\theta$."

Alan: "For $\dfrac{dL}{d\theta}$ to be 0 we have $a\csc\theta(\csc\theta - 2\cot\theta) = 0$. Can $\csc\theta$ be 0?"

Teacher: "Good question, Alan. A common mistake is just to divide an equation by a common factor without thinking whether that could be 0, which can result in a solution being missed. But as $\sin\theta$ is always between 1 and $-1$, $\csc\theta$ has to be greater than 1 or less than $-1$, nowhere near 0."

Bilal: "So $\csc\theta = 2\cot\theta$, or $\dfrac{1}{\sin\theta} = \dfrac{2\cos\theta}{\sin\theta}$ and $\cos\theta = \dfrac{1}{2}$ as we got before."

Teacher: "Good; and yet another way to see this is to think of the vector $PP'$ being resolved into components along $BP$ and at right angles to $BP$. The part along $BP$ is $\delta y \cos\theta$, which increases the distance from $B$ by that amount, while the part at right angles to $BP$ increases the distance by much less when $\delta y$ is small. So again $\delta L$ is nearly $(2\cos\theta - 1)\delta y$. But now we want to look at the same problem in a general acute angled triangle."

Carol: "That sounds difficult! The centre then needs two coordinates and we have to choose both of those for a minimum value of $L$."

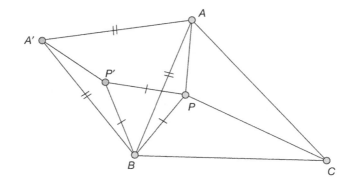

Teacher:  "Yes, it would be complicated that way; but there's another way. In the diagram ABC is the general triangle, and P is a possible position for the cables to meet. Triangle ABP has been rotated through 60° to make A'BP'."

Bilal:  "So AP = A'P' and BPP' is equilateral so BP = P'P."

Carol:  "That makes the total length of cable the same as A'P' + P'P + PC."

Alan:  "And that can't be less than the direct distance from A' to C. So for P to be the best connection point it needs to be on the straight line from A' to C."

Bilal:  "And then, with A'P'PC all straight and BPP' still equilateral, the angle BPC has to be 180° − 60° = 120°, which is what we got before."

Teacher:  "That's right, and by the same reasoning the angles CPA and APB also have to be 120°."

Alan:  "Does that give a way of locating the best P? For ∠APB to be 120°, P has to be on a circle with centre O such that ∠AOB is 240° − that would be the reflex angle − so the other angle is 120°; so the angles OAB and OBA have to be 30° each."

Teacher:  "Yes indeed; and that circle is in fact the circumcircle of the triangle AA'B."

Carol:  "And presumably P is also on the circumcircles of the other two equilateral triangles you can make on BC and on CA."

Alan:  "And aren't there two other lines like AA' that pass through P?"

Teacher:  "That's right. See the diagram, in which A' has been renamed N, and the other equilateral triangles and their circumcircles have been drawn. They all meet at the best location for the cables to meet; and the lines AL, BM, CN all meet in that point too. It is called the Fermat centre of the triangle, after the mathematician Fermat who first raised the problem, though it was his friend Torricelli who solved it."

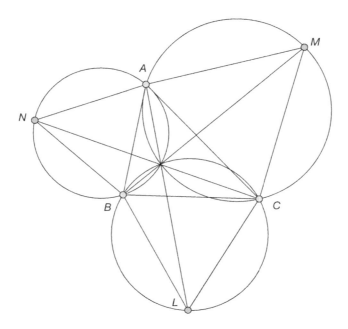

Bilal: "And those lines must all be the same length, which is the total length of cable."

Teacher: "Yes indeed; quite a striking result. There's one other way of seeing why the angles between the cables are all 120°, using your knowledge of physics. If you think of A, B, C as three holes in a smooth horizontal table top, and that three equal weights are hanging below A, B and C on strings that are joined together on the table top, how would the strings look when the system is at rest in equilibrium?"

Alan: "That means you have three equal forces in equilibrium; I think they would have to make equal angles with each other, so the angles would be 120°."

Teacher: "Yes, they would. Now think of the gravitational potential energy of the system, which is a minimum in the equilibrium position. That means the total length of string under the table is as great as possible, which is achieved when the total length of string *on* the table is as little as possible, which is exactly what we have been investigating."

Carol: "Maths is full of interesting and beautiful problems, isn't it?"

Teacher: "Yes indeed; I hope you'll get to enjoy many more. I'm still coming across many that make me stop and think!"

# Index

# Taylor & Francis eBooks

---

## Helping you to choose the right eBooks for your Library

Add Routledge titles to your library's digital collection today. Taylor and Francis ebooks contains over 50,000 titles in the Humanities, Social Sciences, Behavioural Sciences, Built Environment and Law.

**Choose from a range of subject packages or create your own!**

### Benefits for you

» Free MARC records
» COUNTER-compliant usage statistics
» Flexible purchase and pricing options
» All titles DRM-free.

### Benefits for your user

» Off-site, anytime access via Athens or referring URL
» Print or copy pages or chapters
» Full content search
» Bookmark, highlight and annotate text
» Access to thousands of pages of quality research at the click of a button.

REQUEST YOUR **FREE** INSTITUTIONAL TRIAL TODAY

**Free Trials Available**
We offer free trials to qualifying academic, corporate and government customers.

## eCollections – Choose from over 30 subject eCollections, including:

| | |
|---|---|
| Archaeology | Language Learning |
| Architecture | Law |
| Asian Studies | Literature |
| Business & Management | Media & Communication |
| Classical Studies | Middle East Studies |
| Construction | Music |
| Creative & Media Arts | Philosophy |
| Criminology & Criminal Justice | Planning |
| Economics | Politics |
| Education | Psychology & Mental Health |
| Energy | Religion |
| Engineering | Security |
| English Language & Linguistics | Social Work |
| Environment & Sustainability | Sociology |
| Geography | Sport |
| Health Studies | Theatre & Performance |
| History | Tourism, Hospitality & Events |

For more information, pricing enquiries or to order a free trial, please contact your local sales team:
**www.tandfebooks.com/page/sales**